ASIA ANNUAL 2007

ASIA ANNUAL 2007

ENVISAGING REGIONS

Editor-in-Chief
H.S. Vasudevan, Director, MAKAIAS

Issue Editor
Anita Sengupta, Fellow, MAKAIAS

Associate Editors
Suchandana Chatterjee, Fellow, MAKAIAS
Priya Singh, Fellow, MAKAIAS
Kausik Bandyopadhyay, Fellow, MAKAIAS
Kingshuk Chatterjee, Fellow, MAKAIAS

MANOHAR
2008

First published 2008

ISBN 978-81-7304-797-8

Published by
Ajay Kumar Jain *for*
Manohar Publishers & Distributors
4753/23 Ansari Road, Daryaganj,
New Delhi 110 002

Printed at
Salasar Imaging Systems
Delhi 110 035

Contents

ESSAYS

REVIEW ARTICLES

RESEARCH NOTES

Contributors

Najam Abbas Research Associate at the Central Asian Studies unit of the Institute of Ismaili Studies, London.

Kausik Bandyopadhay Fellow, Maulana Abul Kalam Azad Institute of Asian Studies.

Rakhee Bhattacharya Fellow, Maulana Abul Kalam Azad Institute of Asian Studies.

Susmita Bhattacharya Fellow, Maulana Abul Kalam Azad Institute of Asian Studies.

Swapna Bhattacharya (Chakraborti) Fellow, Maulana Abul Kalam Azad Institute of Asian Studies and Reader, Department of South and South East Asian Studies, University of Calcutta.

Deborshi Brahmachari Research Assistant, National Council of Applied Economic Research, New Delhi.

Shantanu Chakrabarti Lecturer at the Department of History, University of Calcutta. Currently Research Fellow at the Institute of Defence Studies and Analysis, New Delhi.

Kingshuk Chatterjee Fellow, Maulana Abul Kalam Azad Institute of Asian Studies.

Suchandana Chatterjee Fellow, Maulana Abul Kalam Azad Institute of Asian Studies.

Amiya K. Chaudhuri Fellow, Maulana Abul Kalam Azad Institute of Asian Studies.

Timur Dadabaev Associate Professor, University of Tsukuba, Graduate School of Humanities and Social Sciences, and Adjunct Associate Professor, University of Tokyo, Graduate School of Humanities and Sociology.

Oleg A. Donskikh Professor, Head of Department of Philosophy, Novosibirsk State University of Economy and Management.

Sreemati Ganguli Fellow, Maulana Abul Kalam Azad Institute of Asian Studies.

Swarupa Gupta Fellow, Maulana Abul Kalam Azad Institute of Asian Studies.

Yulia Guzhvenko Research Assistant at the Centre for Regional Studies, Barnaul State Pedagogical University.

V. A. Lamin Director of the Institute of History, Russian Academy of Sciences, Siberian Branch.

Monika Mandal Fellow, Maulana Abul Kalam Azad Institute of Asian Studies.

Binoda K. Mishra Fellow, Maulana Abul Kalam Azad Institute of Asian Studies.

Arpita Basu Roy Fellow, Maulana Abul Kalam Azad Institute of Asian Studies.

Priya Singh Fellow, Maulana Abul Kalam Azad Institute of Asian Studies.

Krishnan Srinivasan Former Foreign Secretary, Government of India, and Fellow, Maulana Abul Kalam Azad Institute of Asian Studies.

E.G. Vodichev Vice-Director of the Institute of History, Russian Academy of Sciences, Siberian Branch.

1

Introduction: Envisaging Regions

KINGSHUK CHATTERJEE

Among the categories that social scientists frequently play with, that of 'region' seems to have a particular charm of its own. Even though the *raison d'être* of social sciences is to situate human behaviour within the matrices of a generic *human* societal setting, observers have been conscious for long a time of specificities that seem to vary with space rather than time, culture, religion, etc. Before the emergence of social sciences as a discipline, such spatial specificities were conceived of in various ways—the influence of geography, topography, climate, etc. These in turn led to several enduring myths or stereotypes about human behaviour—that hill people are more hardworking than those living in the plains; people living in humid climates get exhausted easily. Another set of spatial stereotypes which was formed quite regularly had a linkage with culture. Probably the best instance of this kind was the stereotype of the Orient as against the Occident, where the Orient was not simply the 'other' in a cultural and epistemic sense, but also a geographic sense—in fact, its cultural and epistemic differences from the Occident were considered to be concomitant with geographical remoteness. Nevertheless, the Orient–Occident binary was primarily cultural in its conception. The category of 'region' was probably the most comprehensive blend between the considerations of space and time, structures, culture, economy, etc.

The present understanding of 'region' is, however, of fairly recent vintage. The concept of 'region' came into vogue only in course of the nineteenth century. European imperial/colonial enterprises around the world had prompted the need to engage with the globe intellectually, in order to understand it better and thus govern more efficiently and profitably.[1] The colonial/imperial adventurers generally required an 'information order', i.e. a composite form of political, social, economic and military intelligence developed by the state, and channels of social communication through which such intelligence could be used in the ruling establishment's engagement with the ruled. The various information orders,[2] which came into being in various parts of the world to facilitate the hegemony of European powers, apparently seemed to disprove a cardinal aspect of European thinking in the age of the Enlightenment, to wit, human experiences are essentially similar. As the diversity of human experiences began to be revealed, these had to be accommodated within the larger epistemic paradigm provided by the Enlightenment. Hence, societies began to be studied as units bound by ethnicity (Aryan, Semitic, Sinic, Australoid, Negroid, etc.), or language (Anglophone, Francophone, Arabic, Sinic, Persian etc.), or religion (Christian, Islamic, Judaic, Hindu, animist, etc.). As European (and, by the second half of the nineteenth century, American) encounters with the outside world became more intense, they became increasingly mindful about other dimensions of social experience, for example, economy, traditions, social structure, political institutions, which had to be factored in to account for the differences and diversity *within* societies. One manifestation of this mindfulness was the invention of the category of 'nation' emphasizing on the centrality of human agency in historical development. Yet occasionally human agency proved an insufficient explanation of congruent behaviour by different 'peoples' within a broader geographical setting; accordingly the category of 'region' was devised to account for behavioural congruency in a particular geographical setting.

Technically, region as a concept pertains to geography, denoting an 'unspecified' expanse of territory, comprising one physical feature or a particular combination of such features and usually considered to be a part of a bigger whole, viz., foothill region, coastal region of a peninsula, peninsular region of a subcontinent, subcontinental region of a continent, and so forth. A region thus is defined typically in terms of a feature or a set of features it comprises of, within a bigger unit with which the region shares some but not all features.

In the social sciences, conceptualization of a region most often pivots around one geographical feature or the other—thus, the Mediterranean region, the Caspian region, the Steppes of Central Asia, the Gulf region. However, the category of 'region' in the social sciences involves some additional connotations apart from the primary geographical one. A 'region' is conceived of in terms of a set of congruous patterns of the impact of the geographical incidence on aspects of human behaviour, i.e. how geographical location impacts on the nature of the economy, society, culture, politics, environment, strategic concerns, and evidently in geopolitics. Thus when a social scientist speaks of, say, the Mediterranean region, the concern is not simply with a cluster of social formations situated around the Mediterranean. The central concern is with particularities such formations develop *because of* their geographical location, viz., the patterns of economic behaviour that are formed, the impact such patterns have on the character of societies or polities in region, the impact of societal and political character on the culture and traditions of the land, etc.

As the study of regions from a social science perspective evolved over the past century and a half, many of the original assumptions pertaining to regional influences began to be challenged. The predominant understanding of the nineteenth-century regionalists tended to revolve around the decisive roles played by the variables of ethnicity, culture and language—hence studies of the Balkans used the Slaves (Serbs, Croats and Bosnians) and Turks; the categories of the Near East, Middle East and the Far East emerged around the aggregative variables of Turks and Slaves, Turks and Arabs and Chinese and Japanese, respectively, operating upon the fixed factor of the 'region'. In British India, regionalists of this kind had a field day: confronted with a civilizational unity amidst widely divergent subcultures, imperialist Indologists like Vincent Smith spoke of a 'unity in diversity' to accommodate both the congruence and the incongruence. By the onset of the Cold War era, as the US-led Western powers began to prepare for a contest with the Soviet Union over global domination, it was considered imperative by both sides to understand the component 'regions' of the globe better. Having left the inventory of knowledge of the nineteenth-century regionalists behind them, the twentieth-century students of regions began to refine it further in the light of structuralism. The discipline of 'area studies' that developed as a result of this—first in the USA, then spreading elsewhere—favours a much greater autonomy to the regional dynamics of a society than their nineteenth-century counterparts ever imagined: the role played by the human agency is downplayed to the point where it is believed to be simply an ancillary variable playing upon the logic of regional dynamics, influencing the outcome of such dynamics but seldom determining it.

Further refinement of the study of regions came about towards the end of the Cold War era, and gained momentum in the post-Cold War period with a new round of integration of the component regions of the globe under the rubric of 'globalization'. One aspect of this refinement has to do with the appreciation that no one region is a self-contained entity in totality, and that regions overlap and even subregions could have a logic different from the regional whole. Accordingly, patterns of behaviour of societies/communities are influenced by the dynamics of not necessarily one region but more than one. Hence, Central Asia is influenced by the regional dynamics of not only the former Soviet Union but also the Perso-Islamic world; India is swayed by considerations of not simply its own immediate South Asian neighbourhood but also of the Indian Ocean region, the Gulf region, the ASEAN region, etc. Few society/community/formations are swayed by only one set of regional or subregional considerations, and regional studies cannot afford to be as deterministic as the original dispensation of 'area studies' had assumed they could. Thus, for instance, the Gulf region may be pivoting around its formidable deposits of petroleum resources, but its location within the matrices of the Arab and Indian Ocean worlds has also to be taken into account in identifying the behavioural dynamics of the region.

A second refinement in the approach to understanding the regional dynamics comes with the appreciation that a region is not simply what *it is*, but also what it is *made out to be*. This position raises the query whether the geographical features that are considered central to the study of regions have any significance in themselves unless they impact on human behaviour in a way, and conversely, if a region can simply be 'imagined' into being, identifying some kinds of human behaviour as coinciding within particular geographic perimeters. These queries have gained considerable significance with the breakdown of nation states, which were often made out to be as kinds of hermetically sealed regional units distinct from every other unit. Indeed, strictly speaking, such positions are not located within the ambit of regional studies yet such interrogations of the parameters of regional studies from a post-modernist standpoint are certainly contributing to the enrichment of the discipline itself.

Pooled together in this volume of the Asia Annual, are contributions which broadly engage with the notion of 'regions' in Asia from the standpoint of various disciplines of social sciences. In their choice of regions under discussion, the contributions have tackled Asiatic Russia, Central Asia, West Asia and South Asia, which, interestingly, comprise the very regions that have attracted the greatest attention in the realm of Area Studies since the Cold War. The essays in this volume have approached the question of 'regions' from the standpoints of history, international relations and economics, which bring out the interdisciplinary character of the imagination of any region.

Oleg A. Donskikh's essay on the notion of 'Eurasia' as a region is factored into the larger issue of Russian identity being premised as much on geography as on culture and history. Donskikh seems to argue that Russia's self-image as 'the shield between Asia and Europe' is laden with a geographic dimension which is frequently lost in comparison with the significance attached to the cultural dimension. As he argues, the other self-images that Russia has historically played with—that of the Christian successor of Byzantine rule since the days of Ivan the Terrible, and Pan-Slavism of the nineteenth century—were associated with the cultural aspects that the Russian establishment wanted to highlight for different reasons. The concept of a 'Eurasian' character for the state stemmed from a definite concern with territoriality which emerged as the Tsarist imperial enterprise ranged from the Baltic to the Steppes, from the Black Sea to the Sea of Okhtosk. With a large body of population which was neither Christian nor Slavic, the emphasis on territoriality became so central that the self-image of Russia had to be cast in a regional rather than cultural mould. As the author indicates, despite the fall of the Tsars and their Soviet successors, that 'regional' element remains crucial to Russia's identity in the modern times.

In their historical treatment of the idea of 'Siberia', V.A. Lamin and E.G. Vodichev have chosen to explore the formation of a 'region'/'sub-region' within that Eurasia. They provide an insight into the historico-political dynamics of the process of integration of the legendary 'cold and gloomy lands' into the Russian state since the eighteenth century. The authors show that while Siberia remained an important source of gold for the Russian monarchy from the sixteenth century onwards, it *became* a region only with the visionary expansion and colonization that began under Peter the Great. Siberia, as we know it today, the authors would seem to argue, came into being principally as a result of the demographic engineering begun by Peter and then continued by Catherine the Great, with the intention of harnessing the economic resources of this region. If the foundation of this demographic engineering lay in the penal colonies that were begun in the eighteenth century, they were certainly not the mainstay of this process of colonization. Still more significant is the authors' indication of the 'Siberian response', i.e. the response of the people who had formulated their own identity in terms of the supposedly 'inhospitable' region that they learned to call their home. The regional identity thus devised proved formidable enough for the central authority of the Russian state to be almost perpetually wary of this particular component region.

Susmita Bhattacharya's essay on the Armenians plays with the category of region in an innovative manner. Her treatment of the Armenians as a *trans-regional nation* tries to account for both the territoriality that comes with being associated with a region, and the potential supra-regional dimension that comes with imagining a nation in terms of the culture of its people. Armenia, as she indicates, is more like a people that live in its diaspora—highlighting the fact that more Armenians are settled abroad than in the present-day republic of Armenia. Yet the societal and cultural attributes of the Armenian people have sufficient congruence around the world to be thought of, and identified, as a nation. Bhattacharya identifies one of the principal indicators of such congruence in the attachment that Armenians have had for centuries, and still have, for the region of 'historic' Armenia. Bhattacharya emphasizes the role played by such imagination of Armenia as a region in the making of the Armenian identity, both in the Republic of Armenia and still more in its diaspora.

Sreemati Ganguli's essay on the Caspian and Trans-Caucasian states provides an account of how the conceptualizations of Eurasia as well as sub-regions have changed to turn 'the former Soviet South' into a new hub of activity which is generating an altogether new set of regional dynamics. Located at the crossroads of Asia and Europe and capable of functioning as not only a trade corridor but also one for energy, the former Soviet South is central to the reimagination of Central Asia. The imagery ranges from that of the Silk Road, which connected Europe with Asia as far east as China, to the North-South Corridor, which can potentially reconfigure the Russian commercial world with the Persian cultural world. This goes far beyond the initial prospects of the opening up of the region which the Area Studies think-tanks of the United States had considered, and which is now generating shivers in Washington raising the prospect of turning this whole region into a Chinese hinterland by edging out even Russia. Ganguli's essay concentrates on the factors that have contributed to such a dynamic reinvention of the region in this manner.

Timur Dadabaev's essay on Japanese approaches to the study of the Central Asian region is an interesting addition to the volume as it brings out the manner in which different imperatives lead to different *readings* about a region. Dadabaev begins by showing the approach of various disciplines to the study of Central Asia, and then moves on to hint how all those approaches were conditioned by the location of observers themselves, viz., Turkish approaches to Central Asia pivoted around claiming the Turkic peoples of the region as part of the Turkic world; the Russians claimed the region in the name of Tsarist and Soviet legacies and historical continuity. The Japanese, Dadabaev argues, move with a different premise altogether, in that they have resolved to explore the cultural and economic past of the region, thinking in terms of the Silk Route, presumably with an eye to developing an independent profile in and of the region.

Arpita Basu Roy's essay on a new regional approach to Central and South Asia with Afghanistan as its link-zone underlines the significance of the location of the observer in the imagination of a region. Beginning with the premise that the dominant principle in defining regions and regional boundaries depends on the basis of the 'purpose' for which regions are to be used, the essay revolves around the vision, hypothesis, strategies and initiatives of a South-Central Asia cooperation from the standpoint of the relative benefits and challenges of regional cooperation for both regions. Basu Roy contends that such re-imagination of Central and South Asia as a region pivots around a new idea about regional division and integration whereby Washington means to turn Afghanistan into a link between Central and South Asia which would then function as a US-promoted transportation and energy corridor bypassing countries like Iran.

Priya Singh's essay on Israel opens up an entirely different dimension to the issue of regions. Confining herself to the binary between *Eretz Israel* (Greater Israel) and *Medinat Israel* (the State of Israel) that has dominated the scholarly discourse on what constitutes Israel, Singh explores both the Biblical and the cultural imaginations of Israel and posits such imaginations against the reality of the State of Israel that came into being in the twentieth century. Singh seems to indicate that while both such imaginations of the region have inspired loyalties in Israel, the hardline position favouring Greater Israel is becoming increasingly chimerical, claiming as it does lands which were originally designated to be part of independent Palestine, and which are now home to a highly numerous Palestinian population. This position (represented in Israeli politics by, *inter alia*, the Likud), therefore, is now being challenged by others (such as the Labour Party and even the Kadima) who believe instead in safeguarding the state of Israel *as it exists*, therefore encouraging an imagery of the land different from the Biblical one.

Shantanu Chakrabarti's essay on the SAARC is an advocacy of retaining the institutional links provided by a regional imagery, even if the historical context of such imagination is different. Since its formal establishment as a regional organization in 1985, the SAARC has been trying to fulfil its role as a regional exercise in confidence-building, as well as a facilitator of regional economic cooperation. Chakrabarti admits that even though the SAARC has failed to fulfil either objective satisfactorily, and in the changed context of a globalized world, revitalization of the organization as a viable economic group rests on the prospects of forging closer linkages between the South Asia and the South-East Asian regions. Nevertheless, he contends that this should not lead to the neglect of the South Asian region itself. He suggests that the organization should continue with its task of greater political engagement—one of its original objectives—along with its attempts to emerge as a key facilitator in forging intra-Asian economic networks.

Swarupa Gupta's essay interrogates in a major way the assumed 'territoriality' latent in our idea of 'regions' by looking at the inter-religious connections between Bengal and its contiguous ethnicities. Gupta explores religious interstices between Bengal and the contiguous areas to demonstrate how these forged connections between the construction of a regional (Bengali) selfhood and ideas about contiguous ethnic identities, thereby redefining the very notion of region in late-colonial Bengal. She further highlights how the imperial strategies of segregation—administrative and cartographic divisions, demarcation on the grounds of physical features, and customs and practices—were subtly transmuted in the delineation of an eastern Indian interregional space. By concentrating on how the rhetoric of religious connection impacted inclusions of some contiguous social groups and geographical areas (and sites), Gupta handles the dynamics of micro-region/subregion/region/trans-region connections, and shows how these informed a wider process of rethinking Indian-ness.

Rakhee Bhattacharya's essay on the economy of north-east India interrogates the character of the integration of the 'peripheral' region with the Indian core. Bhattacharya contends that the region's inclusion in British India was neither organic nor well-intentioned, being driven by colonial goals of extraction of resources from the region. Independent India failed to prove itself any better than the colonial order, by perpetuating the status of the region as 'an enclave economy' dependent on the generous handouts of badly targeted subsidies. The region tended to be clubbed into one single unit and set aside virtually as a peculiarity, distinct from what was taken to be the 'mainstream' of Indian economic development. This in turn ensured a deep-seated misgiving in the region about integration with the Indian 'core'. Lately, though, Bhattacharya argues, New Delhi has realized that India's north-east could play a significant role in the process of India's opening-out to South-East Asia under the rubric of the 'Look East Policy'. Bhattacharya cautions, however, that misgivings about the region's internal ethno-political-economic dynamics may inhibit New Delhi's willingness to allow the region to engage with its neighbours: this may force the region to revert to its previous status of an 'enclave economy'. Bhattacharya proffers the argument that ethnicity can coexist with modernity and the north-east can benefit by rediscovering its lost economic linkages with the neighbouring countries, thus facilitating not simply a successful integration of the north-east Indian subregion into the 'core of the Indian state, but also promoting an organic link between the South Asian and South-East Asian regions for the first time since the colonial era.

In a very subtle way, all the contributors seem to agree on one crucial point: the amorphous character of the category of 'region' itself. The contributors, in their own ways, seem to have come round to the position that the process of the conceptualization of an 'area' or a 'region' is strongly rooted in the historical conjuncture when the concept develops. A logical conclusion which could follow from such understanding of the category of 'region' is that there is little or nothing in the features of a 'region' (barring its geography) which is immutable—a 'region' which is today considered and defined in terms of a subcontinent (say South Asia *vis-à-vis* Asia) may be tomorrow conceived in terms of an ocean (in the given example, Indian Ocean). Does this imply a subtle interrogation of the very discipline of Area Studies? Maybe—because social scientists occasionally have an aversion to the idea that *anything* is immutable in human behaviour.

NOTES

1. Governing efficiently does not necessarily mean good governance. It simply means optimum utilization of resources—which may or may not benefit the people who are being governed.
2. The term 'information order' is inspired by C.A. Bayly, which is sometimes more apposite in bringing out the imperial agenda of European powers, as against the Saidian term 'body of knowledge'. Compare C.A. Bayly *Empire and Information: Intelligence Gathering and Social Communication in India, 1780-1870*, Cambridge: Cambridge University Press, 1996; Edward Said, *Orientalism: Western Conception of the Orient*, London: Routledge and Kegan Paul, 1978.

2

Russia as Eurasia: An Attempt at Self-Identification

OLEG A. DONSKIKH

History is unavoidable, as well as geography, and they stand in correlation through culture. When A. Toynbee asks about the boundaries of such an object as 'France', he asks about these boundaries in space and time. The same comes with concepts like 'Russia' or 'India'. For the citizens of these countries these terms bring the memory of their ancestors, pictures of the native land, customs, and perceptions, experienced in their life, including images of relatives and friends, etc. For strangers, these will be the most-known clichés linked with these countries. For the unbiased observer Russia is presented with the appearance of the Russian State with its specific population (predominantly Slavs, Turks and Finno-Ugrians), religion, customs, etc., united under one authority. An essay on the history of any country normally starts with an indication of its geography, then its population, then of the state, which changed its boundaries up to the present, yet keeping the core territory around the capital city or places related to some significant events. Thus the history of Rus' (the ancient name of the state)—Russia—will start with geography—the huge territory embracing several states and tribes united by one Varangian dynasty since the second half of the ninth century. The curious fact is that the state originated before being populated; as M. Rostovtsev has pointed out, the country, which later became known as Rus', was founded by the Scythians as a trade country on the crossroads between Scandinavia and Greece and through the Steppes from China to Europe:

> The Russia of Kiev was at the same time the last link of an ancient historical chain and the first of a new one. Kievan Russia was the immediate successor of the series of commercial states which had replaced one another in the steppes of South Russia from time immemorial, and at the same time the mother of

the subsequent Slavonic Russian states in Western Russia (the Galicia of to-day), on the upper course of the Dnieper (the modern White Russia), and, most important of all, between the upper Volga and the Oka, Great Russia, the *Russia* of modern times.[1]

Thus the population of the state which came into being in the ninth century recognized itself as (1) the successors of the series of previous states, and (2) the ring of the chain linking North and South on the one hand, and East with West on the other. What is most important is that the national consciousness, from the very beginning of the state, surpassed the boundaries of this state.

Thus, we approach the principal point of the discrepancy between state consciousness and popular consciousness. State consciousness (ideology) is strongly linked with the idea of control over the territory with its population and the collection of levy. The state attitude towards other nations is formed through inter-state relations, which, being dependant on the current situation, are much more dynamic than the popular conceptions. The national consciousness, on the other hand, is linked with prejudice, religion, etc., which are quite steady and can be changed only over generations.

These are concepts which provide the native people with an understanding of their place among other people and form their attitude towards the rest of humankind. It is known, for instance, that in antiquity, this attitude predominantly manifested itself in what could be called 'national egoism', which was based on the conviction that the other people were less human and therefore they were barbarians. O. Spengler stated: 'When Plato is talking about humankind he means Greeks in contrast to barbarians. This coincides completely with the anti-historical style of ancient life and thought.'[2] The same can be stated in relation to countries like the USA which position themselves as bearers of the ultimate truth, which should be shared, and the only possible model of democracy that is fit for every national state in the world. In the case of Russian national consciousness, it can be predominantly characterized by its acceptance of the national and ethnic differences, and its reluctance to impose its will on other people. The Russian people understood themselves as a successive link in the chain of kingdoms and the crossroads from North to South and from East to West. It is has to be taken into account that in some cases the concepts embraced by national consciousness are taken by the state and become the tools of political activity. In other cases, national and state consciousness exist independently, parallel to each other.

In the history of Russian national consciousness, there were at least four significant concepts, which appeared in different times and had different influences and consequences. These are: 'Theory Moscow—the Third Rome'[3]; Russia as a part of Western Europe (Westernization); Russia as the collector of Slavs (Pan-Slavic idea); and Russia as Eurasia. All of these concepts formed a national consciousness on quite a different foundation. 'Theory Moscow —the Third Rome' unites Russia as an Orthodox country with an Orthodox population. Russia, understood as Western Europe, rests on the cultural basis. Russia as the leader of Slavs is formed around the idea of ethnic relationship, whereas the idea of Russia as Eurasia puts geography in the forefront. In this chapter it is impossible to outline them in a series, therefore, only the first and the fourth will be discussed in detail with a mention of the other two where needed.

The 'Theory Moscow—the Third Rome' appeared in the second half of the fifteenth century. It had strong religious roots. The very expression *Holy Russia* rose from the depths of popular consciousness along with the doctrine 'Moscow—the Third Rome'. A.V. Kartashev calls this 'word-revealation'[4]. Rus' saw itself as a successive ring in the chain of Christian States. Moreover, in this situation the question arose again of the position of Russia in world history. The idea was that Christianity had been maintained in the Roman Empire and that after the fall of the First Rome, the Second Rome, Constantinople, had become its indisputable successor. Nevertheless, the betrayal of Orthodoxy in Florence in 1439 had deprived the Second Rome of its importance in world history, and the Great Duchy of Moscow remained the only custodian of pure Orthodoxy (note, however, that Russians always understood their faith to be Grecian).

The creation of the idea 'Moscow—the Third Rome' occurred during the reign of Ivan the Third, the Grand Prince of Moscow during 1462–1505. It should be emphasized that the idea of the Third Rome was connected with the fall of Constantinople rather than with the emergence of the Russian state under the supremacy of the Muscovite Grand Prince. Evidence supporting this can be taken from the fact that at least two more cities, which were politically challenging Moscow at that time, pretended to become the 'Third Rome': Tver and Novgorod.[5]

Significantly, the idea of the Third Rome was proclaimed in the most pure and assertive way, not by politicians but by a monk, Filofei of Pskov, who wrote in his letter to the Grand Duke of Moscow, Vassily III, son of Ivan IV: 'All Christian realms will come to an end and will unite into the one single realm of our sovereign, that is into the Russian realm, according to the prophetic books. Both Romes fell, the third endures, and a fourth there will not be.'[6] There are some significant points in this statement: (1) *eschatology*, about which V. Malinin wrote that 'With Filofei a theory appeared of the world calling on Russia to be not the only Orthodox but also the final kingdom, which was to exist up to the end of the universe';[7] (2) *the mission to keep true Christian belief*: Ivan the Terrible told the Jesuit emissary Possevino that 'russians believe not in Greeks but in Christ; we acquired Christian belief at the beginning of the Christian church, when the apostle Andrew, Peter's brother, came to these lands in order to go to Rome. Therefore we in Moscow accepted Christian belief at the same time as you in Italy and since that time have kept it invariable.'[8] Ostrowski indicates that when Filofei refers to 'the Holy Apostolic Church, which is in place of the Roman and Constantinopolitan and which is situated in the divinely protected town of Moscow, the Church of the Dormition of the Most Pure Mother of God', he means to indicate that the Christian realm in the ideal sense has not moved. It cannot move because it is universal and eternal. Only the capital of its secular protector, which is connected with the physical world, has moved within the eternal abstraction called 'the Church'. In short, the Third Rome theory as formulated by Filofei had nothing to do with *translatio imperii*, and had everything to do with establishing what the grand prince's duties were in regard to the church.[9]

This statement is of special importance in the context of the marriage between Ivan the Third and the Byzantine Princess Sophia Palaeologus, and the declaration of the independence of the Russian church from the Patriarch of Constantinople.[10] J. Meyendorff argues that politically this theory 'had little practical application'.[11] He is definitely right: this idea was much more significant spiritually than politically. Moreover, the Muscovite rulers Vassily III and Ivan IV were eager to avoid any reference to this theory or to the rights of the Muscovite state to the Byzantine heritage in their diplomatic activity. Instead, they tried to prove their primordial rights to govern the Russian state and so a theory was created which traced their origin to Augustus through his brother Prus.[12] At the same time, diplomatic correspondence did not mention the rights obtained through the marriage of Ivan III to a Byzantine princess. Dimitri Stremooukhoff sums up the place of the theory 'Moscow—the Third Rome' in the national consciousness of the Muscovites in the sixteenth century: 'It forms the core of the opinions developed by the Muscovites about their fatherland.'[13] The question is, to what extent was the idea of the

Byzantine successor understood by the Russian tsars in relation to their power?

A comparison of the ceremony of the coronation of the Russian tsar with that of the Byzantine emperor shows a very important difference between the attitudes to the position these rulers held in the Christian world. While the Byzantine emperor was presented during this ceremony as the head of all Christians, the Russian monarch was not. The ceremony was amended twice (first during the reign of Ivan IV in the sixteenth century, and then in the second half of the seventeenth century after prayer books were revised by the patriarch Nikon), and in both cases the Moscow tsars were presented exclusively as rulers over the Russian state.[14]

With the conquest of Kazan Khanate in 1552, the theory 'Moscow—the Third Rome' achieved its completion. Indeed, the Greeks betrayed the Orthodox faith at the council of Ferrara-Florence, and soon afterwards themselves were defeated by the infidel Turks; Holy Russia remained truly Orthodox, and for this fidelity, not only escaped subordination to the Tatars but also annexed their lands. (Berdyaev states that with this concept the Russians acquired a messianic vision, which remained unshaken up to the Communist period.[15]) Therefore, rather than object, it should be noted that of even greater significance is the fact that this idea was accepted by the public around the middle of the seventeenth century and survived for centuries thereafter.[16]

When a distinctive philosophical tradition was emerging in Russia in the middle of nineteenth century, it drew upon resources which had been formed by historical forces, particularly those that clustered around the image of 'Holy Rus' and 'Moscow—the Third Rome'. Although from the beginning of the eighteenth century, with its overpowering Westernization, other values came to the fore: some outstanding thinkers of the third quarter of eighteenth century and the first half of the nineteenth century turned to the values of the Muscovite period in order to find the essentials of Russian national consciousness. Their thoughts and attitudes became crucial to the process of the formation of the emerging philosophical tradition.

Probably the only political outcome of this theory was the striving for Constantinople (Istanbul). Yet this striving was also a continuation of the Russo-Turkish Wars, which were persistently taking place from the sixteenth century up to First World War. The ideological constituent of these wars included the idea of liberation of Orthodox Christians, but in the second half of the nineteenth century, the idea of Pan-Slavic unity under the protection of the Russian Empire was more powerful, especially during the Russo-Turkish War of 1877–8. Curiously though, as soon as the idea of Pan-Slavism became a part of actual politics, allies of Russia in its confrontation with Turkey played, at some stages, an even more important part. For instance, the Prince of Montenegro regarded France as more significant than Russia when the appearance of Russian and French ships in the Mediterranean Sea stopped the Turkish revenge in 1860. This was extremely painful for the Russian consciousness,[17] namely, because of the clash between the ideological and political aspects of the matter.

The concept of Pan-Slavism was formed at the end of the eighteenth century as a reaction against robust Westernization, which, in its turn, arose at the beginning of the eighteenth century in the reign of Peter the Great against the traditional Russian ideology of the Moscow state. That is why these concepts were intimately linked to the history of Russian national consciousness.

The Russian elite experienced the strong influence of Western European culture from the middle of the seventeenth century.[18] A village of German merchants and artisans was founded in Moscow at that time with their own Protestant churches. However, strong opposition against this egalitarian concept arose during the reign of Peter the Great, who openly and vigorously began to transform all spheres of Russian life under the aegis of Westernization. During these reforms even the Moscow Patriarchate lost its head, the Patriarch. For two centuries he was replaced by the Holy Synod which was ruled by the tsar's representative. Thus a lot of things that were regarded as belonging to Western European culture were seen by a majority of the population as bizarre, strange and harmful. Due to this it was the upper layer of society who adopted the idea of Westernization predominantly.

In its turn, the idea of Pan-Slavic unity, from the very beginning, was understood as messianic (partly taking this spirit from the theory Moscow—the Third Rome): the mission was to bring fresh air to the rotten West and to the whole world. One of the most significant enthusiasts of this concept, A. Khomyakov, in one of his poems declared that Russia should present the world with 'the sacrament of liberty and the shine of belief'. However, as Russia was too far from the proclaimed ideal, it had to strive towards it by itself, to become pure and venerable. Yet an anti-Western mood, which was also an important constituent of this concept, came to the fore, and in the course of time, by the end of the nineteenth century, it was undermined from inside by such ideologists as N. Danilevsky and some others. In his famous book, *Russia and Europe*, Danilevsky presented the mission of Russia as to oppose Western European influence. He pictured the Slavic activity primarily in political terms and featured their cultural mission as secondary. The founders of the Slavophil concept did not take the role of the state as something quite significant. On the contrary, Danilevsky regarded its role as crucial. Thus he and his supporters undermined the very core of this concept, and it did not become the ideology of the whole nation. Yet some remnants towards this concept should be traced in Russia's position in relation to the newly proclaimed Kosovo state, when Russia at all levels including UN has been resisting the great pressure of USA and some European countries over Serbia; and, in addition, proposed the project, the so-called 'Southern Stream' which would direct gas pipeline to Western Europe through Serbia.

In relation to these three concepts, it can be observed that (1) as soon as they were impending beyond the ideological sphere and becoming the tool of political activity, they immediately lost their attractiveness and became less convincing for the national consciousness, and that is why the theory Moscow—the Third Rome was not undermined in the course of history; (2) it was also evident that in the course of time these concepts, though linked with one aspect of Russia's life, were embracing, to some extent, all four aspects which have to be touched by the national consciousness—geography, religion, ethnicity, culture. Obviously all of them also related to history, though in different ways. Thus, the theory Moscow—the Third Rome, starting from religion (transition of historical centres of true belief—here history is unavoidably included) linked it with geography (territory of Moscow state), then with ethnicity (old believers thought that the Russians were keeping orthodoxy more truthfully than the Greeks), and then with culture (as opposed to Western European culture). Due to the extension of this theory, Russian national consciousness was imbued with such features as eschatology and messianic inclination. It is interesting to see the process of expanding the concept over its expected boundaries. For instance, Danilevsky in his understanding of Pan-Slavism, included Greeks and Hungarians, the former because they were Orthodox and the later due to the fact that the Slavs surrounded them.

With these considerations one can approach Eurasianism. Eurasianism is a political–social direction of thought which acquired a complete conception around the beginning of the twentieth century. It appeared in Russia during an era of terrible political shocks, but it could be easily argued that its roots date back to the beginning and middle of the nineteenth century, when the basis of Russian religious philosophy was under formation, and Great Russian authors echoed across the globe. In other words, Eurasianism is bound greatly with Russian culture of that period, when that culture reached a worldwide scale.

Eurasianism is a continuation of those questions asked by Russian Slavophils—N. Danilevsky did not become the author of the world's first version of the theory of local culture (elaborated later by such authors as O. Spengler and A. Toynbee) by accident.[19] When a question arose about Russia's role as a shield between Europe and Asia, albeit a one-sided shield, protecting Europe from Asia, it was followed by a deeper question concerning the ratio of civilizations in general and Russia's place among them in particular. Thus, the concept of Eurasianism happened to be founded in geography. Yet at the same time, this concept from the very beginning was linked with the idea of the specific qualities of the Slavic people, plus the eschatological and messianic feeling brought into the national consciousness by the theory Moscow—the Third Rome.[20]

A definite date from which we can count the Eurasian movement is the publication of *Exodus to the East: Premonitions and Performances; Affirmation of Eurasianists*, which made its appearance in Sofia (Bulgaria) in 1921. It included the works of several wonderful authors. The leader of the group was the economist P.N. Savitsky. Later, in *Evraziisky Vremennik*, in his publication *Eurasium*, he points out the goals of the movement:

> Eurasians are the representatives of a new beginning in life and thought; it is a group working for the new attitude to the root questions, which define life . . . Russia takes up a major part of 'Eurasian' territory. The fact that it doesn't so much lie in-between two continents, but is almost a continent itself, doesn't only have geographical value.[21]

Russian culture absorbed aspects of Southern (Byzantium), Eastern (Steppe) and Western (West European) cultures. And further, 'Eurasianists stand out as *the perceivers of Russian cultural peculiarity*.'

This is a direction of thought not in separate countries or economical centres, but in civilizations as a whole. Eurasianism ceased to be a single politically ideological movement near the end of the 'thirties'. However, these ideas still come up in various forms when Russia is in a situation of choice.

It must be kept in mind that there is no particular or distinct understanding of Eurasianism in the realm of ideology or political doctrine. At the same time, there are quite a few definite sets of topics which are normally discussed by Eurasianists in some particular aspect. This observation is also important because it demonstrates the expansion of the concept based upon a single factor:

1. There is no universal culture and, accordingly, there is no universal progressive movement. Eurasianism forced us to change our questioning of the relationship between East and West, and North and South. It was not by chance that at that time (after First World War) in Europe, a conception of local cultures was formed, the founders of which O. Spengler and A. Toynbee as mentioned earlier) observed human history not as a line but as a historical sum of several existing civilizations, when each separate civilization creates its own cultural world and that world evolves in accordance with its own laws. This conception directly contradicts the conception of lineage progress, where all countries must not only follow the same paths during the course of their evolvement, but are also placed onto a single line; moreover, there are leading countries which must be followed by the rest, and there are countries which must be 'pulled up' to the level of the developed countries. In the report of the Constitutive Congress of Social and Political Movement 'Eurasia' 21 April 2001, one of the most well-known modern Eurasianists, A. Dugin, stated:

   > The main principle of Eurasian philosophy is its 'Flowering complexity'. Never in the history of our country have we had a multi-ethnical government. . . . Russians are not an ethnic or racial generality, having monopoly statehood. We exist as a whole because of the participation of many peoples in our course of building a state, including a powerful Turkish factor. Specifically, this approach underlies the philosophy of Eurasianism.[22]

2. Considering the fact that the idea of universal culture (civilization) is denied by Eurasianism, a geopolitical understanding of the centre and periphery is denied too. Naturally, every significant self-sustained culture-civilization becomes the centre; therefore, the ecumene presents itself as the multi-polar whole and not the mono-polar one. For example, P.M. Bitsilli, one of the leaders of the movement discussing the main cultural centres of the old world, stated, 'The imaginative creative role in the Old World was always played by outlying seaside countries—Europe, India, Iran, and China.'[23]
3. Eurasians who lived under specific geographical conditions placed the question of the dependence between landscape and history in a different light. It can be said that from them begins a sequential direction of thought similar to globalism, when any civilization within its borders is viewed as an organic part of

ecumene. The Enlighteners of the eighteenth century loved to discuss the dependence between geographical conditions and the nature of people, but, in addition to these traditional discussions, Eurasians drew out the problems of interaction and stratification of different cultural-geographic territories. 'Considering that to the terms "Europe" and "Asia" we add a certain cultural-historical definition . . . the terms "Eurasia" obtains a meaning in the form of a tense cultural–historic characteristic.'[24]

4. Eurasians presented the idea of anti-scientism in the form of a criticism of positive economics, the laws of which can be formulated. Eurasians also believe that the religious-ideological part of culture is primary, considering that it places goals for economics. The subordination of economy to religious and moral principles in ancient times (and, in part, in the West-Christian civilization up to the new era) changed to militant economics in the nineteenth century. Marxism in its classical variant is a display of this tendency, specific to Western European thinking: 'Eurasians openly declare the primate of culture over politics. They understand that the Russian question is a culturally spiritual, and not a political one.'[25] It is interesting that, for example, the Islamic, Chinese or Orthodox-Russian civilizations do not assume economic determinism. Other than that, individualism is characteristic to Western European civilization, showing itself in liberal ideology, placing the interests of individuals above the interests of the society. It is expressed also in the ideology of political correctness, levelling the ideology of all social groups, no matter what their historical–cultural contents. There is a firm grasp of traditional cultural values. If one talks about Russian civilization as the centre of Eurasia, these values are mainly Orthodox.
5. Eurasianism presumes that the pivot of cultural generality is the religious–ethical part, constituting the most significant factor of unity. Orthodoxy is such a pivot. It is that Eastern element, to which Eurasian culture must return in order to not be crushed by the West. In this way Eurasianism contradicts man-creator against man-consumer. N.N. Alexeev most clearly portrayed this point:

> Great attention must be devoted to Dostoevsky's thought about the fact that modern Western socialism as the idea of the ultimate atheistic organization of earthly life is genetically linked with the Catholic doctrine of world theocracy. Contrary to this some indistinct striving towards otherworld characterizes the basic spiritual Weltanschauung of the East! Let us at least remember the akosmism of Chinese and Indian philosophy, the teachings about the extreme transcendence of the deity of the eastern Gnostics, western apathy to earth's construction, and the neglect to any economism and technology.

> There is no argument, that eastern orthodoxy is much more inverted to the beyond, than western Catholicism. Because of that we have no idea of earth theocracy, although we were alien to the simultaneous, purely suspended idealism.[26]

But orthodoxy must coexist, as it did historically, with alien religions. In the formulation of Eurasian goals, it says, 'It is inevitable that governmental power related benevolently and coexisted with each faith, worshipped by the peoples of Russia–Eurasia, understanding that only faith can serve as a basis for social relations, infused by the spirit of love and a steady amount of human dignity.'[27]

It is necessary to say that the ideological movement of the Eurasianists was not able to produce anything significant in the sense of an actual political movement, and disappeared by the end of the 1930s. This was primarily due to the strong Marxist ideology that characterized Soviet power. Moreover, the leaders of Eurasianism accepted Marxism on the grounds that the Bolsheviks had started to gather together the lands that had belonged to the Russian Empire, demonstrating will, and striving to spread Marxist ideas all over Eurasia and further.

Nevertheless, the cycle of ideas, which had been designed and elaborated upon by the Eurasianists, is much more important than this movement itself. Many political ideologists turned to Eurasianism, some of them taking only particular ideas, others trying to formulate their doctrines, taking into account the wide Eurasian basis. But if Eurasianists themselves differed in some significant points, the recently formed political doctrines are even more different. Eurasianism became the first manifestation of globalistic thinking. It forced political thinkers to take ecumene in its totality instead of discussing actual centres of force. Some of the Eurasian topics became the basis for different political doctrines.

The unity between different interpretations of Eurasianism can be observed only by recognizing that history is not linear and that it is impossible to build a mono-polar world. Prof. I.V. Orlova, Head of the Department of Comparative Research, Institute of Social and Political Research of the Russian Academy of Sciences, formulates this in the following words:

> We think that the most important point in Eurasianism (in addition to the idea of the social, and historical, and cultural, and ethnic unity of Eurasia) is the methodological demonstration of polycentrism and of multi-linear way of social and historical process, the idea of parallel existence and the development of different civilisations, which have their own logic of development, their cultural aim, their own values, goals, and priorities.[28]

The most significant discrepancy in its turn can be found in the attitude towards Orthodoxy. Many contemporary political ideologists cannot accept the idea that Orthodoxy forms the core of Eurasianism. Professor Orlova, listing the main points of Eurasianism, does not refer to Orthodoxy. She names five statements of Eurasianism in the following succession: (1) multi-linear way of historical development; (2) existence of Eurasian civilization; (3) confirmation of the liability to different forms of integration; (4) recognition of independent development as the only perspective for Eurasia, which would be based on its own ideological tradition and modernization without westernization; and (5) synthesis of the national identity of each Eurasian people with the Eurasian identity.[29]

In his turn, the political analyst N. Spassky, when speaking about the Eurasian approach to concrete political actions, names Orthodoxy as one of the significant advantages of Russia:

> We have advantages. This is our mighty state tradition, our great culture, our universally recognised status of the centre of one of world religions (as Orthodoxy at bottom is a world religion), our unique human potential, our results in fundamental sciences, our rich natural resources, our geographical location, our key role in world energetics, and most importantly, our historically developed consolidating mission in the immense Eurasian space.[30]

I think that in this case Spassky's position is more convincing because the single confirmation of the necessity of a multipolar world is not persuasive if, for instance, we would count the American model of the democratic state as the only accepted basis for outer and inner state politics (even in relation exclusively to the progress in economy). The truth is that one of the dominant points of Orthodoxy is the so-called 'sobornost'—collectivism—which does not suppress personality, but vice versa, counts its specifics as a significant property of the whole group. Due to this, the dichotomy of individualism–socialism can be resolved quite harmonically. That is why, not incidentally, Prof. Orlova is adding to her understanding of Eurasianism by the important statement about the synthesis of the West and East.

N. Spassky presents the following Eurasian perspective for the Russian state:

> Russia can survive, strengthen itself, and succeed as a state only if it would be able to actualize its integrative role in relation to the nearby Eurasian territories, if it would become the centre of attraction for all Slavic people and all Orthodox people, and, at last, if it would be needed in its historical mission of the bridge between West and East. But we can well become a real force in the world if we would be able to regulate the balances between USA, China, India, European

Union, Islamic world, helping to avoid wars and through this strengthening our own influence.[31]

The unavoidable 'for Russia movement' from a pro-Western orientation towards a wider world perspective is traced by David Kerr.[32]

The problem is and this was stated earlier, that as soon as any ideological concept in Russia comes too close to politics, it loses its attractiveness and power to convince. The same can easily happen with Eurasianism. It is one thing to oppose the idea of a one-polar world, and quite another to build a multipolar one. From the point of view of Eurasianists, only the second option can be the goal for political actions, yet the concept of Eurasian unity itself should be estranged from concrete deeds; it should stand beyond. The adherence towards multipolar world is not even undermined by the fact that historically Eurasia has been united by one force, by the Steppe, which has been at the same time dangerous for agricultural centres and states, yet attractive for population by the possibility to escape the pressure of the same State. (The cossacks, peasants, who has escaped from their landlords and has formed the buffer states near the borders, provide the most significant example.) The former Steppe, a chain of predominantly Turkish republics,[33] formed the southern regions of the territory of the Soviet Union. The present situation is dramatically different: independent Turkish states form an almost uninterrupted chain throughout Eurasia. This geographical advantage is used to build pipelines, which go in a roundabout way, avoiding Russian territory, but not for ideological reasons. Seemingly the triangle of Russia, China and India will play a much more significant political role in the future. As Sheel K. Asopa indicates, the three powers are opposed to international terrorism and view religious extremism as a threat to their territorial integrity.[34]

It is possible to argue against this position; however, it is true that there is no other way for Russia but to search for its identity and through this identity to acquire its own specific position in the world community. In this search for Russian identity, Eurasianism can play an important and positive role.

NOTES

1. M. Rostovtzeff, *Iranians & Greeks in South Russia*, New York: Oxford University Press, 1922, rpt. 1966, p. 220.
2. O. Spengler, *Decline of Europe*, Novosibirsk: Nauka, 1993, p. 58.
3. In this case the word 'theory' is just tribute to the tradition.
4. A.V. Kartashev, *The Reconstruction of Holy Rus*, Paris: YMCA Press, 1956, p. 29.

5. See D. Likhachev, *National Self-Consciousness of Ancient Rus*, Moscow-Leningrad: AN SSSR Publishing House, 1945, p. 99, also pp. 82–94.
6. Quote from, John Meyendorff, 'Was There Ever a "Third Rome"? Remarks on the Alexeev Byzantine Legacy in Russia', *The Byzantine Tradition after the Fall of Constantinople*, Charlottesville & London: University Press of Virginia, 1991, p. 49.
7. V. Malinin, *Elder of Eliazarov Monastery Filofei* . . . Kiev: Printing Works of Kievopecherskaya Lavra, 1901, p. 616.
8. Quote from D. Likhachev, *National Self-Consciousness* . . . , p. 100.
9. D. Ostrowski, *Muscovy and the Mongols: Cross-Cultural Influences on the Steppe Frontier, 1304-1589*, Cambridge: Cambridge University Press, 1998, p. 230.
10. See also Paul Miliukov, *Outlines of Russian Culture*, Philadelphia: University of Pennsylvania Press, 1948, p. 18.
11. Meyendorff, 'Was There Ever . . .', p. 47.
12. See, for instance, Likhachev, *Natsional'noye samosoznaniye*, pp. 103–4.
13. Dimitri Stremooukhoff, 'Moscow the Third Rome: Sources of the Doctrine', *The Structure of Russian History, Interpretive Essays*, New York: Random House, 1970, p. 120.
14. V. Savva, *Muscovite Tsars and Byzantine Basileuses: On the Problem of Byzantine Influence on the Formation of Muscovite Tsars' Idea of Power*, Khar'kov, 1901, p. 157.
15. N.A. Berdyayev, *Sources and Meaning of the Russian Communism*, Moscow: Nauka, 1990, p. 9.
16. S. Zen'kovskii, 'Russian Old Belief: Spiritual Movements of the Seventeenth Century', *Forum Slavicum*. Band 21. München: Wilhelm Fink Verlag, 1970, p. 39.
17. M.N. Pokrovsky, 'The Eastern Question', *History of Russia in XIX Century*, vol. 6, Sankt-Petersburg: Br. Granat Publishing House, 1913, pp. 3-4.
18. I am not taking into account that city-state of Novgorod, the rival of Moscow was the part of Hansa, famous league of merchants of various free cities of Baltic region, which existed up to the seventeenth century.
19. Some authors see Eurasianism as direct continuation of Slavophils' doctrine —'Yet, despite their seemingly different approaches, Eurasianism in fact was a modification of the Slavophiles' belief that Russia had a unique cultural heritage.' —Dmitry Shlapentokh, 'A Problem in Self-identity: Russian Intellectual Thought in the Context of the French Revolution', *Journal of European Studies*, XXVI, 1996, p. 61.
20. The complex of these ideas was manifested in the famous poem *Scythes* by A. Block.
21. P.N. Savitsky, 'Eurasianism', *Russia between Europe and Asia: Eurasian Temptation*, Moscow: Nauka, 1993, pp. 100, 102.
22. A. Dugin, 'Eurasianism: From Philosophy to Politics.' Paper delivered at constitutive congress of social and political movement 'Eurasia', 2001. See http://evrazia.org/modules.php?name = News&file = article&sid = 734
23. P.M. Bitsilli, '"East" "West" in the History of Old World', *Russia between Europe and Asia: Eurasian Temptation*, Moscow: Nauka, 1993, p. 31.
24. Savitsky, op. cit., p. 101.
25. N.A. Berdyaev, 'Eurasians', *Russia between Europe and Asia: Eurasian Temptation*, Moscow: Nauka, 1993, p. 292.

26. N.N. Alexeev, 'Spiritual Preconditions of Eurasian Culture', N.N. Alexeev, *Russian People and State*, Moscow, 1998, p. 128.
27. 'Eurasianism (Formulation of 1927)', *Russia between Europe and Asia: Eurasian Temptation*, Moscow: Nauka, 1993, p. 223.
28. I.V. Orlova, 'Outlines of Modern Eurasian Theory', see: www.ispr.ru/Confer/EuroAsia/confer9-1.html.
29. Ibid.
30. N. Spassky, 'Strategy for Russia—2008', *Rossiiskaya Gazeta*, 25–07–2006.
31. Ibid.
32. David Kerr, 'The New Eurasianism: The Rise of Geopolitics in Russia's Foreign Policy', *Europe-Asia Studies*, vol. 47, no. 6, 1995, pp. 977–88.
33. Only Turkey itself was outside the Soviet Union.
34. Sheel K. Asopa, *Struggle for Spheres of Interest in Trans-Caucasia-Central Asia and India's Stakes: An Appraisal of India's Central Asia Policy*, New Delhi: Manak Publications, 2006.

3

The Palette of Siberian Images: Gains and Losses for Russia and Siberia

V.A. LAMIN AND E.G. VODICHEV

FIRST LEGENDS OF AN UNKNOWN COUNTRY

The origin of the term 'Siberia' is not clear and is still disputable. Historians, geographers, linguists, ethnologists, journalists, writers and many other specialists involved in the debate have presented different views. Similarly, representatives of different professional groups have their own facts and arguments which they have put forward for consideration by the academic audience. What is really interesting in the context of the contrasting looks of Siberia is that one of the first European perceptions of the northern regions belonging to Siberia, though not identified as Siberia, is probably dated by the time of Alexander the Great's marches to India which took place around 329–328 BC. At that time the invaders collected contradictory data about the regions stretching to the north of the Syr Darya river. The information collected was not encouraging for the continuation of the military campaign. Captive nomads from Middle Asia said that there were just endless plain lands with inhabitants who could hardly be called truly human due to their lifestyle, ways and habits. The territory was described as, being covered with snow for most of the year, and stretching up to icy sea coasts, which were permanently frozen. The country was dark and cold, and only wild people could survive there due to their ability to sleep for several months, waking only for the short period of summer.[1] The region was described as being very poor and not conducive for the continuation of the invasion. Thus, instead of going north, Alexander the Great decided to turn his troops to the eastern (Indian) ocean.

*The research for this essay was supported by the Russian Foundation for the Humanities (Project 07-01-00420a).

The legends of the cold and gloomy lands behind the borders of Europe have a long history. They were, however, far from the reality. Some information about the severe northern climate and the vastness of the territory of Siberia, as well as about the icy coasts of the northern seas, was correct, but the naïve ethnographic description of their inhabitants, native Siberians and other northern people, was an illustration of the inability of ancient Europeans to accept a way of life radically different from their own. This laid down the basis for the fairy tales of Siberia in Europe and in the Arab world, which existed for hundreds of years. Even fifteen years after Alexander the Great's campaigns Siberia was still represented as a wild, cold and depopulated desert on most of the European and Arab maps.

It is worth mentioning that the Russian medieval tradition was not too far from this. The Russian Nestor's Chronicles dating to the end of the eleventh century describe the people of the Northern Urals in a manner which does not differ too much from the first European descriptions of Siberia. In the meantime, the Novgorod Republic, one of the first states on the territory of modern Russia, was very practical in dealing with these 'uncivilized people'. The major activity developed in the state was commerce. Yet in the eleventh century it was clearly understood by the heads of the Republic that setting up commercial relations with the Yugra people might be profitable, and in 1032 the first expedition headed by some Uleb was sent to the Northern Urals and neighbouring regions of Siberia to investigate the possibilities for such contacts. The expedition can hardly be called successful, as most of the Novgorod people did not come back.[2] According to the data available, they could not avoid the temptation of using military means when contacting their potential commercial partners in Yugra. However, those who survived and returned to Novgorod brought new information about the northern people. They were described as hunters and fishermen, and their remote lands were characterized as rich, first of all because of the vast resources of 'the soft gold'—the precious fur of sables, ermines, squirrels and other taiga wildlife. This information led to new marches of the Novgorod people to the Northern Urals and Siberia in the twelfth and thirteenth centuries. Moreover, in 1264, these territories were claimed as a colony of the Novgorod Republic, and marches supported by the militaries to the northern regions became regular. This practice of robbing the northern lands by Novgorod lasted, with limited success, for about four hundred years and stopped only after Novgorod was defeated by Moscow troops in 1471. From the formal standpoint, after this victory, Moscow inherited all of Novgorod's possessions including the territory of Yugra, which, in fact, had never belonged to the Republic.

These pseudo-commercial and *dc facto* military campaigns had a devastating effect on the inhabitants of the peripheral territories of Siberia. However, they had important consequences for the Siberian people as they were changing European perceptions of Siberia. Before the Novgorod expeditions to these lands, they were seen as a region of gloom, cold and was viewed with fear. After the expeditions between the eleventh and fourteenth centuries, Siberia emerged as a country of immeasurable wealth. This was the new Siberian image of long-lasting character that determined the destiny of the region for at least three centuries. The role of Siberia as a reservoir of fur, which was the equivalent of gold (which Russia did not possess at this time), resulted in the incorporation of this territory into the structure of the Russian state.

However, for some time the priorities of the state were different. Up to the end of the sixteenth-century Moscow's foreign policy was driven by other factors. They included making the regime internally stable, protecting the country from the aggressive enemies in the south, and paving the way to Western Europe through the Baltic Sea. The interest in Siberia not as a country of gloom but as a country of wealth re-emerged at the end of the sixteenth century, and its practical implementation was connected with the Cossack Yermak Timofeevich. It should be underlined that the natural incorporation of Siberia into the scope of the Russian influence started long before its official 'conquest'. At this time the Russian state's neutral attitude to Siberia Russian interests were supported by the spontaneous migration of peasants and commercial people to the eastern and northern outskirts of the country, which were never taken into consideration by the Czar of Moscow.

A TREASURY HOUSE OF THE SOFT GOLD

For two hundred years after 'the conquest' of Siberia by Yermak at the end of the sixteenth century, the region's basic role was as the main source of currency for the Russian treasury house. In the beginning of this period, Russia did not possess any deposits of precious metals, and Russian coins were produced by re-minting them from the West European money received through trading Siberian fur on the European markets. The increasing trajectory of the fur supply reached its zenith by the end of the seventeenth century. At this time incomes received from trading with Siberian fur on the international markets covered some 25–30 per cent of all costs in the budget of the Russian state. At the beginning of the eighteenth century the availability of fur started declining. The immediate reaction of the state was to increase the pressure on the aboriginal population of Siberia through the natural taxation system (the so-called *yasak*), and to construct new obstacles for the internal fur trade by strengthening customs regulations. Simultaneously, attempts were undertaken to broaden the territory of the *yasak* system to increase the gross output of the fur supply. However, this did not help too much as at the same time the demand for Siberian fur had started decreasing in the European markets. The European industry was turning more and more towards the more pragmatic cloth and fur was becoming a kind of 'impractical luxury'.

By the end of Catherine the Great's reign (in the second half of the eighteenth century), the period of Siberian's glory as an inaccessible depository of the 'soft gold' had mostly declined. Siberian fur stopped being the major or even an important source of income for the state budget. In 1752 the customs system between Siberia and Russia, previously set by Ivan the Terrible to keep the state monopoly on the export of fur, was liquidated. Concomittantly, by the end of the century the *yasak* taxation system for the aboriginal population was also substituted by its money equivalent.

Substantial changes determining Siberia's future role occurred during the reign of Peter the Great, at the beginning of the eighteenth century. He focused on establishing the Russian monetary system based on local sources of gold and silver on the one hand, and fast development of metallurgy based on local iron deposits, and broadening the structure of export on the other. In the meantime, he made some efforts to develop trade relations with China. Wide activity started across the territory of the country oriented towards investigating local deposits of precious metals, which covered the Urals and the whole eastern part of the state. New manufactures and metallurgy plants appeared in different regions of Russia. Real successes were gained in opening up deposits of metals in Siberia, specifically in the Altai region and near lake Baikal.

However, the first period of industrial prosperity was short-lived. In the 1740s gold deposits were found in the Urals which negatively impacted the Altai and Baikal gold manufactures because the discovered deposits of the monetary metals in these regions were limited and the industry quickly started shrinking. The same processes touched upon Siberian iron manufacturing. The Urals' industry became the economic leader of the country and increased dynamically in terms of volume of production. At the same time, Siberian gold and iron manufacture started declining due to archaic technology, poor investigation of deposits, expensive labour force and lack of support from the state. The quality of Siberian metallurgy products was relatively low and they were too expensive for both internal and international markets. Thus the first generation of Siberian industry was negatively impacted by the developing Urals metallurgy, and this process lasted up to the last quarter of the nineteenth century when the Urals iron metallurgy started to show clear indication of exhaustion.

Siberian industry was sleeping. Old enterprises founded at the beginning of the eighteenth century were hardly managing to survive and no new factories were being constructed. There was some revival of the industrial activity based on local investments only near the town of Kyakhta where international trade with China developed. This industry was oriented on trans-border trade to satisfy the demands of the local population and the neighbours across the Chinese border who were rather primitive. The Siberian tract, which reached Kyakhta at this time, made transport connection with the Urals and central Russia better, also fostering contacts among Siberian cities and towns. However, entrepreneurs from the centre of the country still did not demonstrate any interest in investing in the development of Siberian industry and infrastructure. This situation created a vision of Siberia as a 'bear which is sitting tied to Russia at the time when Russia does not need it at all'.[3]

SIBERIA—A NICHE FOR DEMOGRAPHIC EXPERIMENTS

The main direction of the Siberian development was set by Peter the Great. It was aimed at investigating natural resources and the construction of the mining industry and plants. Such a policy required a substantial labour force, which Siberia never had too much of. In the meantime, the emperor's policy towards the eastern regions was contradictory in terms of the demographic issue. He withdrew a substantial part of the active population from Siberia and sent it to St. Petersburg, which was under construction in the first quarter of the eighteenth century. This labour force was mostly engaged in the construction of dockyards, canals, vessels and the city itself, and was also used for setting up the modern army and navy.

Catherine the Great positioned herself as a follower of Peter the Great. She realized the necessity of compensating the negative demographic changes in the Siberian population connected with the construction of the western façade of the empire. However, the means and instruments used were rather specific. She was the first to extensively use methods of forced colonization of the region by sending there both prosecuted criminals and peasantry. A special decree of the emperor was released, and for a thousand state peasants (a feudal strata of peasants personally dependent on the state), Siberia became a place of involuntary settlement. They were deported to Siberia without any other reasons than the need for manpower in the newly established factories of the mining industry belonging to the state. In addition to the peasantry, the contingents of workers were supplemented by prisoners sentenced to hard labour, sometimes in lieu of capital punishment.

More and more people were being sent to Siberia into exile in the eighteenth and nineteenth centuries. Typically these were people who did not demonstrate much loyalty to the empire. They were a mixture of representatives of different ethnos and nationalities, the majority being of Russians, Ukrainians and Byelorussians. In the nineteenth century a lot of the Polish people who had participated in the Polish insurrections, as well as people from the Baltic areas, accompanied those who were sent into exile from the heartland of Russia. As a result the lack of loyalty to the state that was demonstrated by these newcomers to Siberia was supplemented by their critical attitude towards the Orthodox Church because many of these new settlers were not Orthodox.

All those who were sent to Siberia for hard labour or into exile were supposed to be used for developing Siberian industries and agriculture for the benefit of the state. However, as reported by the officials, the new Siberians did not have much enthusiasm for the task. For example, in 1765, Siberian governor, D.V. Chicherin, reported to the Senate that involuntary settlement in Siberia was infected by the disease of 'laziness' and had not brought any fruits to the state until then. Low engagement and very poor results diminished the enthusiasm for sending people to Siberia to work on the state enterprises. For example, in 1799, the Senate released a decree ordering that about ten thousand people be sent to the Baikal region in order to increase the output of the factories trading with the neighbouring territories of China. In fact, the total number of those who were sent to the region and started working did not exceed six hundred.[4]

There were a number of reasons explaining the failure of involuntary settlement to Siberia. They are diverse in their character. However, what is worth mentioning in the context of this essay is that the negative image of Siberia dominating the country played an important role. For many people Siberia was still 'a country of gloom and cold'. In addition, by the beginning of the nineteenth century in public opinion Siberia became a place where criminals were sent for life. The fact that many of them were sent to Siberia instead of being awarded capital punishment created a vision of Siberia as a region where normal people could hardly survive.

Surprisingly, this image of Siberia was shared not only by the rank and file. It was also shared by the nobles and state administrators who considered Siberia as a huge reservoir for prisoners, as a prison without walls. They could not believe that there were people who might wish to go there voluntarily and of their own will. Historically, such an image of Siberia started to appear in the minds of the nobles by the end of the sixteenth century when the citizens of the city of Uglich who had supported Prince Dmitry (he was murdered as a result of the plot) were sent into exile to the town of Pelym, and a huge bell from the church which tolled when Prince Dmitry was killed 'was punished' by being transferred to the Western Siberia centre Tobolsk. In a way, 'this first prisoner symbolized [the] future destiny of Siberia'.[5]

Russia has never had a deficit of those suspected of lacking loyalty to the regime. As a result the number of people sent into exile in Siberia was growing from year to year. Since they were mostly males, a controversial decision was taken to solve demographic problems. The state police started to depart prostitutes and select imprisoned women to Siberia. This unique method of balancing the two sexes in the east of the country was used until the end of the seventeenth century.

However, despite all these actions, negative for the perception of the region, a new image of Siberia started to appear on the scene. It originated in the minds of the people who tried to escape serfdom and the harsh state pressures constantly experienced in the centre of Russia, and realize their dream of a rich and free life. They dreamed of moving to such peripheral regions where state authority was relatively weak and the territory so huge that there was little chance of their being found and returned to their lords. These people had a specific character and psychological features. They were ready to take a risk and were not afraid of going to 'the country of gloom'. The major difference between these people and the Cossacks headed by Yermak at the end of sixteenth century was that the former were going to Siberia not to conquer aboriginals and nomads but to work on the land for their own benefit. In fact, Siberia became a sort of a filter for such active, risky and capitalist-minded people selecting their best representatives from the Russian feudal system based on serfdom.

The people who escaped and did not return contributed to the newborn image of Siberia as a country of huge lands suitable for agriculture, a country of free people who lived and worked on these lands without any bureaucratic interference, a country which made them rich and happy. Slowly and steadily, over the course of several centuries, this new image began to penetrate the peasants' consciousness. Fairy tales about a country with unlimited lands without landlords started to appear among the peasants by the end of the seventeenth century and spread to the northern territories of Russia close to the Urals. Between the end of the eighteenth and beginning of the nineteenth centuries this picture of Siberia was developed and supported by publications of Russian and foreign journalists, travellers and adventurers who travelled across the Siberian region.

The spontaneous colonization of Siberia, in contrast to the colonization of North America, did not bring a new form of governing. The peasants were more interested in having lands to work on and to escape serfdom, which was the major burden hampering the development of European Russia until its elimination in 1861. Theoretically, there were plans to extend the serfdom system to Siberia. However, fortunately for the region, they were never implemented. The non-existence of serfdom in Siberia became the key and clear marker between European Russia and the eastern outskirts of the empire. This difference was what made Russian peasants conclude that life in Siberia could be much richer and better than in the heartland of Russia.

During the nineteenth century the Siberian economy was steadily developing in the agricultural and industrial sectors, mostly in agricultural products. The development process touched Siberian cities and towns as well as the transport infrastructure. The exploration of gold deposits in the 1840s started to attract investment capital into the mining industry, which required a new labour force and further stimulated colonization. Some newcomers to the region were channelled not into agriculture in the rural areas but into industry, to cities and towns. The involuntary flow of those who were sent into exile to Siberian settlements was still continuing as an instrument of populating of Siberia. In the meantime, free colonization substantially increased and started to dominate the colonization process contributing to the formation of the new entrepreneurial image of the region.

Many experts on Siberia noticed the fact that a peasant from the centre of Russia changed substantially upon his move to the region. He was no longer afraid of the bureaucratic machine and representatives of the administration, had some specific understanding of social and corporate justice and could insist on expressing his opinion. The Russian state, especially its officials in the Siberian region, were becoming more and more suspicious of these features of Siberians which made the traditional instruments of pressure less efficient while dealing with them. The state realized that the Siberian way of 'free thinking' originated in those people who earlier had been sent to Siberia into exile. The share of such people was large, having reached some 10–12 per cent of the Siberian population by the end of the nineteenth century. The first representatives of the state who saw this danger were the Siberian administrators. One by one they started to appeal to the central authorities to stop the inflow of persecuted and sentenced people to the territories they administered on the east of Russia, but this did not help too much.

Another source of potential unrest was found in the Siberian aboriginal population. All the aboriginals were supposed to have been baptized and taken under the ideological and moral supervision of the Orthodox Church. However, this was only theoretical, and the aboriginal population preferred to stay within the frameworks of its traditional beliefs. This demonstrated a passive but stubborn protest against a hostile religion which was logically connected with the state itself. As a result, the demographic profile in Siberia differed from the population in central Russia in many important respects. This contradictory situation stimulated a debate among the Russian elite about the future of Siberia as a part of the empire. The debate crystallized two conflicting and opposing views. According to some theorists, all differences and discrepancies between the region and traditional Russian territory should be levelled as soon as possible. Siberia should be made similar to the rest of the country including the dissemination of serfdom to its territory. Other theorists, comprising intellectuals together with some local administrators, believed that no decisive and offensive actions should be undertaken, as they would stimulate resistance and social unrest. Some experts were sure that there was nothing to talk about as Siberia's fate was already clear, and irrespective of actions to be taken there was no chance of preserving it as a part of the Russian state. They assumed that Siberia's perspective was a replication of the recent history of the North American United States which appeared on the political map of the world as an independent state instead of a former British colony.

There was also an opinion popular among some officials and intellectuals that Russia should not use its limited resources to keep Siberia economically developed. For example, in the middle of the nineteenth century, this system of views was supported by the high-ranking officer of the ministry of the state property, N. Ya. Smirnov, who called against stimulating the growth of the Siberian population. A similar point of view was shared by the famous literary figure, N.B. Gersevanov, who came to the conclusion that Siberia could not give anything to Russia.[6]

The central authorities did not want to believe that the situation was serious and Siberia was becoming a source of social unrest and psychological trouble for the capital. In 1837, Prince Alexander—the future Russian Emperor Alexander II—visited Siberia and travelled across some parts of this extensive region. In his report to his father, Emperor Nikolay I, he made a remark that there was no reason to be troubled because those who lived in Siberia were Russian people devoted to their Czar. He assured the emperor that before his visit 'Siberia was a specific country and now it is Russia'.[7]

Nothing could have been further from the truth. The prince saw what he wanted to see. In the meantime, in 1843, the law on migration, aimed mostly at the state peasants, was adopted by the central authorities. It is necessary to point out that the law was based on the need to resolve the critical shortage of agricultural land in the centre of Russia and not on the need to develop Siberia. It focused exclusively on diminishing the social tensions in the central Russian villages—an acute problem in the rapidly growing rural population lacking free land suitable for cultivation.

As mentioned above, the law on migration touched upon the state peasantry—peasants who were dependant on the state and were considered state property. They were at the disposal of the ministry of state property which administered the migration reform. The reform remained operational for fifteen years. Some 90,000 people migrated to Siberia in this period, mostly to Western Siberia, which meant an annual transfer of 5,000–6,000 peasants. The number of those who migrated within the framework of this migration reform was very limited, as the total population of Siberia (from the Urals to the Pacific Ocean) in the middle of the nineteenth century was equal to about 2.7 million people. There were just three relatively big cities—Irkutsk with a population of some 17,000 people, Tobolsk with more than 15,000 inhabitants, and Omsk, which had some 13,000 people. Obviously the inflow of 90,000 people, who migrated in accordance to the first migration reform could not impact the demographic situation drastically—neither in the cities, nor in the rural areas.

Thus, in the middle of nineteenth century, the image of Siberia was still contradictory. The process of regional development was ongoing but Siberia's resources and economic might were still 'on hold'. The scarce population was the major obstacle in the economic progress of Siberia. The number of those who were looking for a better life and were ready to move to Siberia was substantial. Images of Siberia as a territory of rich and unlimited lands were encouraging these people to move eastward. However, the system of serfdom which kept peasants attached to their landlords' lands and prevented their free exit was the main obstacle. Within the existing legal system the state as such had a direct control over a limited number of peasantry and could not radically impact or change the situation, as the modest results of the implementation of the migration law for state-owned peasants clearly indicated.

Another point was the lack of an integrated vision and a clear strategy in the state and the society about the future of Siberia. Lack of clarity towards Siberia also hindered free migration to the eastern part of the country. The authorities and the political and intellectual elite were not able to project a positive image of Russia as a country whose western and eastern parts were equally important for the state. In a way, the central authorities were afraid of what they had made with Siberia until then and did not know what to do with it in the near future.

SIBERIAN RESPONSE

According to the famous Russian historian V.O. Kluchevskyi, Russian authority 'does not have any limits; it has just threats'.[8] In 1852, the Second Siberian Committee was set up under the umbrella of the central power in order to analyse the current and perspective risks, threats and challenges connected with Siberia as a part of the Russian empire. The establishment of the Committee was inspired by the debates and contradictory views circulating in the society about Siberia's role in the state, the future of Siberia, and need to elaborate new policies and practices connected with the eastern outskirts of the country. The most important issue still was the question whether Siberia would remain a part of the empire or that sooner or later Russia would lose it. Special attention to this issue was given in the spring of 1861 at the special session of the Russian Geographic Society organized by the Second Siberian Committee.

Existing practices concerning the relationship between metropolises and colonies were analysed in this connection. The most impressive examples certainly were the fate of the British colonies in North America, and the most recent case—autonomy for Australia. Most of the experts came to the conclusion that agrarian colonies usually took their independence from metropolises—this scenario was put forward as a universal law of development supported by the historical experience—and Siberia should stay in line with this universal practice. Along this line of reasoning, some of the experts called for a ban of any financial and demographic investments in Siberia: they believed that it did not make sense to do so as Siberia would become independent and appear on the political arena as a competitor to Russia. This was the toughest line taken in the debates. The softer line was also based on the consideration of the future independence of or autonomy for Siberia. However, the supporters of this logic required the continuation of provisional support to Siberia in Russia's state development strategy based on the reasoning that from an economic standpoint, the British Empire had received more gains than losses from the independence of the United States, and the case of Siberia would follow the same logic in the context of Russia.[9]

There were no winners in the debates as the arguments on both sides were based on facts and appeared to be reasonable. However, all of a sudden an unexpected response came from Siberia itself. In May 1865, a leaflet circulating among the students of the Siberian Cadet School, called 'To the Patriots of Siberia', was detected by special services. The contents of the leaflet were based on the assumption that the interests of Siberia would never be in line with the interests of Russia. The unknown author pointed to the special geographic position of Siberia, its specific economic interests and democratic structure of the population, as well as its frontier position which required a peculiar development policy never granted by the Russian state. It concluded that the fate of Siberia should be similar to that of the United States—an independent state based on democratic principles and republican organization of power.

The central authorities were really alarmed. The debates by theorists in the capital of the country did not worry the powers too much. However, the spirit of revolutionary thinking in the territory of Siberia itself seemed much more dangerous to the authorities. Large-scale investigations were organized, which led to the identification of the authors of the leaflet. The immediate threat to the state was exaggerated as no strong and influential organization of plotters was found, and the leaflet was the fruit of the emotions of youngsters dreaming about a democratic Siberian society. The prosecution was organized and became famous as 'A Case for Secession of Siberia from Russia', and a number of people were sentenced to imprisonment. In the meantime, the process of conceptualizing Siberia's fortunes within the Russian state had started taking place, not just in the capital but also within the region itself.[10]

In the light of these events the central authorities began to look at Siberia with doubled attention and concern, trying to identify the first signs of separatism. Siberia got a new image within the metropolis—an image of a colony striving for independence—and has never lost it since that time. The mass exile into Siberia did not lead to an increase in pro-Russian sentiments, but rather polarized the population and radicalized both the 'old timers' and the more creative intellectual section of the population. At the turn of the century, these processes were manifested in an ideology of Siberian provincial consciousness, attributed primarily to Nikolay Yadrintsev and Grigoriy Potanin. Contemporary historians and sociologists were once again in agreement with the proponents of provincial consciousness, seeing such factors as Siberia's insularity and isolation from the rest of the country, the history of tolerance between natives and settlers, and the greater freedom of action and democratic attitudes in the social order, as the starting point in the formation of a Siberian culture.

However, for the first time the situation had gone much further than the identification of socio-cultural differences between the inhabitants of European Russia and Siberia. The formulas posited by the 'provincialists' assumed the characteristics of a socio-political ideology. There was, in the words of A.O. Boronoyev, a Russia-Siberia 'binary pair'[11] and a contradistinction emerged between the whole (Russia) and one of its parts (Siberia). Thus, by the beginning of the twentieth century, Siberia had become a typical example of a region where 'the territory creates a collective consciousness that epitomizes the concept of a "homeland"'.[12]

In general, Siberian 'provincialists' gave more arguments to the central power thinking that Siberia was looking for a chance to declare autonomy or independence. Not just secret police was used as an instrument to suppress the sprouting of the Siberian regionalism. The struggle against the ghost of separatism was carried out with utilization of all possible means and instruments. For some time even the term 'Siberia' was excluded from the official language—a new term 'Asian Russia' was designed to substitute it. Special politics was introduced to dilute Siberian compact settlements consisting of old settlers. They received substantial injections of newcomers to the region. Mass construction of buildings for the Orthodox Church were started to strengthen ideological control over the population. It was done in vain, however, as the Siberian people did not demonstrate any profound religious feelings and concentrated instead on the ethics of entrepreneurship. A high-ranking representative of the Imperial administration, the manager of the Trans-Siberian Railways Committee, A.N. Kulomzin, famously reported after he returned from Siberia in 1896: 'The old-timers do not bother with churches'.[13] Some experts noticed in this connection that the peasants in Siberia in many respects looked more like American farmers than peasants in the centre of Russia.

LAND OF PEACEFUL COLONIZATION

The major event that changed the fate of Russia took place in 1861. It was an agrarian reform which was aimed at the abolishment of serfdom in the country and the introduction of changes in the land property configuration by providing peasants with the right to buy plots of lands from their former landlords. It was good in theory but difficult to implement in a balanced way, especially the second task, as the conditions for purchasing land were tough and impractical. The second half of the nineteenth century was a period of fast growth in the population in Russia. The annual increase of the population was at the level of 1.5 million people, 90 per cent of whom lived in the rural areas where there was a sharp deficit in land for agricultural cultivation. The acute lack of land resulted in social tensions in Russian villages. Even after they had been granted personal freedom after the agrarian reform and abolishment of serfdom in 1861, the peasants were not able to satisfy their desire to purchase agricultural land as it was not available in the required quantity in European Russia. As a result, the process of peasantry marginalization accelerated and the social tensions increased.

Naturally there was a need to decrease the economic tension in the country to prevent social unrest. The solution was found in the chaotic channelling of peasantry migrations to Siberia. The image of Siberia as a paradise with unlimited agricultural lands available for peasants for free circulated across the rural community. There was a spontaneous movement to Siberia from the Euro-Russian countryside, and the flow of migrants increased at the end of the 1860s and beginning of the 1870s. Again, the first reactions of central authorities and the political and economic elite of the country to this process were rather contradictory. Some of them were unhappy with the fact that the peasants preferred to migrate rather than purchase plots of land from the landowners on speculatively high prices. Some others were unhappy that cheap workforce was leaking to the east and their production costs would grow and incomes decrease. Some experts in Siberia also expressed their concern about the fact that excessive colonization of the region might lead to a deficit in agricultural land. In their minds, the availability of such lands in Siberia was limited due to the peculiarities of the climate and the need to maintain good relations with the aboriginal people. However, in principle, Siberians welcomed the migration and colonization process.

A number of calculations were made, and their results confirmed the fact that the natural capacity of Siberia for agricultural populations would remain far below limits for many decades. For example, in the south of Western Siberia the size of the population was estimated at 5–5.5 million people, and it was found reasonable to anticipate an increase in the population by at least twice that number. In Eastern Siberia, from the Yenissey River and to the Pacific Ocean, according to the estimation, lived about 1.2 million people. The density of the population was very low, and it could easily be increased at least eight times. The experts came to the conclusion that seven million people were comfortably settled in the rural areas of Siberia, and at least another 15 million peasants could move there without extending the natural capacities of the region.[14]

In mid-1880s spontaneous migration to Siberia reached a figure of some 80,000 people annually. A special law 'On Free Migration of People from Rural Areas to the State Lands' was released in 1889 which legalized the whole process of migrations. Spontaneous peasantry migration clearly indicated the basic route of the demographic development of the country. In 1891, a State Committee on the Trans-Siberian Railway (which was under construction at this time) made a declaration that peasant migration to Siberia did not bring any risks and threats to the economic standing of Russia. The Committee elaborated some measures focused on regulating spontaneous migrations in order to use migrants as a labour force for the railway construction. However, full legitimatization of the migration process only took place in 1896 when the whole procedure was made easier and more transparent. About 1.4 million people migrated to Siberia in the subsequent ten years. The reform regulating migration to Siberia was named after Prime Minister P.A. Stolypin who managed the reform and who was assassinated some years later. Between 1906 and 1910 more than 2 million people were transferred to Siberia in a well-organized way. After the murder of P.A. Stolypin, the rate of migration decreased but still exceeded 700,000 people between 1911 and 1914.[15] As a result, the rate of growth of the population was higher in Siberia than in other territories of Russia with better climate.

The demographic changes caused rapid economic growth in the region. The southern part of Siberia, close to the Trans-Siberian Railways, was developing quickly as agricultural and industrial territory, and the railways greatly contributed to this process. Between 1910 and 1914, the export of grain from Siberia substantially increased. The share of Siberian butter in Russia's export of this product (an important item of Russian exported goods at the beginning of the twentieth century) was about 88 per cent. Its share of different kinds of meat in the markets of the capital of Russia was equal to 10–12 per cent in 1903–7, and 45–50 per cent in 1908–13.[16]

The country's economic prospects seemed good and the rate of economic growth was high. Siberia contributed much to the overall progress of the Russian Empire. The new image of Siberia presented the region as a territory of rapid economic development. Because of the Trans-Siberian Railways, Siberia came closer to the European Russia. After the railways reached the city of Vladivostok, it took only several days to get to the coast of the Pacific Ocean instead of the several weeks needed before. The authorities directly and indirectly started to exploit and support this image.

However, new challenges appeared on the scene. The agrarian scenario of development was leading Siberia, as well as the rest of the country, to a dead end. The country needed modernization and industrial development. A special commission on colonization and migration analysed the situation around Siberia and came to the conclusion that the authorities should do their best to stimulate economic development in the region by means of industrialization, otherwise the huge mass of population that had earlier migrated to Siberia would transform itself into a kind of explosive which would be extremely dangerous for the region and for the whole of Russia.[17] This call for action, made in September 1917, was too late, but what happened next is another story.

Thus over the course of centuries, the role and significance of Russia in Asia has increased. The Russian Empire expanded to the west and the south, but primarily to the east and north-east: first to the Urals, then to Siberia, which became Russia's internal colony. Territorial expansion into Asia was the result of objective factors. The strategy of creating a continental empire required the borders be moved as far as possible from the central area of the country in order to ensure security. But this led to a historical paradox. In many cases, while Russia was attempting to position itself as a European power, the geopolitical, strategic and economic justification for its place on the world political stage came from the East, from Asia. This was due to the fact that, for all its particular characteristics, beginning in the eighteenth century, Russia attempted to use, albeit in 'prepared' form, European models of socio-economic development. The modernization of the country, which involved increasingly rapid industrial development and the urbanization and bureaucratization of society, required a constantly expanding resource base. The country possessed such resources on a seemingly unlimited scale in the east, in Siberia. Moreover, in contrast to some other newly acquired areas, the eastern regions were not burdened by the traditional forms of Russian economy which hindered the processes of modernization.

The 'eastern vector' in the modernization process at various stages of historical development in Russia was not only predetermined by economic, political, and geopolitical imperatives, but, in contrast to many other strategies, it could actually be implemented. Resources were mined in the east. Various scenarios of socio-economic, demographic, and socio-cultural policies were developed in the east. As a geopolitical and strategic resource and the location of a significant portion of the country's military capacity, for most of the twentieth century the eastern territories had a stabilizing effect on Russia as it pursued its global and international policies.

The experience of the development of the eastern regions and Siberia in particular teaches many lessons which are important both for the current political reality and for the formulation of long-term economic and geopolitical strategies. The main lesson is that the relationship between European Russia and 'Asian Russia'—Siberia—in the past always took the form of a 'home country–colony' dichotomy. The principle of a strictly construed national expediency allowed no significant deviations in favour of a development vector based on the dominant or even adequate consideration of regional expediency; any regionalism was viewed as a potential threat to the foundation of the country and its methods of governance. Such were the laws of the empire.

The empire needed colonies, and the biggest one was Siberia. The empire designed special images of the colony depending on the tasks it had to solve. The images were injected into the Russian society and absorbed by different strata of the population. However, some other images appeared against the will of the central authorities. They circulated among those who lived both in the capitals and in the outskirts of the country, in metropolises and in colonies. The real palette of images of Siberia by the beginning of the twentieth century was not limited by the perceptions elaborated by the state. The images of this huge country inside the country were contradictory, and they contained both gains and losses for Siberia's and Russia's future on the edge of the new epoch. This epoch gave birth to many new images which deserve special attention and a special chapter.

NOTES

1. F. Shakhermaer, *Aleksandar Makedonski,* Moscow: Nauka, 1986, p. 239.
2. I.V. Shcheglov, *Khronologicheskii perechen vazhneishikh dat iz istorii Sibiri,* 1032–1882, Surgut: Severnyi Dom, 1993, p. 16
3. A citation taken from A.V. Remnev and N.G. Suvorova, 'Kolonizatsia Sibiri 18–nachalo 20 vekov: imperio-i natsstroitelstvo na vostochnoi okraine Rossiiskoi Imperii', *Istoriia, antropologiia, kulturologiia. Programmy i izbrannye lektsii. Chast II. Izbrannye lektsii,* Omsk: Omskiy Gosudarstvennyi Universitet, 2004, p. 34.
4. Ibid., pp. 10, 11.
5. A citation of famous Russian historian Petr Slovtsov taken from I.V. Shcheglov, op. cit., p. 47.
6. See Remnev and Suvorova, op. cit., pp. 14, 31.
7. Ibid., p. 31.
8. V.O. Kluchevskii, *Sochineniia v 9 tomakh,* Tom 4, Moscow: Prosveshchenie, 1989, p. 42.
9. N.V. Serebrov (publisher), *Delo ob Otdelenii Sibiri ot Rossii. Sbornik Dokumentov iz Fondov GARF,* Tomsk: Tomskii Gosudarstvennyi Universitet, 2004, p. 11.
10. Ibid., pp. 93–4.
11. A.O. Boronoyev, ' "Sibirstvo" Kak Forma Territorial'noy Identichnosti', *Materialy Gorodskogo Seminara 'Sibir' i Sibirskii Mentalitet,' Saint Petersburg, April 25, 2002,* http: //sibident.narod.ru/text/boronoev.doc
12. Bo Petersson, *National Self-Images and Regional Identities in Russia,* Aldershot: Ashgate, 2001, p. 28.
13. See A.N. Kulomzin, *Vsepoddaneishii Otchet Po Poezdke v Sibir' Dlia Oznakomleniia s Polozheniem Pereselencheskogo Dela,* St. Petersburg, 1896, pp. 123, 124.
14. Shcheglov, op. cit., pp. 423, 424.
15. *Istoriia Sibiri.* T. 3, Leningrad: Nauka, 1968, p. 308.
16. Ibid., pp. 314, 317, 318.
17. Remnev and Suvorova, op. cit., p. 218.

4

Trans-Regional Nation, Nationalism and Identity: A Case Study of Armenians

SUSMITA BHATTACHARYA

ARMENIA: ASIA OR EUROPE

Deep down in history, Armenia has always been a trans-regional nation in transition. The Armenians have made a long journey starting from the prehistoric Armenia of the Haykazuni dynasty, Haykides of 2492/2107–331 BC,[1] to attaining the independent Republic of Armenia in 1991. Because of its strategic location in two continents Armenia has been subjected to invasions by many peoples, including the Assyrians, Greeks, Romans, Parthians, Byzantines, Arabs, Mongols, Persians, Ottoman Turks and Russians. As a consequence, the collective identity of the Armenians today has been formed as a result of the millennia-long evolutionary process that took place in different regions, on various territories, at different ages and stages from historical through modern times.

Today's Armenia (Hayastan) or Republic of Armenia (Hayastani Hanrapetut'yun) is a landlocked, mountainous country between the Black Sea and the Caspian Sea in the South Caucasus, sharing borders with Turkey to the west, Georgia to the north, Azerbaijan to the east and Iran and the Nakhechivan exclave of Azerbaijan to the south. There are different opinions regarding the geographical region the country belongs to. Armenia has been referred to by various sources as an Asian as well as a European nation. For example, the UN classification of world regions[2] places Armenia in West Asia. The *CIA World Factbook*,[3] *National Geographic*[4] and *Encyclopædia Britannica*[5] also place Armenia in Asia. Conversely, numerous sources place Armenia in Europe, such as the BBC,[6] *Oxford Reference Online*,[7]

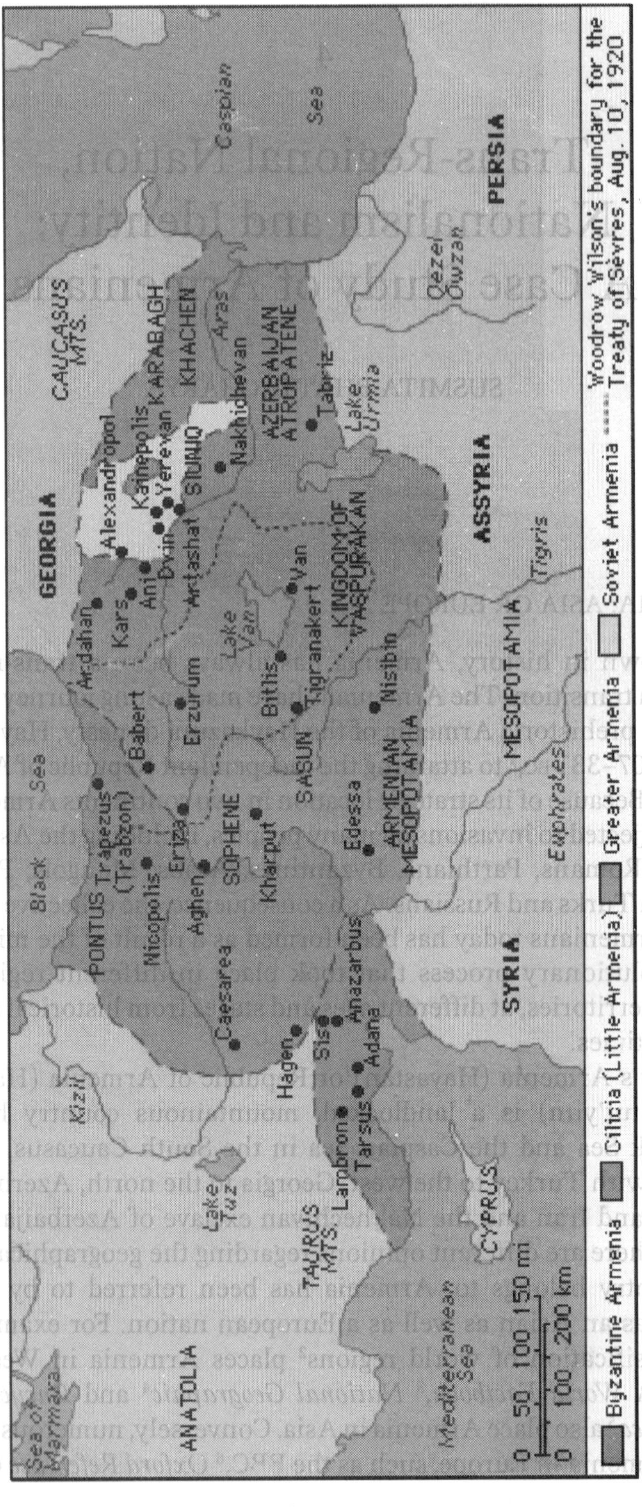

Fig. 4.1: Armenia: Historical Division of Armenia[8]

Merriam-Webster's Collegiate Dictionary[9] (though it also places the historical *Kingdom of Armenia* in Asia), and the *World Atlas*.[10]

The Armenians are quite vocally articulating the boundary between the East and West today. After the post-Soviet turn of events, along with military confrontation with the neighbouring countries, Armenia seems to be getting increasingly disconnected from the 'Caucasus' region. The symbolic remapping of the South Caucasus, shaped by the political expansion of Europe, dilutes the notion of regional belonging and, instead, leads to a polarization of cultural identities between the East and West and Europe and Asia. By reviving the cultural ideal of an 'ancient Christian civilization' in contrast to their neighbours (except for Georgia) who are considered 'Asian and Moslem or nomadic and underdeveloped', the Armenians see themselves as being within Europe.

The Armenian government and its people in general identify themselves as Europeans and part of Europe.[11] Armen Baibourtian, the ex-deputy foreign minister of the Republic of Armenia remarked in a speech: 'Armenia's European aspirations are a manifestation of our strong historical and cultural link to Europe and Europeanness, as well as a national urge to evolve into a free modern society that is able to meet the demands of the new century.'[12] The former Armenian foreign minister, Vardan Oskanian, iterated recently: 'The historical and cultural ties that bind us to Europe and to Europe's neighbors—all of them—are ours to exploit.'[13] On another occasion he said, 'Armenia is in Europe. This is a fact; it's not a response to a question.' Torben Holtze, head of the European Commission's representation in Armenia and Georgia, and ambassador of the European Union with residence in Tbilisi, also stated: 'As a matter of principle, Armenia is a European country.' This debate centring around the question whether Armenia is a European or an Asian country still continues.

A much wider and multidimensional academic discourse, including literatures and debates, has been going on among a large number of Armenian scholars, particularly after the independence of the country, concerning Armenia's place in Asia or Europe, East or West and its Asian or European identification.[14]

ARMENIAN NATIONALISM AND NATIONAL IDENTITY

The Armenian case presents important implications for competing Western theories on the origins of nationalism. It provides powerful evidence of the influence of primordial identity, stemming from ethnicity, language and a sense of shared history.[15] It offers little support for functional or instrumentalist theories, which try to explain nationalism in terms of its utility for state-building or for the advancement of a particular economic or political class.[16] The Armenians form a trans-regional or supra-regional nation, which was subject to suffering, persecution and discrimination at different points of time under alien rules, a fact which played a crucial role in the formation of a sense of unity, oneness or 'Armenianness', and an urge to uphold a strong Armenian identity which is not exclusively bound to a particular territory.

The Armenian national identity has all the traditional components of a European nation:

- a common history dominated by struggle with their Turkish rulers, culminating in the genocide of 1915;
- a shared language and a literary tradition;
- a sense of place, of lands which were historically populated by Armenians; and
- a common religion, the Armenian Apostolic Church.

Besides, a sense and mentality of being victimized has been an important part of Armenian identity for centuries, which intensified after the genocide. Along with the process of learning to adapt to the host lands, the fear of national extinction through assimilation may also have, as suggested by Horowitz and others, been a crucial motivating force generating strong national feelings in the Armenians.[17]

The Armenian Apostolic Church and Christianity have always been important vehicles for the preservation of national identity over the centuries. The intelligentsia, as the bearer of the cultural heritage and the advocate of humanistic values, has time and again emerged as the dominant social force in the nationalist movement, inculcating a strong sense of identity.

MIGRANTS, EXPATRIATES AND IDENTITY

Armenian migrants and expatriates, settled in different regions and corners of the world since time immemorial, have played a crucial role in the formation, strengthening and maintaining of national identity and the national-building process. In the eighteenth and nineteenth centuries, much of the initial learning, research and publications about and by the Armenians, as well as political activism, were done by the expatriate communities in various centres, from the Mekhitarists of Venice and Vienna to the scholars and merchants of Madras and Calcutta.

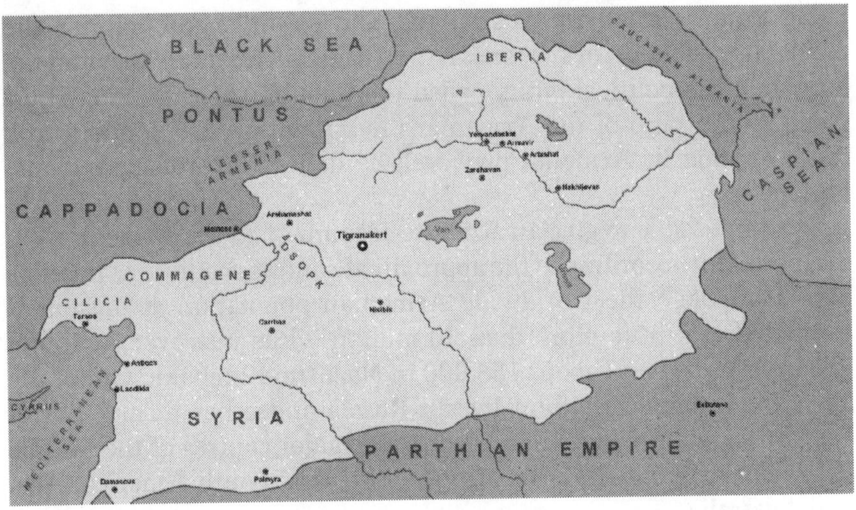

Fig. 4.2: Map of the Armenian Empire under Tigranes the Great 95–66 BC[18]

The Armenians have entered the fourth millennium of their existence as a small fragment of the historical Armenia. But throughout this long period of history, they have enjoyed an independent land of their own, albeit sporadically and for very short spans. The largest in size that it ever was in the long period of its existence was the Armenian Empire under Tigranes the Great from 95 BC to 66 BC stretching from the Caspian to the Mediterranean Seas.

The history of the Armenians is a tragic tale of resistance by sovereign states against stronger neighbours' predatory manoeuvres, and the survival of an ethnic community in the face of suffering and oppression by the alien rulers.[19] As a result, most of the lands regarded as traditional Armenian territory, such as Eastern Anatolia or Nagorno Karabakh, lie beyond the boundaries of today's Republic of Armenia. Present-day Armenia occupies an area of 30,000 sq km in the north-east of the Armenian Highland or Historical Armenia, which included the eastern regions of Turkey and parts of Iran and Syria, and thus retains only less than one-sixth of the territory historically inhabited by the Armenians.

The Armenians are a notable exception, with a larger proportion of the total ethnic community living in the political, cultural and socio-economic regions of the world outside the nation. It is the Armenian–Russians, Armenian–Canadians, Armenian–Argentineans, Armenian–Americans, Armenian–British, Armenian–Germans, Armenian–Kazakhs, Armenian–Lebanese, Armenian–Turkish, Armenian–Iranians, Armenian–Indians, Armenians of

Hong Kong, Armenian–Australians, and so on, who comprise the much larger section of the 'one' nation called 'Armenian', beyond the borders of its political entity called the Republic of Armenia. Thus, going by the ratio of the Armenians living within the Republic and those outside it, Armenia may well be defined as a trans-regional nation.

It is impossible to give an accurate account of all the Armenians in diaspora. But according to the approximate and as accurate as possible data available,[20] the worldwide Armenian population at present is estimated at a little more than 10 million while just over 3 million live in Armenia and about 138,000 in Nagorno-Karabakh. Out of the 10 million, some 3 million live in Russia and other former Soviet Republics, and the rest are settled in the major centres of the Middle East, Western and Eastern Europe, North and South America, Asia and Australia.

Migration and dispersion have been part of the Armenian reality for centuries and each of the progressive relocations from early times opened new chapters in the history of migration and the diaspora.[21] In fact, the migration of the community started when Armenia lost its statehood in 1375, when the Armenian Kingdom of Cilicia fell to the Mamelukes. But a strong sense of national identity among them was formed through an evolutionary process engendered by their experiences in different regions under a number of diverse rulers in different periods of history.

The majority of these trans-regional Armenian communities are Western Armenians, who underwent diverse experiences and processes of evolution. With the flourishing of the trade networks in the tenth century and the consequent economic migrations, the concept of *gaghuth* (colony) and *gaghuthahayutyun* (Armenians of the colonies) was developed. From this period on the migrated people of the community started referring to themselves as living in exile or colonies, and *gaghutahayutiun* was their identity. The Armenian word *spiurk* for diaspora entered into common usage very recently and the difference between *gaghuth* and *spiurk* is a much-discussed topic in the contemporary literature and writings on the diaspora.

The Armenian identity construction process passed through a number of phases. The important periods, which contributed to the evolution, formation and transformation of Armenian nationalism, national identity and national goals are 'Awakening period' and Ease-West divide, the Genocide and post-Genocide period, the Soviet period and the post-independence period.

ZARTHONKH

The conquest by the Ottoman Turks of the western part and the Safavid Persian conquest of the eastern Armenian territories effectively partitioned the Armenians' ancient homeland into Eastern and Western Armenia. A coherent sense of Armenians as a nation with a distinct and distinguished history was spread by patriots, teachers, writers and revolutionaries. Its deep historical foundations took root during the late nineteenth and twentieth centuries, referred to as the period of modern Armenian 'Awakening (*Zarthonkh*)', when Armenian collective identity was metamorphosed from an ethno-religious sense of belonging to a modern nationality.

As mentioned earlier, the embryo of modern Armenian nationalism took shape in two regions and through two parallel trends, namely, Western Armenia under the Ottoman Empire and Eastern Armenia under Persian rule until 1828, when the Yerevan and Karabakh Khanates was annexed by the Russian Empire in 1813 and 1828 respectively. In particular, the Ottoman period was very crucial for the identity construction of the Armenians.

The Western trend based in Constantinople and other centres in Western Europe where the community had settled, and the Eastern trend based mainly in Tiflis (Tbilisi), Tabriz and various centres of the Russian Empire and Eastern Europe, became the catalysts in the intellectual, educational, cultural, religious and political awakening of the Armenians. Each of these two trends had separate origins for their theoretical, ideological and sociological sources, which at first influenced the intellectuals and then subsequently the masses.

The Western component of the awakening evolved around the liberal reform projects influenced by French and Italian thought, constitutionalism and 'Western' nationalism, while Russian and German thought, radicalism and 'Eastern' nationalism influenced the Eastern component.[22] Western Armenian political ideology centred on reform, liberalism and constitutionalism in Constantinople, whereas the Eastern Armenian activists were pursuing revolutionary goals in Tiflis. The religious jurisdictions were administratively divided between the Ottoman and Russian empires as well. All these factors had profound effects on the parallel emergence of Armenian national identity.

The Armenian national *awakening* affected all the crucial elements of identity: language, literature, political ideology, religion and social class. Each of these domains was affected by the East-West divide, and in each case parallel developments took place. For example, the vernacular that emerged was divided between the Eastern and Western dialects. The Western Armenian language was based on the dialect spoken in Constantinople and the linguistic standard of the Western Armenians was influenced by it. It obviously embraced the phonological and lexical influence and elements of the Turkic language. On the other hand, Eastern Armenian was based on the dialect of the Yerevan region, spoken by the Eastern Armenians in Persia and Russian. It had the influence of Persian elements, and later underwent two reforms during Soviet rule, which is still a matter of contention between the homeland and the diaspora.[23] As far as literature is concerned, in the West it was influenced by the realist school, whereas in the East the romantic school was more prevalent.

Books in the vernacular Armenian language were printed. The first bookshop for Western Armenians was founded in Constantinople in 1806. By the 1830s dictionaries, lexicons and books on classical Armenian grammar were being published. Armenians learnt and mastered the art of printing in Europe and became pioneers in both the Ottoman and the Persian states. Armenian-language presses spread out throughout the nineteenth century from the important Armenian-inhabited cities of the Ottoman and Russian Empires into the historically Armenian provinces such as Shushi in Karabakh in 1835 and Van in 1857. Persian Armenians were yet to catch up with their Ottoman and Russian counterparts in setting up new presses in the late nineteenth century.

A large number of schools were established, first in Constantinople, Western Asia Minor and later in other provinces. European teaching techniques were adopted. In the mid-nineteenth century a number of Armenian philanthropic organizations were established to assist in this process and more advanced secondary schools began to come up. These developments changed the West Armenians' attitude towards education. Education was seen by them as the way to reclaim and reform Armenian identity. In the late nineteenth century they started going to Europe for higher study, including the German-run universities in the Russian Empire. A significant number of young people went on to become doctors, nurses and teachers. They seized upon useful ideas and parallel situations at the turn of the nineteenth century and returned home to forge a modern identity for their people.

A similar process was taking place in the Russian Empire as well. In Persia, however, the new educational methods were introduced much later. It was not before the mid-nineteenth century that modern schools were created in Tabriz and New Julfa which then spread into the provinces by the end of the century. In all the three empires the schools were primarily under the aegis of the Armenian Church, though by mid-century they had become agents of secularization.

Armenian newspapers also played a vital role in standardizing a literary version of vernacular Eastern and Western Armenian for the first time in the middle of the nineteenth century. The first Armenian newspaper had been published in distant Madras in India in 1794, followed by several European sites, but soon newspapers were being published in the inner diaspora of the Ottoman Empire, in Constantinople and Smyrna. Tiflis and other cities in the Russian Empire followed suit a little later, while the Persian Armenian cities lagged behind until the end of the nineteenth century. Alongside vernacular newspapers, and sometimes in them, novels in the two written Armenian dialects began to be published around mid-century, and grammar and textbooks of Eastern and Western Armenian were prepared. By the 1860s Armenian newspapers were dealing with a variety of topics including the difficulties and oppressions faced by their compatriots.

Armenian theatre, a genre imported from Europe, like the press and literature served to inform Armenians about their historical past and recreate a common identity. National myths were formed. During this period the Armenians contributed to various fields of Ottoman and Persian culture like music, art, theatre, literature, journalism and science.

Simultaneously various reforms in the religious sector by the Russian and Ottoman Empires strengthened the Armenian Church as a unifying administrative framework for the Armenians of the two empires and effectively enforced and extended the religious aspect of their identity. In Tsarist Russia, the regional Catholicate of Albania was abolished leaving the Catholicate of Etchmiadzin as the sole communal representative of the Armenians. By a statute in 1836, the Russian Armenians' religious and communal privileges were defined and the Armenian Church's rules were regularized everywhere, whether in the Caucasus or Moscow or the Crimea. The *millet* system of organizing the Armenian community of the empire by religion through the Armenian patriarchate of Constantinople consolidated the political power around the Armenian Church.

The administrative reforms, adoption of a constitution for the community in 1863 by the Ottoman Empire and the Armenian National Assembly also invoked a political consciousness among the Western Armenians. The Persian Armenians also, like their compatriots in the Ottoman Empire, were allowed to form communal autonomous organizations in the judicial and civil spheres through their churches. Regular councils with the participation of laymen were formed and assemblies held, and diocesan constitutions were created at the beginning of the twentieth century.

As the Armenians started communicating among themselves through newspapers and books, learnt about their past history and worked together in common institutions, their horizons expanded beyond their immediate surroundings. The Armenians in the provinces, which formed the greater part of historical Armenia, became more accessible, and by the 1870s they had become the focus of attention and interest for Armenians in the different centres of all three empires—Constantinople, Tiflis and Tabriz. The cultural and educational institutions also made efforts to these areas. Ethnographic, literary, cultural and educational concerns were soon supplemented by economic and political ones. In the 1860s this became part of an evolution in the Armenian political consciousness from purely cultural romanticism to realism tinged with romanticism, which called for action.

The second half of the nineteenth century witnessed the emergence of a political identity among the Armenians as they partially overcame their tripartite imperial division through the unifying forces of schools, common publications, national ideology and new international organizations. They strove to create conditions of greater freedom and equality, and participated in various reform movements. Both of these East and West trends coexisted in the Armenian national identity and in the nationalist-revolutionary programmes of the Armenian intelligentsia. The experience of the community in all the three political domains made them politically conscious and encouraged them to fight for their cause, and they became part of the national movement of the same nation.

In order to defend themselves against oppression in the provinces and ultimately to achieve Armenian self-rule, the Armenians organized themselves into political parties. As a result, in 1885 the first political party, Armenakan Party, was formed in Van, followed by the Hnchakian Party in 1887 in Geneva, the Armenian Revolutionary Federation (ARF) or Dashnaktsutiun in 1890 in Tiflis, and finally, the Armenian Democratic Liberal Party in Istanbul in 1921 (its roots go back to the Armenakan Party).[24] All these parties became engaged in revolutionary activities and instilled a new nationalistic attitude. They formed branches in the three empires ruling over historic

Armenian territories, as well as in many other countries with Armenian colonies. All of them believed in achieving the right to Armenian self-rule, but only the Hnchakian Party initially demanded outright independence. The two later parties added socialist ideology, filtered through various Russian revolutionary movements, to nationalist goals.

By the beginning of the twentieth century, despite the different social, economic, cultural and political currents, the different dialects and different lifestyles adopted by the two regions, the Armenians had developed a sense of belonging to a common nationality with a common destiny. The Eastern Armenian (Russian) intellectuals writing in St. Petersburg, Moscow and Tiflis made their subject and their cause the Turkish Armenian peasant's struggle to protect his family, goods and property. The imagined communities became culturally and administratively more real.

THE GENOCIDE

The Armenian political parties that emerged in the late nineteenth century were mainly concerned with the liberation of Western Armenia. Their ideas were further fuelled by the demands for autonomy and reform for Armenia that were being made in the European and Russian diplomatic notes of the time. This rising Armenian nationalism was in sharp conflict with the emerging Turkish nationalist ideology. The Ottoman State under Sultan Abdul-Hamid II responded by carrying out the Armenian Genocide of 1915, when almost the entire Armenian population was erased from Western Armenia, which put an end to all hopes of an independent Armenian state in Western Armenia. Given the importance of the notion of an independent Armenia, it is clear that the events of 1915 had the most profound and traumatic effect on the Armenian national identity.

Although dispersion and exile have been a near constant in Armenia's two and a half millennia history,[25] in the twentieth century the number and nature of the community profoundly transformed after the genocide and deportations between 1915 and 1920 the most significant millennial moment. The Armenians lost, as is generally agreed, one and a half million of its population and their homeland in eastern Anatolia. While transforming the identity of the survivors, this radically shook the sense of collective national identity of the Armenians which had evolved over a period of more than one millennium in their historic territories. It has become a dominant characteristic feature in defining 'Armenianness' in the twentieth century by adding a new dimension to the identity construction: the collective memory and politics of the survivors and the generations thereafter. They began to rebuild their lives and communities by establishing schools, churches, social and cultural organizations, spots teams and various other diasporic Armenian organizations in various countries in different regions of the world, wherever they had sought refuge. Maintaining the elements of Armenian identity such as language, religion, customs and traditions became the sacred objectives of these communities.

The genocide was the great 'equalizer' of identity.[26] It made everybody a victim, a survivor, and therefore a member of a community of the victims of genocide. This sense of victimization and notion of injustice became a central element of the Armenian collective consciousness. The fear of losing identity through the dangers of cultural assimilation in foreign lands developed.[27] 'Armenianness' acquired additional layers of identity after 1915.

Immediately after the genocide, the Armenian cause became very much territorialized, focusing on getting back the homeland. The genocide contributed to the perpetuation of an anti-Turkish attitude in the popular Armenian culture and the negative Armenian perception of the Turks. It engendered an identity politics related to it. The Armenians worldwide have been constantly making efforts to get recognition by different governments as a means of putting pressure on Turkey, and this politics of genocide recognition has affected the Armenian political identity.

This highlights the continuing division in the evolution of Eastern and Western Armenian identity in the twentieth century. Although the genocide is a 'pan-Armenian wound', it physically affected only the Western Armenians. It did not permeate and become the central element of Armenian identity in the Eastern Armenia till 1965. It entered the Russian and Soviet Armenian consciousness as a 'learnt injustice' rather than an 'experienced reality'. The survivors developed a stronger sense of national consciousness. Having been on the verge of annihilation, the Western Armenians developed a powerful will to survive. Once the sense of being a victim eased its debilitating hold on the Armenian psyche, martyrdom, mixed with rage and a national cause, drove subsequent generations to pursue national goals. Apart from physical decimation and dispersion, the genocide overshadowed most of twentieth-century Armenian life as a whole. Jenny Phillips,[28] studying Armenians in Boston, suggests that they have a root paradigm of an endangered people. They henceforth

Fig. 4.3: Map of the Democratic Republic of Armenia, 28 May 1918–2 December 1920[29]

lived as if they were constantly threatened, whether as individuals or as a group.

During the First World War and the genocide many Armenians fled Ottoman Empire for the relative safety of the Russian Caucasus. With the declaration of independence of the Republic of Armenia on 28 May 1918 by the members of the nationalistic ARF, immigration continued in anticipation of starting a new life in a land of their own. But the short-lived first independent Armenian state of the twentieth century could not fulfil their dream and Armenia became a part of the Soviet Union.[30]

THE SOVIET PERIOD

When Armenia entered the Soviet system there emerged a new version of the East-West identity, with the Armenian Revolutionary Federation (ARF or Dashnaktsutiun) leading the anti-Soviet or pro-free, independent unified Armenia movement. The Ramkavars, Hnchaks and their supporters, on the other hand, took an opposite stand regarding Soviet Armenia. They believed that Armenia should be supported, no matter who ruled it. This view maintained that the diaspora would soon die out through assimilation and physical threats and that the republic was the only viable long-term solution for an Armenian future. But from the 1970s onwards, the two sides became less diametrically opposed and began to take similar stands, particularly regarding the state of Armenia.

From 1920 to 1945 the Armenian identity was in turmoil. When in response to the Soviet government-initiated repatriation from 1946 to 1949, over 100,000 diaspora Armenians immigrated to Soviet Armenia they experienced the difference in the East-West Armenian identity. They were referred to as *aghpar* to mark them as 'other', which seemed to be a misunderstanding by the Eastern Armenians of the Western Armenian pronunciation of the word 'brother' (*yeghbayr*). The first president, Levon Ter Petrossian, was born in Syria in 1945. Although he was only a four-year-old when his family was repatriated to Armenia in 1946, and grew up as a Soviet citizen, he was quite often referred to as '*aghpar* Levon'.

Though the Soviet regime was ostensibly anti-nationalist, in reality the Soviet nationality policies contributed to a powerful feeling of a territorial nationalism. Long years of Soviet rule made the small territory of the Armenian state demographically more Armenian than it had been in the previous several centuries. One of the most highly educated populations in the Soviet Union, the Armenians knew their history, language and culture more thoroughly than most of their predecessors. The ruling elite were all Armenian; a considerably powerful Armenian intelligentsia was forged. In Armenia the nationalist feelings were the strongest and the national causes have always been dominant factors determining the behaviour of all social groups and political activists in Armenia and in the diaspora community, from dissidents and intellectuals to the established communist elites in the country. In the late 1950s and 1960s, following the Stalin era, the growing demand for greater national and personal expression exploded in the form of a new nationalism. All these factors contributed in furthering the consolidation of a sense of intense nationalism and identity, which ultimately led Armenia to declare its intention to become a sovereign and independent state, and on 23 August 1990, it entered its second period of independence in the twentieth century.

Three issues in 1988 stimulated a broad-based national movement in Armenia: firstly, environmental threats from a nuclear plant at Metsamore, close to Yerevan; secondly the pervasive corruption and arrogance of the local Communist regime; and thirdly and the most volatile issue concerning the fate of mountainous Karabakh (Lernayin Karabakh in Armenian, Nagornyi Karabakh in Russian), an Armenian-populated enclave in Azerbaijan.

Most importantly, two significant events, the Karabakh movement of February and the devastating earthquake of December, marked the year 1988 as a watershed in the evolutionary process of the Armenian national identity, and placed the Soviet republic at the centre of the concerns and collective consciousness of the communities scattered over all the regions in the world. As such, the 'homeland' became the focus of their activities, acquiring a more concrete dimension rather than being an abstract notion in the background of diasporan identity. After 1988 there were unprecedented contacts and possibilities of cooperation between the two entities. The Armenian diaspora has been actively involved in the process of reshaping the economic, political and cultural life of Armenia since the earthquake of 1988.

POST-INDEPENDENCE

At the initial stage, when Armenia became independent in 1991, there was a great deal of enthusiasm, excitement and anticipation in Armenia and among the communities settled in different regions over the impending reunion of Armenians in the homeland. On an emotional and abstract level the people of Armenia were devoted to the idea of one Armenian nation and one Armenian people (*Hai zhoghovurd*). During 1991–2 many diaspora Armenians went to the homeland either to settle there or to help with the state-building process by volunteering their skills to the country on a short-term basis, be it for weeks, months or even a year. It was seen as a matter of 'duty' for diaspora Armenians to go to help the homeland in any way they could. The need to unify, protect and strengthen the Armenian nation was the driving force that persuaded diverse social groups to sink their differences and cooperate with the government functioning in Yerevan. The Armenian NGOs and donors[31] have been playing a significant role in the economic, social and political development of Armenia.[32]

The most visible manifestation of Armenianness among these two entities was in the form of a series of high-level appointments of government officials from the diaspora following the independence of the country. The most notable were Armenian–US citizens. Jirair (Gerard) Libaridian was appointed as an advisor to President Levon Ter Petrosian in January 1991; Raffi Hovannisian, a 32-year-old US-born lawyer, was appointed as independent Armenia's first foreign minister in October 1991; in January 1992 Sebouh Tashjian of California was chosen as minister of energy; and Vartan Oskanian was appointed deputy foreign minister in November 1994. He was promoted to foreign minister in February 1998. Such appointments were seen as a clear signal that the new post-Communist government of Armenia was reaching out to the diaspora, extending a hand of cooperation to bridge the gap between them. The press and much of the political rhetoric in Yerevan and in the diasporan communities reflected this spirit of cooperation between the two 'wings' of the nation.

On a practical level, however, various issues, concerns and questions were raised.[33] There did exist diametrically opposite views on certain issues,[34] which though expressed directly by two parties Armenian Revolutionary Party (ARF) and Armenian Pan-Nationalist Party (ANM), reflected the division and prevailing tension among the Armenians as a whole both in the Republic and in the various corners of the globe: (i) independence from the Soviet Union in pre-independence days; (ii) relations with Turkey; (iii) the Armenian Question and the Armenian Cause; (iv) genocide recognition of lost lands in Turkey; (v) reunification of Karabakh with Armenia, followed by Nakhechivan and Akhalkalak; (vi) political ideology such as liberal democracy, market relations and privatization of state assets or mixed economy and social democracy; (vii) form of government—with strong a presidency or strong parliament; (viii) Citizenship relating to dual citizenship; and finally (ix) the diaspora's role.

The last one is based on the Armenians' conception of nation. One side believes that though Armenia and the diaspora are two entities of the same nation, the latter should not meddle in the state's internal political affairs. The other side opts for 'one nation, one homeland' and argues that since nation is indivisible, its politics should be a symbiosis between the two entities. Hence it is legitimate for diaspora-based 'pan-national' parties such as the ARF to have a direct say in the affairs of the homeland. Some in the diaspora believe that the president should be regarded as the leader of all Armenians. For example, Dikran Voskuni, the editor of the popular newspaper *Nor Gyank* (New Life), based in Los Angeles, in relation to the former president once said that 'Ter Petrosian should be, feel and act as the President of all Armenians'.[35] But others insist that the diaspora is a separate polity in its own right and cannot be represented by the leadership in Yerevan.[36] Besides, some Armenian scholars have raised the issues of orthography, notions about homeland, the pure or real Armenian, *hai* (Armenian people) and *hayastantsi* (people from Armenia).[37]

But the recently growing number of returnees from the Western countries, who are settling there for business, study or volunteer work, shows that in Armenia something has radically changed, and that it is slowly becoming a new and real homeland for members of the diaspora. The homeland is no longer an abstract place of longing and nostalgic myth, but rather a social reality, at times with frustrating encounters and conflicts. The focus is rapidly changing to an idealized homeland on that soil.

In the twenty-first century, one point is very clear, that the Armenians are not a homogeneous monolithic community. In spite of the 'ruling assumption' of helping Armenia, there are heterogeneity and diversity of opinions and affiliations within and between the expatriate Armenian communities throughout the world. They speak in two dialects and have two churches and Catholicos—the Armenian Apostolic Churches in Etchmiadzin, Armenia and in Antelias, Lebanon—and three religious denominations, namely, Apostolic, Catholic and Protestants. They are affiliated to different political parties such as Dashnak, Hnchak and Ramkavar. They have origins in different countries, regions and cities and different, socio-economic backgrounds and different degrees of assimilation in the host countries. They have different ideas about Armenianness (*hayutyun*) and the fatherland (*hayrenikh*). 'There are ambivalences within this trans-regional community regarding their place in and relations with Armenia.'[38]

Nevertheless, overlying these divisions are very strong ties—practical, symbolic and emotional—which bind the Armenians around the world to each other and to the idea of an Armenian people or nation. They continue to identify themselves as Armenian (*hay*), consider themselves as part of the Armenian nation (*azg*), and believe that they share a common origin and history. Institutions like family, churches, political parties and charitable and cultural groups form trans-regional links and provide continuity in a fluid world and the intellectually and politically active elite construct a framework of ideas which informs about private as well as public constructions of belonging. Until recently there was no centre and periphery in the Armenian world, and it is only with the independence of the former Soviet Republic of Armenia in 1991 that there has been an increasing focus on one place as a symbolic homeland.

This strong sense of Armenian identity is distinctly reflected through their interaction, activism, engagement and contributions in the sustainable developmental process of post-independence Armenia.

They are ideologically and materially involved and implicated in the national projects of their homeland.

CONCLUSION

After the emergence of independent Armenia, quite a deluge of literature, debates and discourses have dealt in detail with the issue of Armenian identity and the diaspora's relations with Armenia, which reflects the aspirations of both entities of the trans-regional nationality to see their newly independent real or imagined homeland emerge as a thriving nation.

Krikor Beledian has made a distinction between *spiurk* (the Armenian term for diaspora) and *gaghuthahayutyun* (the Armenian term for Armenians of the colonies).[39] He further states that an Armenian is a person who constantly asks who he or she is. The question of identity is itself part of the Armenian identity. In his view land is no longer one of the basic elements of the Armenian identity.[40] Aram Veeser opines that the Armenia that is indispensable to all Armenians is not a territory but a concept.[41] Khachig Tololyan argues that since identity is relational, the most important first step is to change one's feeling of identity as personal to a feeling of identity as communal, and then acting for that community. It requires involvement and the necessity to act as one. In his logic,[42] to be a true member it is not enough to claim that one is an Armenian, one has to accept certain responsibilities and duties for the nation (*azg*) and the Armenian Cause (*Hai thad*). He also makes a distinction between the Armenians: (a) the 'diasporics'; (b) the 'ethnics'; and (c) those Armenians who are assimilated in all but name.[43]

It is the 'diasporics' who share the view that despite all its shortcomings and borders, the Republic of Armenia must survive and the trans-regional Armenian communities must help it to survive and thrive. They must translate the subjectivity to agency, and the internalized sentiments and beliefs about one's identity and origin should be transformed into externalized participation in helping Armenia.[44] For the majority, the Republic of Armenia is the homeland. As Razmik Panossian[45] points out, though Armenia is only 20 per cent of the 'greater Armenia' in its landmass, it still remains the only tangible homeland for the Armenians.

In recent years the Kocharian government through its proactive policy has attempted to overcome these differences and encourage greater dialogue and cooperation between these 'two wings'. The government so far has organized three Armenia diaspora conferences in Yerevan to address different issues, the first in September 1999, the second in May 2002 and the third in September 2006, in which participants from various regions and homeland discussed socio-economic developments, culture, science, education and issues related to Armenia-diaspora organizations and structures. The conferences provided both 'wings' opportunities to deal with each other on multiple levels, both institutionally and individually. The arguments propounded by the diverse social and political groups of both entities reflect the strong national feelings and deep sense of belongingness to the nation, concern for it and the zeal to take part in the developmental process of the nation. Despite the profound divisions and differences, a sense of belonging to the same nation—of being or feeling Armenian still prevails. And all these developments on the part of the government and the diaspora manifest the coherent sense of Armenian identity, which is trans-regional.

Today a very small community of the Indian Armenians is concentrated in Calcutta with their three churches and chapels, a hundred and eighty-seven year old school and old-age home. Even this minute section of the Armenian diaspora did not miss the focus and activism on the part of both entities of the same nation in their strive to revive the worldwide Armenian identity, which culminated in 2005 in the visit of His Holiness, Catholicos Karekin II, accompanied by the then President of the Republic, Ashot Kocharian, Archbishop Aghan Baliozian and other dignitaries to Delhi, Chennai, Mumbai and Calcutta.[46]

NOTES

1. 'Patriarchs, Kings and Rulers of Armenia', available at *http:// www.armenianway.com*
2. Composition of macrogeographical (continental) regions, geographical subregions, and selected economic and other groupings: Geographical region and composition, United Nations Statistics Division, available at *http://unstats.un.org*
3. 'Country Profiles: Armenia', The World Factbook, Central Intelligence Agency, available at *https://www.cia.gov/library*
4. 'People and Places, Armenia', available at *http://www3.nationalgeographic.com*
5. 'Armenia', available at *http://www.britannica.com/eb/article-9108699/Armenia*
6. 'Country profile: Armenia', available at *http://news.bbc.co.uk/2/hi/europe/country_profiles/1108052.stm*
7. Website: *http:// www.oxfordreference.com*
8. 'Armenia: Historical Division of Armenia', available at *http://concise.britannica.com*
9. Armenia—Definition from the *Merriam-Webster Online Dictionary*, available at *http://www.m-w.com/dictionary/armenia*

10. 'Country Details', available at *http://worldatlas.com/webimage/countrys/europe/am.htm*
11. 'European Movement in Armenia', available at *http://www.europeanmovement.am/AboutArmenia.html*
12. Speech by Mr Armen Baibourtian, Deputy Foreign Minister of the Republic of Armenia 'A Foreign Policy for a Small State: Armenia's Case', 31 October 2007, Japan Institute of International Affairs, Tokyo, available at *http://www.armeniaforeignministry.com*
13. Vartan Oskanian, minister of foreign affairs at the 'European Neighbourhood Policy' Conference in Brussels, Brussel', Belgium, 3 September 2007, available at *http://www.armeniaforeignministry.com*
14. John Borneman and Nick Fowler, 'Europeanization', *Annual Review of Anthropology* 26, 1997, pp. 487–514; Irene Bellier and Thomas Wilson, 'Building, Imagining and Experiencing Europe: Institutions and Identities in the European Union', in *The Anthropology of European Union*, ed. Bellier and Wilson, Oxford: Berg, 2000, pp. 1–30; Alexander Kavkaz Iskandaryan, *Rossiya: Migratsiya lega'lnya i nelegal'naya*, Yerevan: KISMI, 2004; Ashot Voskanian, 'Preface', in *Armenia on the Way to Europe*, ed. A. Voskanian, Yerevan: Antares, 2005, pp. 6–17; Levon Abrahamian, 'Armenia and Armenians between East and West', Conference paper at the 3rd Armenian Diaspora Conference in Yerevan, September 2006.
15. Anthony D. Smith, *The Ethnic Origins of Nations*, New York: Blackwell, 1987.
16. E. Gellner, *Nations and Nationalism,* Ithaca, New York: Cornell University Press, 1983; E. Hobsbawn, *Nations and Nationalism*, Cambridge: Cambridge University Press, 1991.
17. D. Horowitz, *Ethnic Groups in Conflict*, Berkeley, CA: University of California Press, 1985.
18. Source: *http://www.wikipedia,org*
19. C.J. Walker, *Armenia: The Survival of a Nation*, rev. 2nd edn., London: Routledge, 1990.
20. Data available at *http://www.armeniadiaspora.com.* Also see R.H. Dekmejian, 'The Armenian Diaspora', in *The Armenian People: From Ancient to Modern Times*, vol. 2, ed. R.G. Hovannisian, New York: St. Martin's Press, 1997.
21. Rouben Paul Adalian, 'The Historical Evolution of the Armenian Diasporas', *Journal of Modern Hellenism*, no. 6, 1989.
22. R.G. Hovannisian (ed.), *The Armenian People: From Ancient to Modern Times*, vol. 2, New York: St. Martin's Press, 1997, chapters 4–7; R.G. Suny, *Looking Toward Ararat: Armenia in Modern History,* Bloomington and Indianapolis: University of Indiana Press, 1993.
23. The first reform was done in 1922 by Manuk Abeghian who changed the orthography and several letters characteristic of Classical Armenian, also known as Mesrobian Armenian, and they are not used in Eastern Armenian.
24. Louise Nalbandian, *The Armenian Revolutionary Movement*, Los Angeles: University of California Press, 1963.
25. Suny, *Looking Toward Ararat.*
26. Razmik Panossian, 'The Impact of the Genocide on Armenian Identity', *The Armenian Weekly,* 73(16), April 2007.
27. D. Horowitz, *Ethnic Groups in Conflict*, Berkeley: University of California Press, 1985.

28. Jenny Phillips, *Symbol, Myth, and Rhetoric: The Politics of Culture in an Armenian-American Population*, New York: AMS Press, 1989.
29. Source: *http://www.answers.com*
30. From 1922, as part of Transcaucasian SFSR, and as Armenian SSR from 1936.
31. Armenian Health Alliance (AHA), Armenian General Benevolent Union (AGBU), Armenian Relief Society, Aznavour Pour l'Armnie, the Armenian Assembly of America, the Lincy Foundation, the Armenian American Mammography University Centre, Medical Outreach of Armenia, Organization for Developmental Services in Armenia, the United Armenian Fund have all played an important role in providing assistance and guidance to aid Armenia's post-Soviet transition.
32. Armine Ishkanian, 'Diaspora and Global Civil Society: The Impact of Transnational Diasporic Activism on Armenia's post-Soviet Transition', in *Central Asia and the Caucasus: Transnationalism and Diaspora*, ed. T. Atabaki and S. Mehendale, London: Routledge, 2005.
33. Masih Joseph and Robert O. Krikorian, *Armenia at the Crossroads*, Amsterdam: Harwood Academic Publishers, 1999.
34. Stephan Astourian, 'From Ter-Petrosian to Kocharian: Leadership Change in Armenia', Berkeley: Berkeley Program in Soviet and post-Soviet Studies Working Paper, 2001.
35. *Nor Gyank*, 7 August 1997.
36. Krikor Beledian and Khachig Tololyan, 'Fresh Perspectives on Armenia Diaspora Relations', *Armenian Forum* 1, no. 3, Autumn 1998.
37. Ibid.
38. Razmik Panossian, 'Between Ambivalence and Intrusion: Politics and Identity in Armenia-Diaspora Relations,' *Diaspora: A Journal of Transnational Studies* 7, no. 2, 1998; Susan P. Pattie, 'Longing and Belonging: Issues of Homeland in the Armenian Diaspora', available at *http://www.transcomm.ox.ac.uk.*
39. 'Fresh Perspectives on Armenia-Diaspora Relations'.
40. Ibid.
41. Aram H. Veeser, 'International Nationalism: Living Lack, Muzzled Cohort: A Response to Anahid Kassabian and David Kazanian', *Armenian Forum* 1, no.1, Spring, 1998.
42. Khachig Tololyan, 'Rethinking Diaspora(s): Stateless Power in the Transnational Moment', *Diaspora: A Journal of Transnational Studies*, 5, no.1, 1996.
43. 'Fresh Perspectives on Armenia-Diaspora Relations: Khachig Tololyan and Krikor Beledian Speak with *Haratch*', *Armenian Forum*, 1, no. 3, Autumn, 1998.
44. Ibid.
45. Panossian, 'Between Ambivalence and Intrusion'.
46. Mother See of Holy Etchmiadzin Information Services, Vagharshapat, Republic of Armenia.

5

The Strategic Significance of the Former Soviet South as a Region in the Post-Cold War Era

SREEMATI GANGULI

The disintegration of the USSR in 1991 and the eventual end of the Cold War brought about a 'tectonic shift' in global politics. The singular authority of the USSR was replaced with the formation of a number of new independent sovereign states in the region. And it must be duly noted that a focus on the post-Soviet space as a centre of gravity for geo-strategic goals, which include geopolitical and geo-economic interests of the major global and regional powers, was activated against this background. A number of scholars termed the entire post-Soviet space as the Eurasian region. Some analysts of the Central Eurasian Studies Society used the term 'Central Eurasia' to include the entire Black Sea region and the Caucasus in the West—through the Middle Volga region, Central Asia and Afghanistan—and onto Siberia, Mongolia and Tibet in the East. Robert M. Cutler proposed a 'mega-regional' scale of analysis to include all of Russia, China and the whole of South and South-West Asia from India to Turkey, as well as a 'Greater Eurasia' which includes the European Union also. For Alexander Dugin, a grand 'Eurasian Empire' stretches from Dublin to Vladivostok, which includes those regions beyond the political boundaries of the CIS but are geopolitically vital for Russia. For Zbignew Brzezinski, who maintains an ideologically opposite stance as against Dugin, the Eurasian region extends from Lisbon to Vladivostok.

Considering Eurasia as a mega-area of analysis, this essay tries to focus on that part of the region that the five Central Asian republics of Kazakhstan, Kyrgyzstan, Tajikistan, Turkmenistan and Uzbekistan and the three republics of southern Caucasus—Georgia, Armenia and Azerbaijan. This region is termed as the Former Soviet South or the Southern Tier. The region has emerged as a critical factor in the security and economic considerations of South Asia, the Middle East and Europe. The dictionary definition of a region is a large land area that has geographical, political or cultural characteristics which distinguish it from others, whether existing within one country or extending over several ones. A region is often generally construed as 'sub-systems of states linked by geographical relationship, mutual interdependence and subjective perception of belonging to a distinctive community.'[1] Authors like Sheila Page define a region as a 'group of countries which have created a legal framework of cooperation covering an extensive economic relationship, with the intention that it will be of indefinite duration, and with the possibility foreseen that the region will evolve or change'.[2] But a region may also be marked by conflict, or by a mixture of agreement and disagreement—as the states share 'the interdependence of rivalry' as well as 'the interdependence of shared interests'.[3] There are other theories that present different views on analysing a 'region'. From the neo-realist perspective, states of a region need to share some complementarity of interests, division of labour and a shared responsibility to achieve a specific desired aim. But more specific to this discussion may be the 'World Systems Theory', as analysed by Cantori and Spiegel.[4] This theory describes a region as 'the total interaction of relations within that region' and analyses the factors that delineate a region like foreign relations among the states of the region, geography, socio-eco-organizational factors, historical background and, interestingly, the role of external powers that provides the relevant gestalt or the 'intrusive system' to influence the subordinate system or the internal dynamics within the region itself. We will not use the theoretical framework and parameters of this particular theory, but the main argument of this discussion follows the same logic, as the article wants to show how the global powers react to the internal dynamics of the region under consideration, and in the process, how the region has become a centre of global attention.

This region is increasingly viewed as strategically sensitive, engulfed by a host of security problems, both internal as well as external. The strategic sensitivity of the region is all the more acute because of its proximity to other strategically significant regions like the Black Sea and the Persian Gulf, two vitally important waterways for energy trade, making the region vulnerable to the geopolitical manoeuvrings in the Middle East. This factor is crucial for the US involvement in the region, for the US moves to contain Iran and promote Turkey. Having Afghanistan in its neighbourhood has also lent credibility to its strategic significance to the world as the Central Asian Republics, if not the whole region, are victims of terrorism, religious extremism and narcotics trafficking across the border from Afghanistan. But the real factor is the presence of Russia as the traditional power in the region, which has opened up new scopes for clashes of interests and new equations in power-relations.

This article tries to focus on those three issues that have proved crucial in making this region the centre of global attraction—the estimated and exploitable reserves of energy and the related issue of securing viable routes to link the energy-producing region to the world market; the potentials of the region as a trade corridor between Asia and Europe; and the problems of insecurity emanating from separatism, drug-trafficking, religious extremism which have internal sources and external encouragement.

SILK ROAD INITIATIVES

The disintegration of the USSR in 1991 and the emergence of independent countries rekindled the interests of regional and global powers in the region—for its economic resources as well as for its potential of becoming a trade corridor between China, South Asia, the Middle East and Europe. New initiatives to build roads, railways and energy pipelines were floated by major global and regional powers to exploit the resource-potentials of the region as well as to use it as an interconnecting bridge between Asia and Europe. Interestingly, all these initiatives are termed as 'Silk Road Initiatives' so as to reformulate the concept of the old Silk Road that connected China, India, Central Asia and the Middle East some four thousand years back.

The first such initiative was the Transport Corridor-Europe-Caucasus-Asia (TRACECA) which was established in 1993 in Brussels under the European Commission-funded TACIS Programme. The Basic Multilateral Agreement for the Programme was signed at the 'TRACECA Summit-Restoration of the Historic Silk Route' in Baku in 1998 and the TRACECA Intergovernmental Commission was set up in Tbilisi in 2000. The member countries of this programme are Armenia, Azerbaijan, Afghanistan, Bulgaria, Georgia, Kazakhstan, Kyrgyzstan, Moldova, Iran, Romania, Turkey, Ukraine, Uzbekistan and Tajikistan. Turkmenistan is still not a signatory of the MLA, though it participates in the TACIS TRACECA Programme.[5]

Another initiative was mooted in August 2005 during an international symposium in Urumqui on regional economic cooperation on the development of a New Silk Road from Liyanyungang in China to Rotterdam in the Netherlands. This initiative[6] was formerly known as the New Eurasian Continental Bridge. The Meet was jointly hosted by the UNDP, the China National Coordination Mechanism of the New Eurasia Continental Bridge and the Chinese ministries of commerce, railways and civil aviation. This corridor, it was decided, would cover sixteen countries with multi-modal transport systems like highways and roadways.

The North-South Transport Corridor is another such initiative, jointly promoted by India and Russia. This corridor, stretching from Mumbai to St. Petersburg, was initiated in 2000 by a tripartite agreement between India, Iran and Russia. The trade and connectivity potentials of the corridor have attracted eleven more members—Armenia, Azerbaijan, Belarus, Bulgaria, Kazakhstan, Kyrgyzstan, Tajikistan, Ukraine, Turkey, Oman and Syria. In 2000, a proposal on the revival of the Silk Road in the Region was mooted by President Askar Akayev of Kyrgyzstan, Heydar Aliyev of Azerbaijan, Robert Kocharian of Armenia, Prime Minister K. Tokayev of Kazakhstan and the foreign ministers of Iran and Turkey during their annual meet.[7]

During her visit to Afghanistan in October 2005, the US Secretary of State Condoleeza Rice promoted a broad idea of the 'revival of the fundamental basis for the Silk Road' in the Central and South Asian region to create new areas of cooperation like trade, transport, energy, democracy and communications among the states in the region.[8]

Another Silk Road Initiative is being promoted by the Central Asia Regional Economic Cooperation (CAREC), which comprises Afghanistan, Azerbaijan, China, Kazakhstan, Kyrgyzstan, Tajikistan, Uzbekistan and Mongolia. The CAREC Initiative has agreed to an eighteen billion dollar strategy to set up a network of roads, airports, railways and seaports to make the region a vital transit route for trade between Europe and Asia—a modern-day equivalent of the ancient Silk Road. The plan is called the 'Transport and Trade Facilitation Strategy' and is financially supported by ADB, EBRD, IMF, UNDP, the World Bank and the Islamic Development Bank.[9]

The main beneficiaries of these initiatives will be the countries of the region, rich in energy resources, minerals and other natural resources but faced with the problem of connectivity to the global market. These countries are landlocked and the existing rail and road transport infrastructures do not provide intercontinental reach. The Silk Road Initiatives try to offer these states more investments to restructure their economic systems as well as better access to the global market. Data shows that all these initiatives are expected to bolster the scale and value of trade in the region, for example, the volume of inland trade will double in size between 2002 and 2015, as the experts in Azerbaijan predict; the overland route from China to Europe is expected to lessen the transport time from the present 20–40 days (along seaborne routes) to only 11 days and to reduce the transport costs from $167 at present to $111 per container; and the North-South Transport Corridor will reduce the time of delivery from India to Russia by 10–12 days and cut operational costs by around $2000 per container.[10]

All these economic initiatives, which try to promote economic interaction among regions within a broader perspective to achieve a sort of an economic integration, also cater to the interests of the external powers that are involved. The EU's interest in developing the region's economic potentials and in connecting the region to the European market through the multi-modal transport corridor is reflected through its TRACECA Initiative. China's involvement in the Central Asian economic scenario is amply demonstrated by the two initiatives it promotes. This, along with Japan's 'Eurasian diplomacy' in the 'Silk Road Region' declaring its involvement in the region's economy and energy sectors, points to the Eastern direction of the Silk Road, a fact often overlooked by the West. The inclusion of Afghanistan in the US-backed Initiative is notable as it tries to create a fully integrated Greater Central Asia–South Asia region. For the US, the Initiative helps it to achieve its regional goals—to strengthen democratic stability and economic reforms, to foster regional security and cooperation on the war against terrorism and drug trafficking and to promote economic growth and cooperation in the region. All this corresponds to the US' global strategy. The North-South Transport Corridor provides India with an alternative route to get connected with the region as India lacks direct connectivity due to its strained relations with Pakistan and the instability in Afghanistan.

ENERGY

After the disintegration of the Soviet Union, the region has gained prominence and attracted attention because of its virgin wealth of energy. The changes in the geo-strategic scenario in the Middle East since the First Gulf War of 1990–1, the sanctions on Iraq, the worsened relations between the US, Iraq and Iran and the Iraq War of 2003 led to insecurity in the export of energy from the Middle East and have provided the ideal backdrop for the growing pre-eminence of this region. After 1991, the energy-rich countries of the region, namely, Kazakhstan, Turkmenistan and Azerbaijan, opened their energy sectors to global bidders and the data shows the extent of involvement of these companies. In 1993, TengizChevroil got a forty-year joint venture in Kazakhstan; in 1997 Kazakhstan signed a Production-Sharing Agreement (PSA) with Texaco (US), ENI (Italy) and British Gas for the Karachaganak oil and gas condensate field; and for the Northern Caspian Shelf another PSA was signed by Kazakhstan and the Kazakhstan Caspishelf Consortium, an alliance of Agip (Italy), British Gas, British Petroleum, Mobil, Shell, Statoil, Total (France) and Kazakh partners. Also, the Chinese National Petroleum Company (CNPC) formed a joint venture with Aktobemunaygaz for the Zhanazhol gas plant in which CNPC has a 60 per cent share. In 1999, AgipKCO (a consortium of Agip, BG, Exxonmobil, Shell, TotalFinaElf, Impex, ConocoPhilips) and KazMunayGaz signed an exploration and development contract for the Kashagan field.

In 1991, Azerbaijan signed a joint agreement with Amoco, Ramco, BP, Statoil, Unocal (US) and Mcdermott to develop the Azerbaijan sector of the Caspian; in 1994, it signed the 'contract of the century' — a thirty-year, $7.5 billion deal to develop the Azeri–Chirag–Guneshli fields with the Azerbaijan International Operating Company (AIOC) comprising the State Oil Company of Azerbaijan Republic (SOCAR), Amoco, BP, Statoil, Pennzoil, Mcdermott, Ramco, TPAO and Unocal. It also signed a PSA with Caspian International Petroleum Company for Karabagh and entered into another agreement with SOCAR, BP, Statoil, LUKoil, Nefitran International Company and Turkish State Petroleum Company for the development of the Shah Deniz oil and gas condensate.

Turkmenistan provided exploration concessions in the Cheleken offshore project to Larmag Energy and development rights in the Kaimir and AK-Patlauk oilfields to Bridas (Argentina). In 1996, Turkmenistan signed an agreement with Petronas (Malaysia) to develop three oil and gas deposits, an Exploration and Production-Sharing Agreement with Monument Oil and Gas (Britain) for Nebitdag oilfields and three contracts for the upgradation and reconstruction of the Turkmenbashi refinery with three foreign consortiums. In July 1998, Turkmenistan signed a deal with Mobil and its partner Monument Oil and Gas for the exploration and development of the Garashsyzlyk field.

However, Russia, the traditional power in the region, is also in the reckoning. In Kazakhstan, the state Kazakh company KazMunayGaz and Gazprom formed the KazRosGaz Company, with a 50 per cent share each, and the company later became the monopoly gas exporter of Kazakhstan. Russia and Kazakhstan signed another agreement on the joint development of three oil and gas fields in Kurmangazy, Khvalynskoye and Tsentralnoye on a 50:50 basis. Lukoil has a 50 per cent share in the Turgai Petroleum joint venture in Kumkol and a 40-year PSA with KazMunayGaz for Tiub-Karagan Oilfield signed in 2004. Russia signed a 25-year agreement with Turkmenistan in 2003 for the supply of two trillion cubic metre of gas.

The energy resources of the region and its landlocked-ness have made the routing of pipelines from the region to the world market the single most important issue in the related energy politics. The energy-rich countries of the region need diversified markets for energy and diversified pipeline routes to reach there, as they desperately need foreign exchange to carry out economic reforms, repay external debts and restructure their domestic economic infrastructure, as energy is their only viable exportable item. The existing energy network is of Soviet origin with new modifications in the post-Soviet era, and much of that network has come under Russian control, for example, Kazakhstan transports most of its oil through the Soviet-built Atyrau-Samara or the Druzhba Pipeline and the newly-built Tengiz-Novorossisk Pipeline and for Turkmenistan, the main gas export pipeline still remains the Soviet-built Central Asia-Centre Pipeline.

However, in the post-disintegration scenario, there emerged the need for the regional and extra-regional powers to diversify export routes to carry the energy resources of the region to the global market, so that Russia cannot command unilateral control over the transport network, and thereby cannot exploit unilateral economic and political advantages from the energy-producer countries. And thus, the politics of the construction of new pipelines has been intertwined with the competition for gaining political and economic influence in the region. The most important and most hyped pipeline to be built in the post-Soviet era is the Baku-Tbilisi-Ceyhan pipeline. Another is the Baku-Tbilisi-Erzurum natural gas pipeline and most significantly, both these pipelines bypass both the Russian and Iranian territories. Kazakhstan joined the BTC pipeline in 2006. The success of Kazakhstan's oil swap deal with Iran boosted the prospects of a 2080-km-long pipeline project from Uzen (Kazakhstan) to the island of Kharq (Iran) via Turkmenistan. The Atasu (Kazakhstan)–Alashankou (China) pipeline, completed in 2006, has offered Kazakhstan the huge Chinese market. For Turkmenistan, the 200 km long pipeline from Korpeje-Kurkui (Iran) still remains the only non-Russian pipeline to the global market, despite its attempts to patronize diversified pipelines like the Trans-Caspian Gas Pipeline, Trans-Asian Gas Pipeline, the Trans-Afghan Gas Pipeline and the Trans-Iranian Gas pipeline. For Azerbaijan, the Soviet-built Baku-Supsa pipeline was the only outlet to the outside world before the BTC pipeline became operational.

The alliances and complex interrelationships revolving around the energy pipelines reveal the new Caspian strategic interdependencies. For the states in the region, particularly for Georgia and Azerbaijan, the BTC pipeline provides an alternative pipeline route, much sought after, which bypasses Russia and thereby limits their economic and political dependence on that country. Kazakhstan and Turkmenistan, on the other hand, are trying to retain as many options available to them. The BTC pipeline project provides some gains for Turkey in the energy politics: Azerbaijan's dependence on Russia as the sole transport link will be attenuated, Turkey will gain from transit revenues and other spin-off benefits, the mounting load of tanker traffic on the Black Sea straits and the related eventual possibility of ecological disasters can be reduced through this alternative route and, most important, Turkey will be able to present itself as the provider of an alternative route to the CARs, bypassing Russia.

Iran acts as the effective provider of alternative routes for the CARs in the southern direction. But lack of financial capital and the US sanctions (under the 1996 Iran and Libya Sanctions Act that prevents US companies from investing in Iran) hinder the prospects of its ambitious projects like the Trans-Iranian Gas Pipeline (Turkmenistan-Iran-Turkey).

The EU is a relatively new entrant in the Central Asian energy sphere. According to the data published during the 2005 London Summit between the EU and Russia, in the near future, Russia will supply 50 per cent of the natural gas requirements of the EU states, which explains the dependence of the EU on Russia for its energy requirements. But, prompted by the Ukrainian gas crisis of January 2006 when Russia turned off its gas supplies to the Ukraine to press for higher prices for Russian gas, and the associated potential high levels of risks involved in dealing with Russia, the EU has intensified its search for alternative gas sources and has identified Kazakhstan and Turkmenistan as potential partners. The EU has already initiated a Caspian-Black Sea Energy Dialogue or the Baku Process. During the first visit of the EU Energy Commissioner Andris Piebalgs to Kazakhstan in May 2006, it was revealed that the EU was seeking long-term supply contracts with Kazakhstan and Turkmenistan as well as promoting a string of energy pipelines to

Europe, like the Trans-Caspian Pipeline and the Trans-Caucasian Pipeline, which circumvent Russia. But certainly all these initiatives have not gone beyond the preliminary planning rounds. Also the strained relations between Turkmenistan and Azerbaijan and the actual amount of gas that Turkmenistan will be able to deliver to Europe after fulfilling its commitments to Russia and China, may prove to be substantial roadblocks in the EU's plans in Central Asia. Also, the proposed Yamal-Europe (Russia–Germany via Belarus) and the North European gas pipeline (Russia–Finland–UK via the Baltic Sea) ensure EUs enhanced dependence on Russian energy.

In August 2006, Japanese Prime Minister Junchiro Koizumi visited Central Asia where he initiated the 'Central Asia plus Japan Dialogue', and Japanese Foreign Minister Taro Aso outlined Japan's Silk Road diplomacy. Both these initiatives have a strong component of energy cooperation with the region. Experts say that Tokyo's recent initiatives are prompted by Beijing's express desire to get a monopoly over the pipelines from Central Asia, with the intention to re-export energy to Asia-Pacific Rim countries to secure for itself economic as well as political clout over others. Japan has also initiated an ambitious plan for a pipeline from Central Asia to the Indian Ocean via Afghanistan and Pakistan, thus bypassing both Russia and China. This plan aptly accommodates US geo-strategic imperatives to attenuate the growing Russian and Chinese influence in the region.

There is a latent, not very express, rivalry in this Central Asian energy sphere between Russia, the traditional power, and China, the increasingly emerging one. To fuel its own economic growth, China desperately needs energy imports, so it has made huge investments in Kazakhstan, Turkmenistan, and recently, Uzbekistan (Aral Sea), and has plans to enter into the hydropower sector in Kyrgyzstan and Tajikistan as well. Also, apart from the just completed the China–Kazakhstan gas pipeline, two more Chinese pipeline projects, one each with Kazakhstan and Turkmenistan, are in the offing. There has been, at the same time, an increasing range of cooperation between Russia and China in this sector—Russia is the fifth-largest oil exporter to China; they are planning to build an oil pipeline from Angarsk (Siberia) to Daquing (China), as well as two other gas pipeline projects to reach China. The aforesaid China–Kazakh oil pipeline has the potential to undercut the geopolitical and geo-economic significance of the Washington-backed BTC pipeline.

The geopolitical rivalry for the control of the energy flows of Central Asia and of overall Eurasia is evident in this project. The China–

Kazakh pipeline is geopolitically significant from the standpoint of an emerging Eurasian initiative towards some form of greater energy independence from Washington. Its geo-economic importance lies in the fact that half the oil pumped through this pipeline will flow from Russia, since there is insufficient output from Kazakh fields. This focuses on China–Kazakh–Russia energy cooperation, a nightmare scenario for Washington. Also, China has opted for the first time to secure a source of imported energy which is unlikely to be vulnerable to US aircraft carrier battle-groups, as is the case with oil imports from the Persian Gulf and Sudan.

In May 2001, Dick Cheney, the then US Vice-President, recommended in the Administration's seminal National Energy Policy Report that 'the President make energy security a priority of our trade and foreign policy', singling out the Caspian basin 'as a rapidly growing new area of supply'.[11] The main thrust of US policy towards Central Asian energy has been to promote 'the development of multiple export routes', with the US emphasis being on those routes that bypass Russia, Iran and China. So the US has given priority to geopolitical considerations over commercial viability in determining pipeline routes in the region. This point is most relevant in two US-backed pipeline projects—the BTC and the TAGP. In the first project, the US has used Turkey to outmanoeuvre Russia and Iran against the prevalent estimates that the BTC is the most costly and least viable energy route out of the Caspian. In the second case, the US has promoted Pakistan as a potential transit route as well as market for Central Asian energy and initiated a pipeline project which verily bypasses Iran.

Rajan Menon, the noted analyst, commented that the perimeter of the former Soviet Union constitutes 'Russia's geo-strategic, as opposed to legal, boundary'.[12] To preserve its vital (geo-strategic) interests in the region in the post-Soviet era, Russia took to three courses: security cooperation, economic cooperation and energy cooperation. According to the Russian ministry of foreign affairs, Russian interests in the Central Asian energy sphere include the exploitation of the Central Asian hydrocarbon potentials (mainly of Kyrgyzstan and Tajikistan) which will provide Russia decisive leverage over the whole region; and the use of existing Russian export pipelines and promotion of its energy companies to ensure their maximum possible shares in relevant projects. For example, Russia signed 25-year-long energy cooperation agreements with the four Republics except Kazakhstan in 2003, whereas with Kazakhstan, it has a fifty-five year Production-

Sharing Agreement for Kurmangazy the gas field. Russia is the main investor in the virgin gas fields of Uzbekistan and Kyrgyzstan as well as in the hydroelectric power scenario in Kyrgyzstan and Tajikistan.

SECURITY

It is to be noted that there is significant diversity of security parameters within the region—the states of the South Caucasus are mainly a part of the Caucasian security complex, and are much more vulnerable to events happening in the Northern Caucasus area (consisting of the Federal Regions of Daghestan, Chechnya, Ingushethia, Northern Ossetia, Kabardino-Balkeria, Karachai-Cherkessia and Adygea of Russia) than the Central Asian Republics. Also, these states can be, to a certain extent, linked to the security logic of the Wider Black Sea Region. On the other hand, the problems of insecurity in Central Asia have their roots in the Ferghana Valley area and in Afghanistan. Also India, Pakistan and China are more involved in the Central Asian Republics, both economically and strategically.

The Southern Caucasus region has become potentially one of the most unstable regions in global politics due to a series of unresolved or 'frozen' secessionist conflicts between Armenia and Azerbaijan over Nagorno-Karabakh, and in the secessionist territories of Abkhazia and South Ossetia in Georgia. These conflicts bear the risk of reactivation of these into explosive crises, thereby leading to a deterioration in the fragile security environment of the region. The Nagorno-Karabakh conflict has drawn Russia and Turkey into opposite camps, supporting Armenia and Azerbaijan respectively. Regarding the Abkhaz conflict, Russia reportedly, supports the Abkhaz separatists through its military base in Gudauta and the Russia-led CIS peacekeeping force. There are risks of military spillovers from the Chechen conflict into Georgia, such as the possible dangers of inter-ethnic and inter-communal violence from frictions among ethnic Georgian, Ossetian and Kist-Chechen communities in the Pankisi Gorge area in the northern Georgian sector which borders Chechnya.

Threat perceptions in Central Asia focus on challenges like religious extremism, terrorism, separatism, drug trafficking, etc. The threat of a recurrence of the Tajik separatist conflict of 1992, the growing clout of religious militant groups like the IMU as was evidenced in the armed infiltration of IMU fighters from Tajikistan into Kyrgyzstan and Uzbekistan in 1999 and 2000, and the clandestine support they get from the Chinese Uighur separatists as well as the growing support radical Islamist groups like the Hizb-ut-Tahrir enjoy in the Ferghana Valley and the menace of drug-trafficking all this forms the insecurity scenario in Central Asia. There is no denying the fact that there is an obvious Afghan angle to this: Robin Raphael, the then Assistant Secretary of State for South Asia, told the US Senate in 1996 that 'Afghanistan has become a conduit for drugs, crime and terrorism that can undermine Pakistan, the neighbouring Central Asian states and have an impact beyond Europe and Russia'.[13] Later, a UNI report from Moscow said, 'after burning their fingers in the Chechnya conflict, Afghanistan- and Pakistan-trained mercenaries are seeking fresh pastures to exploit their brand of fundamentalism, with Tajikistan, Kazakhstan and Kyrgyzstan emerging as their new hot-spots'.[14] Also, economic stagnation, weak law-enforcement systems, growth of armed political movements, unprotected borders, poor financial systems and limited institutional capabilities to make use of local resources have made the republics increasingly vulnerable from narco-trafficking across the border from Afghanistan. According to the UN Regional Representative Office for Drug Control and Crime Prevention, approximately 65 per cent of the drugs from Afghanistan follow this route: Afghanistan–Tajikistan–Kyrgyzstan–Kazakhstan–Russia–Europe. A 2002 US State Department report[15] mentioned another permanent route: Afghanistan–Turkmenistan–Uzbekistan–Kazakhstan–Russia–Europe.

The scenario of insecurity in the region has been one of the prime factors in the involvement of regional and extra-regional powers there. Iran and Russia do share some common important interests—neither wishes to see the growth of unhindered American presence in the region, nor do they want to have a growing Turkish influence in the region as Turkey has cultural and linguistic links with most of the states of the region, like Azerbaijan, Kazakhstan, Kyrgyzstan, Uzbekistan and Turkmenistan. Also, the Russian policy of favouring Armenia over Azerbaijan serves Iranian interest as Iran is wary of the secessionist feelings of the Azeries in Southern Iran, who seek to join with Northern Azerbaijan. But the limited appeal of the Iranian brand of Shiite Islam and the fear of export of radical religious ideas have contracted Iran's chances of involving itself in the regional security scene. Turkey's involvement in the region has been more or less pro-West in character: In the Caucasus, it has a strategic partnership with Georgia, it has also taken the role of a virtual guarantor of Azerbaijan's security through supervising the building of Azeri military forces and maintains close[16] military ties with Georgia, though it has very poor relations with Armenia.

Turkey also maintains military assistance programmes with all the Central Asian states, it was actively promoted by the West as a model for secular liberal democracy to the newly independent states of the region after the Soviet disintegration, but Turkey's advantages of being such a model or of promoting pan-Turkism in the region have been checkmated by its limited ability of providing financial and technological assistance to the states.

However, it is to be noted here that the principal powers that are involved in the region are the US and Russia. Whereas the US has concentrated on the region to ensure that 'no Eurasian challenge emerges, capable of dominating Eurasia and thus also of challenging America', Russia, on the other hand, came belatedly to the realization of its vital stakes in the region and to claim the space as its natural 'zone of vital interest': The US' Eurasian geo-strategy purports to forestall, as Brezezinski has expressly put it, the 'worst-possible scenario':

1. An eventual emergence of an assertive 'single entity' in the Eurasian middle space, comprising Russia and the new Republics in the post-Soviet space;
2. An extension of Russia's assertive influence or 'control' over the Eurasian South; and
3. Russia's 'alliance' with China in the East.

On the other hand, Russia rediscovered its strategic stakes involved in the region after its initial pro-West euphoria. The latter part of the post-Soviet era for Russia has been characterized by salvage operations, to rescue the remnants of past influences in the post-Soviet space as well as to stall intrusions by external forces in the process.

The US war on terror in Afghanistan and the establishment of its military bases in the neighbouring Central Asian states—Khanabad, Kokaydy and Tuzel in Uzbekistan, Manas in Kyrgyzstan and Kulob in Tajikistan—the ongoing process of expansion of NATO that has reached the Central Asian Republics, the formation of joint operational-strategic structures by the US armed forces under the USEVCOM and USCENTCOM, the setting up of peacekeeping battalions in Central Asia (CENTRAZBAT) and in the Caucasus (CAUSBAT), the West's support for the so-called Colour Revolutions in Georgia, Ukraine and Kyrgyzstan and the Andjan events in Uzbekistan have all led to increasing clashes of interests between the US and Russia in the region.

As a centre of competitive engagement of external powers, the region is also a witness to competitive regional security initiatives: the US promotes the Georgia–Ukraine–Uzbekistan–Azerbaijan–Moldova (GUUAM) that has become GUAM, now with Uzbekistan not being a part of it; there is the Shanghai Cooperation Organization (SCO), promoted chiefly by China and consisting of Russia, Kazakhstan, Kyrgyzstan, Uzbekistan and Tajikistan as members and India, Pakistan, Iran and Mongolia as observers; and Russia attempts to reinforce the Collective Security Treaty Organization (CSTO), which has Russia, Belarus, Armenia, Kazakhstan and Tajikistan as members. Whereas GUAM was initiated as an anti-Russian grouping, the SCO and the CSTO, despite having undercurrents of competition, have something in common—anti-terrorism drives and putting up a sort of anti-US grouping in the region. NATO is also involved in the region through its Partnership for Peace Programme, in which all the eight states in the region are members, and through its role as the leader-in-charge of the International Security Assistance Force (ISAF) in Afghanistan since 2003. The latter exercise prompted NATO to actively involve itself in the region for military transit and other supportive facilities and that is why Central Asia, along with the Caucasus region, was designated as an area of 'special focus' in the June 2004 Istanbul Summit of NATO.

CONCLUSION

The region under discussion is a new entrant in global politics, in the sense that the states in the region became sovereign entities only after the disintegration of the USSR in 1991 when they became individual actors. For the greater part of the nineteenth and the twentieth centuries, they had belonged to the Russian and the Soviet security systems. But this discussion has not followed their individual journeys towards nation-building, restructuring of their economies and becoming confident actors in the world arena. It has tried to analyse how and why the region assumed strategic significance in the post-Cold War era. The virgin newness of the region, which has emerged from the Soviet fold for the outside world to cultivate for its own geo-strategic ends, as well as its economic potentials, attracted global attention. More significantly, the region offered the external powers, both regional and global, a new area of competition over economic resources and strategic advantages. The region presents itself as a connecting land route between Asia and Europe, limiting the distance and time and thereby the costs of trade between the two continents. The economic logic of various Silk Road Initiatives is based on this basic premise. But it is quite obvious from the choice of routes, and of members, that the powers involved in these initiatives use this geo-cultural concept of the Silk Road to achieve their own geopolitical gains. Interestingly, not all these initiatives are trade routes, like, for instance, the BTC pipeline which is termed as the 'Silk Route of the 21st century', or the NATO-sponsored 'Virtual Silk Highway' to provide satellite access to the Internet and to the European Scientific and Educational networks in the states in the region, or the 'Silk Road Strategy Act' of 1997 by the US Congress for providing considerable sums of money to Armenian and Georgian non-proliferation export control development programmes.

The hitherto untapped energy resources of the region have been another important factor for the global attention it enjoys. The energy politics played by the external states provides ample proof of the geo-economic significance of the region. Again, the involvement of not only Russian but also other international companies in the extraction and development of oil and natural gas in the area, the choice of pipeline routes and the preference for non-Russian ones by the other external countries show that this is not just a geo-economic exercise, based purely on economic logic. But the geopolitics of energy is the most important point, as each power wants to use the leverage of energy to gain a foothold in the region and, in the process, outbid the other powers. It is quite obvious that each power, involved in either the Silk Road Initiatives or the energy-politics, offers its own scheme to the region as the best option available to it, which strategically excludes other competitors. For example, each and every Silk Road Initiative, except the North-South Transport Corridor, has excluded Russia from its programme. Also, the pipeline routes, initiated by the EU and the US, avoid Russian territory and in most cases geopolitics prevails over economics. For instance, the logic of economic feasibility was bypassed in determining the BTC route although the alternative route through Iran made more sense economically. However, it was not politically acceptable because of US–Iran hostilities.

The region has become a centre of global attention in the last fifteen years with so many interests involved for various reasons. Whether the involvement of the powers and clashes of their interests actually constitute a 'Game' or not is not within the purview of this essay, but what this essay stresses is that there is a definite clash of interests among the powers, as is quite obvious from the foregoing discussion. But simultaneously it must be admitted that in this post-Cold War world, conflicting interests do not force nations to remain in isolation; they interact to engage others, to balance between mutual conflicting and cooperating interests—all in an attempt to pursue their own goals. For example, states do cooperate with each other in the energy sphere in this region. The US and Russia concentrate on energy cooperation as is evident from the Joint Statement of the May 2002 Summit which announced a new energy dialogue to 'enhance global energy security and international strategic stability' through measures like creating a Russian–American Working Group on Energy Cooperation. Also, at the 2006, the G-8 Summit under Russian Presidency, the G-8 nations arrived at decisions covering the reliability of the energy infrastructure, diversification of production and supplies of energy resources, development of energy-saving technologies and alternative energy sources with the hope that these decisions would help 'improve the global energy security system', which involves cooperation in this region as well. Turkey's interests in providing alternative routes notwithstanding, one should note that Russia supplies 60 per cent of Turkey's natural gas and 20 per cent of its oil requirements. Moreover, the inauguration of the 750-mile-long Blue Stream gas pipeline, the world's deepest undersea pipeline which connects Southern Russia to the Northern Turkish city of Samsun, accentuates Turkey's dependence on Russia for its energy requirements. There is cooperation in the security sphere as well, as is evident in the Russian offer of help to the US during the Operation Enduring Freedom in Afghanistan in 2001 or in the CSTO's proposal to establish a Eurasian Advisory Council which would include representatives from the CSTO, the SCO, NATO, the EU and the Eurasian Economic Community.

The strategic significance of the region lies as much in its economic potentials as in its geopolitically sensitive location. But the prime factor has been the context. The post-Cold War era which began with the disintegration of the USSR, serves as the contextual reference for this discussion. New possibilities and new challenges for the region, the involvement of new powers and the new dimensions in their rivalries and cooperation while balancing their interests—all this characterizes the era.

NOTES

1. Fulvio Attina, 'Regional Cooperation in Global Perspective: The Case of the "Mediterranean" Regions', Jean Monnet Working Papers in Comparative and International Politics, April 1996.
2. Sheila Page, *Regionalism Among Developing Countries*, Basingstoke: Macmillan, 2000, p. 5.

3. Barry Buzan, 'The Southeast Security Complex', *Contemporary Southeast Asia* 10, no. 6, June 1988, p. 2.
4. Louis J. Cantori and Steven L. Spiegel, *The International Politics of Regions: A Comparative Approach*, Englewood Cliffs, NJ: Prentice-Hall, 1970.
5. See *www.traceca-org.org/docs*
6. 2004 International Symposium on 'Regional Economic Cooperation Along the New Silk Road', available at *http://www.undp.org.cn*
7. See 'Outlook for the Caucasus and Central Asia: Is it the Silk Road or the Great Game?' Available at *http:// annualmeeting.weforum.org*
8. Allan Lee Boyer, 'Recreating the Silk Road: The Challenge of Overcoming Transaction Costs', *China and Eurasia Forum Quarterly* 4, no. 4, 2006.
9. See 'New Silk Road Flourishes with 8-Country Plan', available at *http:// www. kazind.com/newsarchives*
10. See 'The New Silk Roads: Transport and Trade in Greater Central Asia', available at *www.silkroadstudies.org*
11. Cited in Lutz Klevemann, 'Oil and the New Great Game', *The Nation*, February 2004.
12. Rajan Menon, 'After Empire: Russia and the Southern Near Abroad', in *The New Russian Foreign Policy*, ed. Michael Mandelbaum, New York: Council on Foreign Relations, 1998, pp. 121–2.
13. Robin Raphael, 'Testimony to the Senate Foreign Relations Sub-Committee on the Near East and South Asia', 11 May 1996, cited in Ahmed Rashid, *Taliban: Islam, Oil and the New Great Game in Central Asia*, New Haven: Yale University Press, 2000, p. 178.
14. Cited in Mahendra Ved, 'Afghanistan and Cross-border Terrorism in the CIS', paper presented at the International Seminar on 'The Afghanistan Crisis: Problems and Prospects of Peace' organized by the Himalyan Research and Cultural Foundation, Indian Council on Social Science Research, November 2000.
15. See 'International Narcotics Control Strategy Report, 2002', available at *www. state.gov./g/int/rls/nrcrp*
16. Zbigniew Brezezinski, *The Grand Chessboard: American Primacy and Its Geostrategic Imperatives,* New York: Basic Books, 1997, p. 35.

6

Conceptualizing Central Asian Regional Studies in Japan: Approaches, Perspectives and Issues

TIMUR DADABAEV

Research into the Central Asian (Kazakhstan, Kyrgyzstan, Tajikistan, Turkmenistan and Uzbekistan) region is considered to be a minor field, not only in Japan but also in other countries outside Central Asia. Even when the importance of the region is well understood in the international community, the small scale of its local economies, its perceived ability to play only a limited role in international affairs, and its close geographical proximity to large countries like China and Russia result in the lack of interest and enquiry into it. Not a great deal of research has yet been done on Central Asia, and, moreover, very few researchers or organizations have studied it as a single region. Depending on the political and other considerations, the Central Asian region is often considered to be part of either the larger Eurasia, South Asia or Turkic world.[1]

Yet, the international significance of Central Asia is exemplified by the immense regional energy resource deposits, its geographic location, being at the crossroads of various transport and energy corridors, its economic and demographic potentials and regional importance in terms of the stability not only of Asia but also of Europe. These keep scholars' and practitioners' attention on the region. The high integration potential of the regional states further increases their international standings and brings to light the importance of conceptualizing it as a single region. Because of these reasons, the realization for enhancing research into this region and treating it as one regional unit as opposed to the approach where Central Asia is researched as a part of other geographic areas and spaces has gained ground in the academic community in recent years. Accordingly, this essay poses the following questions. What is the place of Central Asia in various academic disciplines and studies? How is Central Asia currently treated by scholars and what are the problems with current approaches to it? What are the challenges and alternatives available?

In order to answer this set of questions, this study will use the case of Central Asian studies in Japan. This essay employs the case study of Japan mainly because there is a genuine steady interest and ongoing debate among Japanese scholars about the role and the place of Central Asia as a region and how studies into it in particular should be posited. Structurally, this essay will first briefly outline the history of the question of how and why Central Asian studies witnessed significant growth in Japan. By doing so, it will attempt to contribute to the understanding about the areas that attract Japanese scholars to Central Asia. The second part will highlight the specificities of Japanese approaches to Central Asian research by focusing on the language choices of scholars and their perceptions about Central Asian geographic belonging. The third part will then highlight the general modern trends in Japanese studies on Central Asia by emphasizing the apolitical nature of such research and its inner orientation. And finally, the concluding remarks will touch upon the major problems, challenges and tasks of Central Asian research in Japan.

JAPANESE RESEARCH ON CENTRAL ASIA

Historical Research

Historical studies are the starting point for Japanese research into Central Asia. Although the number of newly enrolling students into the departments of history in general and specializing in Central Asian history in particular is falling in recent years, this is still the most developed field in Japan. While the number of Central Asia-focused historians in Japan is not very high, their findings are often competitive and frequently exceed those of their colleagues elsewhere, including research findings of Central Asian scholars based in the region and outside of it.

As provided in the brief yet very thorough and informative account of Central Asian history by Hisao Komatsu, the first steps in Japanese enquiries into Central Asia started with the travels of Japanese diplomats (for instance, Nishi Tokujiro) and officials stationed in Russia to the Russian Turkestan.[2] In their writings they attempted to depict the realities of the lives and values of the people in the Russian-dominated territories of what is now Central Asia. Such attempts are also very similar to the descriptions of diplomats and officials of similar, little-known territories (aside from Central Asia) during their extensive travels. Later in the twentieth century, further efforts were made by Japanese officials, diplomats and scholars alike, to enquire about the state of affairs in Soviet-era Central Asia. There were few such attempts in the 1930s and 1940s. Yet these attempts were mostly encouraged and predisposed by the expansionist ambitions of imperial Japan. These efforts ended with the Japanese defeat in the Second World War.

Studies of Central Asia as a part of the orient were more successful and fruitful. These studies include those of Eastern Turkestan, especially of the pre-Islamic period. The trend set by these scholars largely shaped the mindset of many academicians and the public at large about the historical, cultural and social connections between Japan and Central Asia through the Silk Road. At a later stage, with new studies of what is currently Central Asia, the idea that there is more to the notion of Central Asian history than the connection and development through the Silk Road was mooted, which largely emphasized the importance of understanding Central Asian history through understanding the mutual interaction and integration of the nomad and settled societies.[3]

The more recent studies on modern history focus on a variety of subjects connected to Central Asia. These include the period from the Russian conquest, and the subsequent relations of Central Asia and Russia, to the various uprisings in Central Asia (like the Andijan uprising led by Dukchi Ishan) and the policy of National Delimitation.[4] In addition, the Perestroika period encouraged various studies of the current affairs of Central Asia, producing a number of studies covering both Central Asian regional developments and country-by-country analyses.

There are several reasons for the intensive development of historical studies into Central Asia, mentioned above, in Japan. Firstly, aside from the politically motivated studies of the early period, there is the deep appreciation and interest that both scholars and the general public have for the Silk Road in Japan. Central Asia comprises one section of the Silk Road, symbolized by cities such as Samarkand, Bukhara and Khiva which flourished because of the traffic of people travelling along it. In addition, the nomadic lifestyles of the people along the Silk Road served as an additional source of inspiration for those interested in the region, leading them to enquire about the essence of these nomadic and settled lifestyles. Furthermore, Japanese archaeologists and historians with an interest in this history have produced fine studies, maybe some of the best in the world. Naturally, successful studies produced followers who further developed this field. Secondly, because Central Asia was a closed area during the Soviet period, research fields other than history were restricted for political reasons. Access to the region was limited and analysis of social conditions in the various areas of Central Asia was not encouraged by the Soviet government, which tried to use the Central Asian republics as a showcase and role model for an 'Asian form of socialism'. The possibility of unrestricted research into the societies of Central Asia produced fears of unwanted results among the Soviet authorities.

Even in the aftermath of their independence, the majority of the regional countries preferred the foreign scholars to work on historical themes as opposed to those involving modern issues and problems of societies. For Central Asian governments, history remains the object of their pride and admiration—something that they want told, distributed and glorified not only by local but also by foreign scholars. Each of the regional states attempted to re-shape and rebuild its history emphasizing its pre-Soviet history and making efforts to encourage studies into it. Therefore, they opened up access to new primary sources symbolizing the fact that historical research would be welcomed by the governments. On the contrary, for the majority of regional governments, and especially those that are more conservative in their attitudes to the freedom of research, studies into contemporary social problems are often not very rewarding.

Area Studies

Conceptually defined, the second field to take up Central Asia was Area Studies, a new discipline compared to the study of history. There were a few periods of development in the area of Area Studies too. It initially approached Central Asia as a part of the Soviet Union, but after the collapse of the latter, it began to study it as an independent region. In terms of its aims and methodological contribution, Area Studies had several targets. Firstly, there was the task of understanding the region and its specificities. Naturally, due to political restraints, scholars in this group first specialized in Soviet, Turkish, Chinese or other area studies, with minor focus on territories that are now referred to as Central Asia. Under Soviet rule, access to modern Central Asia was very limited mainly due to political constraints, while the infrastructure was more or less well developed. With the demise of the Soviet Union, part of those specializing in larger geographic units zoomed in on smaller localities and specific regions. In this sense, the collapse of the Soviet Union presented these scholars with both opportunities and new challenges and frontiers.

In addition to the studies of countries and local specificities, another group of studies focuses more on certain issues and problems as opposed to countries and regions. Such topics include studies of minority groups settled across Central Asia,[5] community life in this region,[6] the research of the forms and shapes of everyday Islam,[7] enquiry into such notions as democratization, popular participation in the governance,[8] the region-wide problems of water resources,[9] and border delimitation or cooperation.[10] The distinct feature of these types of studies is that they focus on their research targets by crossing the geographic or disciplinary boundaries. The primary aim of these studies within Area Studies is to understand, explain and contribute to problem solving.

Owing to these features, the field of Area Studies has been popular over a considerable period of time with students, scholars and practitioners. However, the major flaw with it is that by using multidisciplinary methods, and by focusing on the subject and not on certain boundary-defined geographic spaces or disciplines, it is very difficult to conceptualize these studies and place them within the net of other similar or related studies. For many discipline-based scholars, this approach of Area Studies specialists represents an attempt to cover a bit of everything while compromising on the depth of the study or its academic value. In this sense, in Japan, Area Studies, to a great extent, serves the function of a cushion between discipline-dominated specialists and the general public. In this sense also, this field is very successful in attracting the attention of people at large to the Central Asian region, making the task of expansion of the discipline-oriented studies, mentioned in the next section, and a wider dissemination of their tasks easier.

Central Asia as a Case Study

A third type of study frequently observed in Japan on the Central Asian region uses Central Asia to provide detailed case studies to test certain theories of certain disciplines and to discuss some broader themes, using the distinctive features to be found in this region, rather than attempt to study and understand Central Asia itself. An example of studies of this type are the few studies by agricultural economists or agriculturalists into the issue of agricultural cooperatives or soil pollution.[11] Similarly, a certain number of environmentalists studied the problem of the Aral Sea as a case study to understand the general nature of water-related catastrophes in the world. Related studies by environmental scientists were on water problems from the point of view of the water quality, water reserves available in the mountainous areas of Central Asia, or the impact of global warming on the change in natural cycles.[12] Law scholars are often preoccupied with the introduction of a new law system emerging in the post-Socialist societies.[13] For them, the study of the society is a secondary variable, their primary focus being the newly established legal system. Very often, they are preoccupied with understanding and introducing specific legal cases, and once they achieve their task, they move on to a completely different set of countries, thus again prioritizing the comparative studies of legal systems as opposed to in-depth analyses of correlation between the society and the legal systems being constructed. The important point about all of these studies is that they have provided a wealth of detailed information which is essential to complement studies in other fields.

JAPANESE APPROACHES TO STUDYING CENTRAL ASIA

Two aspects in researching Central Asia seem to be of crucial importance. Firstly, the language choices of scholars studying this region largely influence the outcomes of their research. Secondly, the issue of how to academically conceptualize the Central Asian region among other regions is an important factor in understanding the logic behind many developments in it.

Language Choice and Central Asian studies

International (including the Japanese) scholars of Central Asia have employed a number of languages to study the historical background as well as the ethnic and religious constructs of societies in the region. Initially the main languages utilized by them in the course of their studies were Russian, Turkish, Chinese, Arabian and Persian. These were the languages through which Soviet-era Central Asia was approached and researched. Accordingly, during the period of Soviet rule, scholars who studied Central Asia as part of the Soviet Union used the Russian language. In many cases they first acquired some knowledge of Russian and then spent a period of study within the educational and research institutions in Moscow, Leningrad (St. Petersburg) and other cities. A limited number of them were then given permission to travel to or live in Central Asia for a short period of time. Naturally, for the majority, guidance was provided by their Russian or Moscow-based 'supervisors' and the degree of expertise of these 'supervisors' differed from each another. Even when foreign scholars managed to visit Central Asia in person, their behaviour was closely watched over and their interests, academic contacts and fieldwork significantly controlled. In certain cases, these controls were applied in order to prevent foreign scholars from gaining access to certain, even non-sensitive information, while in other cases, the informants and academic contacts were intentionally guided to provide biased information in order to distort the realities of life in Central Asia. Very few writings, managed to avoid these challenges and manipulation, and they form the solid basis of modern Central Asian studies.

Another group of scholars considered Central Asia, even in Soviet times, as an integral part of the Turkic culture and area and therefore used the Turkish language as the language of access to information. The Turkish language presented an opportunity for many scholars not only to access information written in Turkish language by those Central Asians who had either immigrated to or worked in Turkey, but also offered a chance for them to learn the grammatical and phrase constructs of Turkish, which is very close to the languages of peoples in Soviet Central Asia. It was they who, after the collapse of the Soviet Union, could easily adopt their linguistic skills and learn local languages fairly easily.

In addition to Russian and Turkish, there were a variety of languages used to access Central Asia. As mentioned earlier, Chinese was one such language, which was used to gain access to and study the Chinese part of Central Asia although the common languages of the people residing in these areas are Turkic in their nature. Those scholars who considered Central Asia in terms of its Arab or Persian cultural heritage used the Arabic and Persian languages to understand the history and traditions of these peoples. This is especially true for those scholars who work on written sources.

The situation regarding languages of access to the Central Asian region owed to the fact that during the Soviet period access to the region was either through Moscow or through a country with close cultural links to it. Although such a variety of linguistic approaches offered a multiplicity of research outcomes and viewpoints on the region, it also resulted in two major problems. Firstly, these foreign languages used by international scholars were not necessarily very useful for pursuing research at the local level. They may have provided access to experts on the region or written research sources but were unfit to serve as an intermediate tool of communication in the interviews in the field. For instance, the answers of respondents and the people at large in the Russian language will differ significantly from the answer to the same question in a local language because the terminology used in the latter would normally imply certain notions which are non-existent or disregarded in the Russian or other alternative languages.[14] In addition, perceptions narrated in Russian will differ from those in local languages because there is a difference between the same notions used in various languages. Consequently, using these languages for research often unavoidably coloured the results and these languages served as a 'double filter' on the way to the information.

Regional Affiliation

Language choice has a casual relation with the treatment of the region by many scholars. As partly indicated earlier, various scholars, according to their main language of access to the region, analyse different aspects of these societies from different perspectives. This, however, creates confusion among scholars of Central Asia in Japan about how to regard the regional affiliation and value system of Central Asia. Some would consider Central Asia to be part of Russian research, while others would include it in Europe or South Asia. In addition, such uncertainty about how to consider Central Asia among other 'Asias' is evident not only among individual scholars but also among institutions. For instance, in certain institutions, Central Asia is classified as part of the Middle East, while in others as Western Asia, the Slavic world or even Europe. With new US-suggested initiative to include Central Asia into South Asia (the concept of Greater Central Asia) and consider it to be part of the latter, only added to the confusion. When Central Asian scholars from outside Japan witness such confusion, the natural reaction is strong resentment of such artificial divisions. While many Central Asian scholars recognize the commonalities in the mentality and lifestyles of people in Asia, the majority of them reject approaches which consider Central Asia to be part of South Asia or the Slavic world. Although certain literature indicates that Central Asian regional identity is somehow linked to the Eurasian one and to the notion of Eurasianism, there are a considerable number of scholars who emphasize the notion of the Central Asian region as being a separate geographic and geopolitical space. At the same time, the fact that the Central Asian region is often studied in combination with or as a part of other regions indicates that Central Asia still has to be evaluated as a unitary region. This largely implies that while Central Asia appears on the geographic map of the world, it has yet to be drawn into the intellectual and research map in Japan and internationally.

TRENDS IN JAPANESE RESEARCH ON CENTRAL ASIA

There are several trends in the Japanese research, which are not limited to but included into the following two main groups. These are dominance of apolitical research themes and striving for fundamental raw data.

Apolitical Nature of Research

The first trend to be emphasized here is the apolitical nature of the studies on Central Asia in Japan. In the main, these studies are not influenced by political considerations. There are a very few studies which have a political agenda. Even fewer studies are funded by or conducted through the guidance of politically motivated institutions or agencies, as is the case with many funding institutions in Europe and the US. In addition, studies which start with certain political assumptions, or attempt to prove them, are non-existent. In particular, special agendas such as democratization of the studied societies or human rights are neither given priority nor ignored. Even those funds that come from the government do not have preconditions or political tasks to be achieved through such funded research. The same can be said about private funding which comes from internationally known funds like the Toyota Foundation, the Sasakawa Foundation, the Tokyo Foundation, the Matsushita Foundation and many others. The Japanese-government affiliated Japan Society for the Promotion of Science (JSPS) also funds a great number of research projects and individual researchers. Yet no political agendas are normally put forward. Rather there is an atmosphere of almost absolute research freedom in the research institutions and among individual scholars.

The approach is extremely important and efficient and the academic merits of the research projects are given primary importance while the remaining aspects are respected but not prioritized. Such an attitude is not only a good sign of the open-minded approach of the scholarly and funding communities in Japan, but more importantly, it offers greater opportunity for scholars funded by these institutions to penetrate the societies being studied. Moreover, such an impartial policy offers greater opportunity for Japan-based scholars to engage their Central Asian counterparts, even if those from the most repressed societies. This does not imply that Japanese funds or the Japanese government supports repression. On the contrary, the approach to these projects from the point of view that enhanced academic exchange and common research activities will eventually result in stronger academic potentials and active civil society institutions.

The second trend within this group is partly connected to the apolitical nature of research in Japan, namely, its complete detachment from policy. On the one hand, academic objectives and less policy-binding and non-conditional research objectives make these studies more attractive for the academic community, for the reasons explained above. On the other hand, such absence of policy in the research objectives of many studies raises many questions about the applicability of those studies for the purpose of the improvement of local conditions or living standards of the population. It is certainly not compulsory to have a policy direction in all fields of research, but in some the excellent results achieved by Japanese scholars could well be harnessed for wider policy choices and perspectives. Large-scale surveys or heavily invested studies into environment might potentially benefit Central Asian countries by providing the data, which for various reasons, they cannot obtain on their own, and by transferring know-how and expertise from technologically superior Japanese institutions to their counterparts in the field.

Among the many reasons for the apolitical nature of the studies and their weak policy orientation is the fact that in its imperial past, Japan had already employed research to satisfy its political ambitions and achieve certain colonial goals. This became a lesson for many Japanese scholars and practitioners about the dangers of such approaches which prevent them from using their research findings and projects even for the sake of contributing to the societies they study. This emphasizes the dilemma that the Japanese academic community studying Central Asia is facing at the moment, which, on the one hand is purely research-oriented and on the other hand is striving to use its knowledge and expertise for the good of the studied societies.

Normative and Inner-Oriented Trends of Japanese Research

In the long list of tendencies, which are not limited to the ones mentioned in this essay, another is a paradoxical tendency in Central Asian studies in Japan: the number of studies increases annually, covering a great number of areas and disciplines, yet the scope and amount of data available on the various subjects is still very limited.

A great number of studies have been done on particular themes concerning phenomena in the region, but there is even greater number of subjects which await study. There exist a vast number of studies concerning the particular states, their governments and government–society relations, but there is an urgent need for Japanese scholars to move from a classical normative pattern of focusing mainly on these aspects of Central Asia. Much more needs to be done in terms of research which focuses on the non-state actors at the local level in order to look at various issues from the perspective of the ordinary people living in Central Asia.

This problem also brings to light the existing gap between the topics and the research themes that Japanese researchers consider important and what their Central Asian counterparts attribute importance to. At first glance, studies about Central Asia by both groups of scholars seem to be following the same direction, and in some sense this is certainly true. However, there is a fundamental difference in the logic behind and the purpose of the various studies conducted in Japan and Central Asia. On the one hand, studies by Japanese scholars generally tend to place a greater emphasis on understanding Central Asia and the way various institutions and life cycles work there. On the other, Central Asian scholars are more concerned with policy-related topics as well as the relationships between the region and other places, such as Japan, Asia and the world. Their interests also extend to the kinds of changes that have already occurred, or need to occur in those relationships.

Obviously, such differences between the objectives of the studies are connected to the trends indicated in the previous section, and they are also connected to the differences in the backgrounds and standpoints of researchers in the Japanese and Central Asian settings. However, this also highlights the potential area for fruitful cooperation, which again can benefit both local and Japanese scholars. In addition, if and when this difference in perspectives and research interests lessens, both sides will be able to discuss questions from the same standpoint: promoting the exchange of ideas and dialogue between the academic communities and contributing to the economic, social and political development of the respective Central Asian societies.

CONCLUSION

There are a great number of challenges and new tasks that Japan-based scholars of Central Asia need to embrace in order to increase efficiency and international recognition of their studies. Among them, in the light of the issues already mentioned, two challenges seem to be of particular importance. These remain the necessity of avoiding the biases associated with the notion of 'double filters' in studying Central Asian societies; and increasing the number of studies that will shift away from normative approaches and seek new angles from which to look at the region. Central Asian studies in Japan, need to consider Central Asia not in terms of being part of a Russian, Turkish or Middle Eastern-Arab sphere of influence, but rather as an individual region. This will eventually result in more attention being paid to local-based indigenous knowledge, ways of thinking, lifestyles and values.

In addition, knowledge of local languages needs to be given primary significance when approaching these societies. Even these days there is a pattern of thinking among foreign scholars that Central Asia can be studied through an adequate knowledge of Russian, Turkish, Chinese or some similar language. While recognizing the value of these languages for Central Asia-focused scholars in Japan, there is a growing tendency of studying local languages, which is the only tool that can enable scholars to reflect on the local perspectives. The main problem of many studies done in the Russian, Turkish or Chinese languages is that Central Asia is often misrepresented, either because of intentional or unintentional stereotypes towards Central Asians or because of the existence of a linguistic 'double filter', making it very difficult to catch and correctly interpret the peculiarities and specificities of certain expressions and languages. With the recognition of this fact, the number of those proficient in Central Asian local languages and those who use local languages for their research (such as Uzbek, Kazakh, Kyrgyz, Turkmen, Tajik and Uighur) has increased dramatically among Japanese scholars in the recent years. This is largely a sign of the increasing opportunities for language study and study abroad that have come with the independence of the former Soviet republics. The number of Japan-based Central Asian language programmes is very limited and has yet to be increased. Enhancing the local-language capacity of Japanese and Japan-based scholars of Central Asia further will remain the task and the challenge to avoid the 'double filter' misrepresentation of local societies.

Second, broader, socially based research themes are necessary, rather than those centred around the notions of state or the government. Research which looks at local forms of communities, such as how people in Central Asia understand various issues, the structure of formal and informal networks and lineages and others, is potentially a perspective frontier for future studies. From the point of view of policy, studies which deal with transnational, region-encompassing issues, on the one hand, and those concerned with raising the latent power of local communities and other non-state actors on the other, seem to be of special importance. As an example of the former, scholars could probe, through specific case studies, the feasibility of regional integration and the possibility of transforming the national sovereignty into regional sovereignty over certain issues in Central Asia. A theme associated with this type of study is research into the ways to achieve sustainable development in the region without over-reliance upon the government.

Third, to conduct such research effectively, it is essential to facilitate and maintain enhanced cooperation between Japanese and Central Asian scholars. One way to achieve this, which is being exemplarily practised in recent years, is joint field-based research expeditions and teams which broaden the participation boundaries to include participants from Japan and Central Asia on an equal footing.

Finally, many Central Asian issues have traditionally been discussed within the various disciplines, such as International Relations, Economics, History, Cultural Anthropology and Environmental Studies. However, the analysis and solution of the many problems facing Central Asia require a multidisciplinary, multifaceted approach. Discussions confined within the various disciplines are often limited in their academic tools and the scope of their coverage. In this sense, the problem-solving approach, when a problem or an issue is approached from a variety of disciplines and fields of knowledge within the same expedition or fieldwork, seems to be a better way to explore post-Soviet Central Asia.

NOTES

1. For Turkish perspectives on Central Asian research, see Ismail Turkoglu, 'Central Eurasian Studies in Turkey', in *Research Trends in Modern Central Eurasian Studies (18-20 Centuries): A Selective and Critical Bibliography of Works Published between 1985 and 2000*, Part 1, ed. Stephane A. Dodoignon and Hisao Komatsu, Tokyo: Tokyo Bunko, 2003, pp. 99-126. For the North American view on Central Eurasian research, see Laura L. Adams, 'Research Trends in Sociology', in Dodoignon and Komatsu, *Research Trends in Modern Central Eurasian Studies (18-20 Centuries)*, pp. 87–98.
2. For a brief description of Central Eurasian studies in Japan, see Komatsu Hisao, 'Central Asian Studies in Japan', *Asuno Toyogaku*, no. 13, pp. 4–6 (available in print and online at: *www.ioc.u-tokyo.ac.jp*). For a more detailed account see Hisao Komatsu, 'Modern Central Eurasian Studies in Japan: An Overview 1985–2000', in Dodoignon and Komatsu, *Research Trends in Modern Central Eurasian Studies (18-20 Centuries)*, pp. 127–45.

3. See Mano Eiji, *Chuou Ajia no Rekishi (A History of Central Asia)*, Tokyo: Kodansha, 1977; Mano Eiji, 'Retrospect and Future Issues in Inner Asian Studies', *Annals of Japan Association for Middle East Studies (AJAMES)* 17, no. 2, 2002, pp. 33–44.
4. For instance see Hisao Komatsu. 'Andijan no . . . to Ishan (The Andijan Uprising and Ishan)', *Toyoshi Kenkyu* 44, no. 4, 1986, pp. 1–31.
5. For example, see Nurbulat Masanov, Erlan Karin, Andrei Chebotarev and Natsuko Oka, *The Nationalities Question in Post-Soviet Kazakhstan*, Tokyo: Institute of Developing Economies, 2002; Natsuko Oka, 'Soren ni okeru Chyosen jin kyousei ijyu (The forced deportation of Koreans in Soviet Union)', in *Kaihou no Hikari to Kage* (Lights and Shadows of Liberation), Tokyo: Iwanami Shoten, 1998, pp. 65–90; Natsuko Oka, 'Deportation of Koreans from the Russian Far East to Central Asia', in *Migration in Central Asia: Its History and Current Problems*, ed. Komatsu Hisao, Obiya Chika and John S. Shoeberlein, Osaka: The Japan Center for Area Studies, National Museum of Ethnology, 2000, pp. 127–45.
6. See Yoshida Setsuko, 'A Field Report on Economic Transition: Lifestyle Changes in a Village of Northern Kyrgyzstan', *Central Asia Monitor*, no. 4, 1999, pp. 1–7; Yoshida Setsuko, 'Zayakutachino' Shyudanka (Collectivization of Sayaks)', *Shyakai Jinruigaku Nenpo*, no. 26, 2000, pp. 169–85; Timur Dadabaev, *Mahalla no jitsujo: Cyuuou Ajia no Shyakai no Dentou to Henyou*, Tokyo: University of Tokyo Press, 2006.
7. For instance, Hisao Komatsu, 'Central Asia', in Haneda Masami and Miura Toru (eds.), *Islamic Urban Studies: Historical Review and Perspectives*, London/ New York: Kegan Paul International, 1994, pp. 281–328.
8. For instance, Uyama Tomohiko, 'Kazakhstan no keni shyugi taisei (Authoritarian Regime in Kazakhstan)', *Roshiia Kenkyu (Russian Studies)*, no. 23, 1996, pp. 91–109.
9. I. Kobori and M.H. Glants (eds.), *Central Eurasian Water Crisis: Caspian, Aral and Dead Seas: Water Resources Management and Policy*, Tokyo: United Nations University Press, 1998; Tsuneo Tsukatani, Kristina N. Toderich and Umerzak M. Sultangazin, 'Daily Water Flow Database from Aral Basin', *Discussion Paper*, no. 526, Kyoto: Kyoto Institute of Economic Research, Kyoto University, 2001.
10. For instance, see Timur Dadabaev, *Towards Post-Soviet Central Asian Regional Integration: A Scheme for Transitional States,* Tokyo: Akashi Shoten, 2004.
11. See, for instance, *Survey on Agricultural and Rural Development Based on Population Issues: The Republic of Uzbekistan*, Tokyo: The Asia Population and Development Association (APDA), 2003.
12. See, for instance, Chiyuki Narama, Yuichi Shimamura, Saichi Nakayama and Kanatbek Abdrakhmanov, 'Recent Changes of Glacier Coverage in the Western Terskey-Alatoo Range, Kyrgyz Republic, using Corona and Landsat', *Annals of Glaciology*, no. 43, 2006, pp. 223–9.
13. For instance, see *Uzbekistan Minpou Jiten (Dictionary of Civil Code of Uzbekistan)*, Nagoya: Center for Asian Legal Exchange, Graduate School of Law, Nagoya University, 2004.
14. For differences in the use of language in social research and concrete examples, see, Timur Dadabaev, 'Uzbekistan: Post-Soviet Realities', in *Values and Life Styles in Urban Asia*, ed. Takashi Inoguchi, Miguel Basanez, Akihiko Tanaka and Timur Dadabaev, Mexico City: SIGLO XXI Editors, 2005, pp. 207–34; and Timur Dadabaev, 'Post-Soviet Realities of Society in Uzbekistan', *Central Asian Survey* 23, no. 2, 2004, pp. 141–66.

7

The New Regional Approach Towards South and Central Asia: An Assessment

ARPITA BASU ROY

'Regions', regionalization and regional organizations are all a product of and a reaction to the changing economic and political world order. A region implies a sense of world. It is much more likely that the sense of region or the nature of regionalism or the structure of a regional organization will change over time, as conditions, and the perception of them, change within the region and outside. Not all the actors even within a region, or indeed a regional organization, need share the same perception or motivation. They are likely to use the idea or the structure for different purposes or apply different emphases. The actors and their roles, taken together, make up the essence of the region. A region is part of the world and for some it may be the whole world. More usually, it is seen to be part of the world in which there are other regions variously conceived and constituted. In them, geographical realities assert themselves, but they are most readily conceived and created in political and economic terms.[1] There are no 'natural' regions; they are constructed, deconstructed and reconstructed—intentionally or non-intentionally—in the process of global transformation by collective human action and identity formation. Since regions are social constructions, there are no 'given' regions, nor any given regionalist interests, but interests and identities are shaped in the process of interaction and inter-subjective understanding.

The focus of this essay is the region of Central and South Asia and the recent attempt to renew the linkages between the two regions involving Afghanistan. At issue is a region reaching across Central and West Asia to the Indian subcontinent, with shared roots and whose parts, to a large extent, intersect in Afghanistan. Depending on the historical context and perspective, the two major regions of Asia, i.e. South Asia and Central Asia, have been either linked or separated. In recent times, obstacles to integration frequently proved difficult to overcome and separating forces have overpowered the integrating trends. It is being argued that the fault line between Central Asia and South Asia has incurred significant economic and political costs for the countries on either side of the line and even globally. It has provided fertile ground for illegal drug production and fermentation of extremist political ideologies and movements, and it has deprived the region of the benefits of integration and the movement of people, goods and ideas. Moreover, it has isolated their bridge, which is Afghanistan, for decades and suppressed its economic development. In view of the transformation that is taking place in the region, the essay discusses the benefits of such cooperation for the region. The discussion revolves around the vision, hypotheses, strategies, initiatives of a South–Central Asia cooperation from the standpoint of the relative benefits and challenges of regional cooperation for both regions as such cooperation involving Afghanistan hinges upon establishing a Central–South Asia Regional Cooperation Organisation in future. The essay argues that such cooperation can be achieved by means of what is more generally known as the Contractualist or Functional theory (Interest-based theories) of International Relations as advocated by Robert O. Keohane and which had been labelled as 'Neoliberal Institutionalism'. Theoretically it can be argued that states are rational egoists who care for their absolute gains and it is the international regimes that help states realize their common interests. And this rationalizes the cooperative initiatives between South and Central Asia involving Afghanistan as a bridge.

The essay also delves into the American approach and its role in such cooperation. The dominant principle in defining regions and regional boundaries have generally been made on the basis of the 'purpose' for which regions are to be used. This essay also analyses the 'purpose' of Washington's new approach to Central and South Asia. It is also very important to note that in 2005, the USA launched its Central Asian Infrastructure Integration Initiative programme whereby it was recognized that a 'secure and prosperous Afghanistan, which anchors Central Asia and links it to South Asia is essential to the future of economic success'.[2] By practising a new approach based on a new idea about regional division and integration, Washington intends to implement the idea of turning Afghanistan into a link between Central and South Asia to integrate them into a single region. This is to be accomplished with the help of US-promoted transportation and energy corridors which will cross Afghanistan to tie Central and South Asia together. The essay seeks to explore the idea that 'South and Central Asia is a region of great strategic importance where American interests and values are engaged as never before' and how such a new regional approach will boost Washington's regional ambitions and its global position. It will attempt also to study the important conceptual distinction between the Greater Central Asia project (initiated by the Central Asia-Caucasus Institute) and the conception of a new single South and Central Asia region held together by Afghanistan, initiated by the US administration. By way of conclusion, the essay argues that in such South–Central Asia cooperation, where several challenges impede the process, the 'hegemonic-stability theory' may apply and then reinforce the role of the hegemon (in this case the USA) in the formation of international regimes and further substantiate the claim of the stabilizing effects of power concentration. It also takes note of the possibilities of maintaining the regime even if the role of the hegemon is diminished in future.

THEORIES OF COOPERATION AND THE SIGNIFICANCE OF ECONOMIC COOPERATION FOR SOUTH AND CENTRAL ASIA

Regimes may be the result of the direct imposition of institutional arrangements on subordinate elements coerced into compliance. Imperial and feudal systems are said to be illustrative of such regimes. In an alternative conception, a dominant power may exert leadership in the formation and preservation of regimes which serve its interests but are also widely accepted in the international system. Thus Robert O. Keohane develops a regime concept based on hegemonic stability, cooperation and collaboration. Focusing on the world political economy of the two generations after Second World War, Keohane defines hegemony as possession of a preponderance of material resources—raw materials, sources of capital, control over markets and a competitively advantageous position in the production of goods in great demand. Central to Keohane's concept is what he terms as cooperation after hegemony at a time when the hegemonic power had declined in power and influence.[3]

The neo-liberal or interest-based theories of international relations, which have come to represent the mainstream approach to power differentials, argue that international regimes help states realize their common interest although they portray the states as rational egoists who care only for their absolute gains. Neo-liberals have drawn heavily on the economic theories of institutions that focus on information and transactions of interests that underlie different types of regimes and that affect the likelihood of a regime being created in the first place.[4]

The purest representatives of the neo-liberal regime theory may have two approaches. The first, 'contractualism', which studies the effects of international regimes on the ability of actors to cooperate in situation resembling the prisoner's dilemma, develops a functional argument to explain the creation and maintenance of regimes. The second, situation-structuralism, building on this perspective takes into account the full spectrum of strategic situation in which actors might cooperate through regimes. It analyses the implications of these different constellations of interests (or 'games') for both regime formation and the institutional form of the regime.

It is rational to cooperate when states have common interests, although it is another matter how states can overcome the uncertainty about their partner's objectives and fear of defection.[5] The basic argument for any kind of regional cooperation revolves around the idea of potential gains for the people of the region. On the other hand, the price of non-cooperation could also be large: lost economic opportunities, a heavy toll extracted from the spread of disease, natural disasters and environmental destruction, as well as conflict and insecurity. In the case of Central Asia, cooperation would ease the barriers placed by the new borders between the republics and allow people to connect throughout the region and beyond with trade and investment, linked infrastructure, shared water and energy, common environmental, health and disaster protection, and a free flow of ideas and knowledge. Furthermore, the region faces real opportunities. It is today surrounded by some of world's the most dynamic economies. The people of the region enjoy commonalities of history, culture and language, conflict among the new nations has been avoided and new avenues for trade and access to world markets and knowledge are opening up. All these reflect the shared conviction that borders that divide are borders that lack a human face, and only increased cooperation can help the Central Asian states expand trade, especially with distant countries. International donors have started cooperating on transport investment programmes, which will improve old transit routes and create new ones throughout Afghanistan. This could greatly facilitate trade across the region from Iran to Pakistan to Central Asia, provided security and peace are fully established and maintained in Afghanistan. Bridges have been constructed between Afghanistan and Tajikistan, and more are under construction with

US assistance, including a bridge across the Panj River: groundbreaking took place in 2005. Today, Afghanistan offers vast business opportunities to its Central Asian neighbours due to the flow of foreign and military assistance into the country.

Central Asia's landlocked location requires the five countries in the region to maintain good relations with neighbouring countries for international trade (markets and supplies), for transport and transit routes beyond the region and to major international shipping ports, and for dealing with external threats from terrorism, the drug trade and human trafficking. The immediate neighbours, Afghanistan, China, Iran and Russia, have become important partners in many of these areas. Except for Afghanistan, their relative size and wealth offer opportunities to obtain investment capital as well as access to new technologies, and expanding markets for Central Asia's natural resources, agricultural products, other raw materials and some manufactured goods. At the same time, Central Asia's relations with its neighbours reflect complex national interests and risks which can spark tension in bilateral relations and in regional organizations and programmes. Regional organizations have been created and are gaining in strength.[6] Increased cooperation would help the CARs expand trade, especially with distant countries, take a more active part in global production networks and related trade in manufactured products, and diversify trade in terms of geographical distribution and commodity composition.[7]

For South Asia, apart from the general issues of cooperation like trade facilitation and transport, investment trade and business potential, sharing the benefits of water; countering the narcotics trade and transportation of energy,[8] increased cooperation regarding the TAPI natural gas pipeline, renewable sources of energy, and agriculture and agro-industrial development are also important. However, the primary interests revolve around greater trade in energy between the energy surplus countries of Central Asia and the energy deficit countries of South Asia, notably India and Pakistan. Another positive impact of integration is that region-wide organizations could facilitate cooperation, which among other objectives, would discourage interference in Afghanistan.

It is believed that Afghanistan, like all countries in the region, will benefit from the payment of transit fees and duties. Its neighbour Iran will be able to reclaim its traditional vocation as a moderate trading state looking Eastward as opposed to its present role as a militant Shia state fighting for influence in the Arab lands to its west. Moreover the reopening of the ancient east-west trade corridors across Pakistan will break its isolation.[9] It can thus be argued that since the countries of these regions can find common interests and derive absolute gains through cooperation, a wholehearted effort towards such cooperation should be pursued and encouraged. It can also be argued that after such a South–Central Asia regime is created, it can be maintained even without the effort of the hegemon. According to Keohane, regimes are more easily preserved than created. Hence it can be argued that after such a regime is created and established, the hegemon's role, in this case the USA, can also be bypassed to a certain extent. In Keohane's words, 'Cooperation is possible after hegemony not only because shared interests can lead to the creation of regimes, but also because the conditions for maintaining existing regimes are less demanding than those required for creating them.'[10] Moreover, whether or not there exists a hegemonic power, international regimes, in Keohane's formulation, depend for their existence on perceived interests which are common or complementary in nature. International regimes arise from shared interests. The greater the incentives for cooperation, the more likely it is that such regimes will survive the decline of a hegemonic power.[11]

At present, for the creation of this regime, apart from the countries of Central and South Asia and the USA, key international institutions like the Asian Development Bank, the World Bank, the IMF, the UN and the EU are active players in the region. It is worthwhile to note that such South–Central Asia cooperation is also regarded as a formidable obstacle to economic and other integration of the countries of the region with the Shanghai Cooperation Organisation (SCO). That is, the resistance of the USA and the European Union is becoming even more determined and better organized as is evident from the many recent economic moves and diplomatic manoeuvres. Hence the strategies of USA's moves as an extra-regional hegemon in the region need to be analysed.

VISION, HYPOTHESES, STRATEGIES INVOLVING THE SOUTH–CENTRAL ASIA COOPERATION REGIME

It is envisioned that Afghanistan will play a greater central role as a fulcrum of cooperation and trade in the strengthening of the entire region. And the success of Afghanistan's political and economic transformation after years of war, turmoil and neglect depends very much on strengthened regional economic cooperation and integration. At one time this region, including Afghanistan, stood at the very centre of the world economy, epitomized by the Silk

Road that served as the main trade link between East and West. As a consequence of these longstanding trade and transport economic ties, which encouraged population flows across Afghanistan's borders; the people of Afghanistan share an immensely rich mosaic of cultural, ethnic and linguistic affinities with their neighbours. Afghanistan's strategically important central location allows it to act as a focal point for facilitating greater economic cooperation and integration across the region. It is expected that this vision can be achieved in this region as well. A stable and flourishing Afghanistan can serve as an extraordinary opportunity for the region and the world at large.

The basic assumptions in favour of regional cooperation involving Afghanistan lie in the centrality of Afghanistan in the region. Located at a point where four of the most populous and resource-rich regions in the world converge—South Asia, Central Asia, the Middle East and the Far East—a stable Afghanistan is a unique and unprecedented opportunity not only for the people of these areas, but also for the entire world. Afghanistan's economy is transforming and the climate for business has somewhat improved for the new and returning investors in many sectors. It has been declared as a fully functioning, free market economy. The government has shown its commitment to developing a competitive, export-oriented private sector, setting a rapid pace for expansion and fuelling private investment opportunities. So a pro-business environment is being highlighted. Afghanistan is approaching a critical turning point where an improving political, social and economic situation will have far-reaching implications. The economic interdependencies that will emerge in an increasingly open regional market system will give each country in the region a greater stake in the stability of its neighbours. Trade and investments are likely to be the main drivers of economic growth in Afghanistan in the foreseeable future. The focus on investment projects with a regional component as well as inter-regional trade will enable Afghanistan and its neighbours to move from the economic periphery to the very centre of a new but at the same time ancient world economic region. Afghanistan provides investment opportunities in important sectors like transport and logistics, energy and mining, and agriculture. This area has a 'first mover' advantage.[12] The existence of a nexus between security, politics and development and economic development is inexorably linked to a secure and stable political environment which makes it possible to attract investment and fully develop the country's human and natural resource potential. It is believed that trade and economic cooperation have the potential to contribute substantially in bringing together this entire region.

Some of the strategies of achieving such cooperation have been (a) cooperation on a step-by-step basis (for example, a number of opportunities for increased cooperation in the areas of energy, trade, development of natural resources and transport were discussed at the Kabul Conference in 2005); (b) cooperation via bilateral and multilateral interaction, as effective regional cooperation must be based upon a more extensive and more frequent exchange of information, between governments concerning their efforts in reforming the policies and regulations that determine the economic environment in their countries, between regional organizations and international donors concerning the projects and programmes that they are planning and implementing, and between businesses and private sector organizations, concerning the commercial opportunities that are becoming available. Continued regular meetings among the regional countries at the ministerial level, such as the Kabul and the Delhi conferences, are necessary to accelerate the momentum towards greater regional integration. It is being stressed that the role of the government and the private sector must be fully appreciated and reflected in economic policies in order to establish an environment where the enormous economic potential of the region can begin to be realized; (c) Cooperation via working groups through subregional bodies like the strengthening and increased integration of existing regional and subregional bodies like SAARC, ECO, SCO and CAREC, which will provide a basis for the countries of the region to participate more effectively as a region in the international economic forums and institutions, such as WTO, the United Nations and the international financial institutions. It is argued that only in this way can the economic interests of the region be fully and consistently represented.[13]

INITIATIVES TAKEN TO ESTABLISH THE REGIME

Regimes are created by states as instruments to achieve certain goals through multilateral negotiations. With the aim of creating an ongoing mechanism for pursuing Afghanistan's greater economic cooperation throughout the larger South and Central Asian region, the Kabul Conference on Regional Economic Cooperation brought together government ministers and senior official from 11 countries in December 2005.[14] The outcome of the conference is embodied in the Kabul Declaration, which identified a number of specific goals to be achieved. It is held that there has been progress in achieving these goals but challenges remain and much needs to be done. The Second Regional Economic Conference on Afghanistan took place in Delhi nearly one year after the Kabul Conference. It represented an important milestone in Afghanistan's progress towards greater political and economic stability. Co-hosted by the governments of India and Afghanistan, it aimed to build on the success of the Kabul Conference by strengthening the process of economic cooperation and integration within the region and extending the framework for greater cooperation in areas such as improved border management, strengthening trade and transit agreements, new power purchase agreements, and expanding opportunities for cross-border employment arrangements, all of which offer the prospect of substantial economic benefits for the region as a whole. A particular focus of the second conference was the identification of practical Afghan projects which will be commercially attractive for potential private investors and businesses from regional countries. The back-to-back business conference also provided an opportunity to present potential private investors with a number of viable commercial initiatives of regional importance.[15]

In an effort to facilitate Afghanistan's economic cooperation with all of its Central Asian neighbours, UNDP, together with the World Bank and the Asian Development Bank, sponsored the Conference on Regional Economic Cooperation in Bishkek in 2004. Government and private sector representatives from the five republics, Afghanistan, Iran and Pakistan participated in plenary sessions and small discussions to identify actions on topics such as how to expand trade, how to capitalize on Afghanistan's location as a land bridge between Central Asia and Iran on one side and South Asia on the other, and how to enhance access to Afghanistan's reconstruction efforts for firms in all of these other countries.

The Regional Economic Cooperation Conferences held at Kabul (2005) and New Delhi (2006) offered an important opportunity for the international community to continue supporting collaboration in this regard by removing impediments and identifying areas of potential cooperation to promote mutually beneficial ties. These conferences have been considered largely successful in the attempt to reach out to the region and acknowledging Afghanistan's importance for regional growth. The key areas where it was agreed that mutually beneficial initiatives could be undertaken included trade facilitation and transport; investment trade and business potential; electricity trade and energy development; sharing the benefits of water;

countering the narcotics trade; and transportation of energy.[16] The new opportunities for increased cooperation and integration that were on the agenda for the Delhi Conference include the TAPI natural gas pipeline; renewable sources of energy; and agriculture and agro-industrial development.

The Afghan government has also showed its interest in sharing the benefits of Afghanistan's centrality to advance increasingly close and mutually beneficial economic relationships with its neighbours and with those countries beyond the immediate neighbourhood. The Afghan government, with the assistance of the international community, is paying particular attention to streamlining transit and customs procedures which are currently adding unnecessary time and costs to trading activities. There is considerable activity underway to construct new and more efficient fully integrated border posts which will incorporate new systems to facilitate trade, including the computerization of customs.

AMERICA AS A HEGEMON IN THE REGION

America, positioning itself as a global hegemon, has great interest in Central Asia because of geopolitical as well as geo-economic considerations. It is interesting to note that 'South and Central Asia is a region of great strategic importance where American interests and values are engaged as never before' and such a new regional approach will boost Washington's regional ambitions and its global position. Halford Mackinder,[17] an expert on geopolitics, described Central Asia as part of the Heartland and a key to global domination: who rules the Heartland commands the World-Island (Eurasia and Africa), and who rules the World-Island commands the world. Even if one does not agree with the Heartland theory, one should recognize that Central Asia is a strategic region from which two great powers (Russia and China), whose interests often clash with American interests, can be influenced. The region also borders on Iran, which is described by Bush as one of the 'axis of evil' countries. America, on the one hand, promotes the local countries' 'independence' (interpreted as independence from Russia, China and Iran), while on the other, it encourages stronger cooperation with the United States and the West.

America, which resolves to remain as one of the key world powers remains as one of the world's main consumers and importers of energy resources. And the Central Asian countries can be described as smaller states which produce and export oil and gas, and this explains

America's approach to Central Asia. The United States, being the leading industrial power and the main oil importer, accounts for a quarter of the world's oil consumption and imports about 60 per cent of the oil. The American government must ensure uninterrupted supply of adequate amounts of oil at acceptable prices. Significantly, the annual oil consumption is 7.5 billion barrels of oil,[18] while in 2004, America's proved resources were 21.3 billion barrels. Since different sources offer different estimates of the Caspian oil reserves, the Energy Information Administration of the US Department of Energy offers its own estimation of between 17 and 44 billion barrels.[19] So it can be assessed that the proved Caspian reserves are equal to America's proved reserves; at best, they are twice as much.

It has been interpreted by Atajan Iazmuradov that there are two main reasons for America's new regional approach: the changes on the American domestic scene triggered by the Afghan and Iraqi developments and the geopolitical changes in Central Asia that undermined the US's position there.[20] This was why the US Administration armed itself with the 'Greater South Asia Project' rooted in the Greater Central Asia Project devised by the Central Asia-Caucasus Institute of the Johns Hopkins University. The new focus of USA on Central Asia is a marked departure from the 1990s when it was primarily a bystander interested in the region but unwilling to get involved. After 11 September 2001, the USA has emerged as a principal power in Central Asian affairs. With the troops' presence in Kyrgyzstan, Tajikistan and Afghanistan after the defeat of the Taliban, all the signs point to a long-term military stay in the region.[21] The USA, a major player in the region, projects that its foreign policy goals for the twenty-first century as winning the war on terror, finding outlets for energy supplies, achieving prosperity through economic cooperation and exploiting democratic opportunities in the region. It foresees that its policies will champion change and reform to produce a more stable, prosperous and integrated region.

Russia and China on the one hand continue to endorse US-led operations which are aimed at defending Afghanistan against insurgency; but on the other, a long-term US military presence anywhere in the region is unacceptable for either country both of whom see the Americans as trying to cut them out of spheres of traditional influence. Moscow sees the promotion of democracy by the USA and NATO as a pretext for continued, even accelerated interference in its former republics. The Chinese seem mostly engaged in using diplomatic means to thwart an open-ended US military presence in the region. India has emerged as an important player in the region and has friendly relations with the regime in Afghanistan. It has worked hard to win the confidence of the post-Taliban government in Kabul. New Delhi has contributed $565 million towards Afghanistan's reconstruction—making it the sixth largest contributor—divided among infrastructure repair, humanitarian assistance and institutional and human resource development, all these drawing regular complaints from Pakistan which accuses India of harbouring sinister motives like intelligence gathering from its consulates in Kandahar and Jalalabad and also of fostering insurgency inside Pakistan's Balochistan.

The effort to establish such a regime is often criticized as an anti-SCO initiative. It is being argued that the SCO started extending the geographic limits of Central Asia to include South Asia when it granted Pakistan observer status in 2005 and established contact with Afghanistan, only to come face to face with a now evident counter-strategy. The alternative strategy, it is argued, is to pump Central Asian energy resources out of the SCO-zones. The economic content of such 'anti-SCO' plans, it is believed, is limited to two main projects in which the political motives outweigh the economic common sense. Both concern pipelines leading to Indian Ocean ports via Pakistan and Afghanistan and the idea is to prevent the SCO from coming together in an oil and gas bloc by whatever means and at whatever price.[22]

The concept may face criticism from various quarters but the 'Greater Central Asia' concept is nevertheless gradually taking shape in the US, a role which the two countries of Pakistan and Afghanistan owe to considerable US presence there, particularly the us military presence in Afghanistan.

AMERICA'S NEW APPROACH AND THE GREATER CENTRAL ASIA PARTNERSHIP

America's new approach to Central Asia, initiated by the US State Department, and the working project Greater Central Asia Partnership published in March 2005 by the Central Asia-Caucasus Institute of the Paul H. Nitze School of Advanced International Studies at the Johns Hopkins University are closely connected. Frederick Starr, who happens to head the Institute, in an essay entitled 'A Partnership for Central Asia' outlined the project, where he mildly criticized the US policies. He said, 'The geographical delineations used by the U.S. government prevent policy makers from recognizing Afghanistan, Kazakhstan, Kyrgyzstan, Tajikistan, Turkmenistan, and Uzbekistan as comprising a single region' which, he was convinced, 'has impeded the development of a coherent Central Asian policy'.[23] Starr offers an alternative project devised by his institute based on the new regional approach to Central Asia, Afghanistan, and South Asia as a single Greater Central Asia region linked to South Asia by including Afghanistan into Central Asia, and by describing it as South Asia's natural extension. The argument for such cooperation is that Afghanistan is Central Asia's natural outlet to the warm seas, therefore, transport infrastructure, railways in particular, as well as transit gas and oil pipelines, is an absolute necessity. To realize the new regional approach, a new regional institute, the Greater Central Asia Partnership for Cooperation and Development (GCAP) with a forum status, should be created. The author believes that it might be effective in the spheres of security, administration, democratization, economy, transport and trade, agriculture and anti-drug efforts, as well as in religion, culture and education.[24] From the very beginning, the project has been described as an 'open project' in which the United States, the Central Asian countries, and Afghanistan can cooperate with the members of the counter-terrorist coalition, as well as regional actors, namely, India, Pakistan, and Turkey, and Russia and China. Starr has taken the trouble to emphasize that the project is not directed against the interests of the two latter states, and that they might even profit from it.[25] This is in contrast to the opinion of others who consider it to be an anti-SCO move.

So both the institute's project and the US Administration's new regional approach stress the need to integrate Central and South Asia economically by stitching them together with transportation and energy corridors across Afghanistan. There seems to be an obvious parallel between the restructuring of the US State Department, effected within America's new approach to the region and that part of the work done by the Central Asia-Caucasus Institute, which compares the structures of the US Defense and State Departments[26] and recommends instituting the post of Assistant Secretary of State for Greater Central Asia.[27] However, it should be stressed that some of the institute's propositions and recommendations were left beyond the scope of the new American regional policies. There is also an important conceptual distinction between the US's regional approach and the institute's project. The institute concentrated on setting up a Greater Central Asia linked to South Asia as a single and interconnected region. This means that the institute came forward with a conception of a new region it called Greater Central Asia linked to South Asia, while the US State Administration went further to formulate a conception of a new single South and Central Asia region held together by Afghanistan.

It is being argued that the US had lost much of its influence in the region following the revolution in Kyrgyzstan and the Andijan events in Uzbekistan, and this required the American leaders to seek a new regional approach. Within the US, the conception was prompted by the growing dissatisfaction with the results in Iraq and Afghanistan. Therefore, this regional project was devised as an answer to the challenges described above whereby the world community's attention would be favourably directed towards Afghanistan, a US protectorate. Such a regime is intended to receive more support at three levels: inside the country, in the Greater South Asia region, and in the international community.[28]

CONCLUSION: CHALLENGES OF REGIME FORMATION AND THE LIMITED UTILITY OF HEGEMONIC STABILITY

Theories of collective action show that a group of states benefiting from a regime does not guarantee that they will 'supply' it. In this connection, according to Keohane, the contractualist theory incorporates power considerations where hegemons often play a crucial role in the formation of international regimes.[29] What is more, he bases his argument for the robustness of regimes in part on the difficulties of 'regime' creation in the absence of hegemonies. The justification for the role of a hegemonic stabilizer is reflected to a great extent in the hegemonic stability theory originated in economist Charles Kindleberger's work on the Great Depression.[30] Kindleberger argued that for the world economy to be stabilized, there has to be one stabilizer. What concerned Kindleberger was not the institutionalization of international politics or the strength of regimes but the creation and maintenance of what David Lake termed as 'the international economic infrastructure'.[31]

The difficulties in regime creation in the case of South and Central Asia seem to be numerous. There are several impediments to such cooperation, the glaring one being the political and economic instability in Afghanistan. The problem of instability and lack of security within Afghanistan remains a major obstacle and has the potential to impede any progress towards regional cooperation. While the vision for such economic cooperation and the initiatives taken so far are commendable, yet much remains to be achieved. Many analysts are apprehensive about the prospects of such cooperation. Marvin Weinbaum is of the opinion that to envision a newly viable geo-economic entity emerging anytime may soon probably overstate the compatibility and common interests at present among regional states. The idea of a greater region is complicated by their different political systems. The Central Asian Republics, according to him, are often held to be more nationalist than regional in their attitudes. There is an arena of competition among regional players. As a result, the Central Asian republics, together with their southern neighbours, according to Weinbaum, are likely to fail for the foreseeable future to measure up to their regional responsibilities.[32] Conflict and tensions within the countries of the region, as the India–Pakistan impasse, remain another major impediment in the success of the regime.

Economic considerations encourage states to pursue strategic trade policies, but important political considerations also motivate them. As noted earlier, the absence of an international government encourages states to be more concerned with how they fare in relation to others—their relative gains—than with how they fare individually—their absolute gains. Often pursuit of relative gains may interfere with the logic of comparitive advantage and free trade. In the case of South and Central Asia, it may happen that states may be prone in the economic as well as military sphere to 'forgo some of the benefits of cooperation or economic exchange in the short run, in order to assure security, broadly defined, over the long run' as suggested by Mastanduno.[33] And relative gains and states' concern for position in their relations with others also shed the light on the reasons why United States, the principle advocate of free trade in the post-Second World War era, has increasingly engaged in trade practices which makes it look less like a hegemon and more like an 'ordinary country' (hegemonic decline).[34]

Hence, the rational justification for the US acting as a hegemonic stabilizer in this case will lie in the fact that often groups of rational actors do not act on behalf of their common interest, which amounts to a failure to provide the group with a public good (Olson 1965).[35] Kindleberger had thus argued that only an outstanding economic and political power with the capacity and willingness to lead would supply and support the infrastructure that permits international exchange to take place. As stated earlier, regimes are more easily preserved than created. It can thus be argued that after such a regime is created and established, the hegemon's role, in this case the USA, can also be bypassed to a certain extent. Therefore, the possibilities of hegemonic decline should not be ruled out at a later stage when the regime is established. Thus the overwhelming presence of the US in the creation and maintenance of regimes becomes legitimate and becomes the possible explanation for the formation, if not the persistence of regimes, where unilateral actions need to be taken by a stabilizing power.

NOTES

1. Nicholas Tarling, *Regionalism in Southeast Asia: To Foster the Political Will*, London and New York: Routledge, 2006, p. 18.
2. Remarks at Eurasian National University, Speech of Condoleezza Rice, US Secretary of State, at the Lev Gumilev National University of Kazakhstan, 13 October 2005, available at <*http:www.state.gov/secretary/rm/2005/54913.htm*>.
3. Robert O. Keohane, *After Hegemony: Cooperation and Discord in the World Economy*, Princeton: Princeton University Press, 1984, p. 32.
4. Andreas Hasenclever, Peter Mayer and Volker Rittberger, 'Interests, Power, Knowledge: The Study of International Regimes', *Mershon International Studies Review* 40, 1996, pp. 177–228.
5. Ibid.
6. Shabir Ahmad Khan, 'World Interest in Central Asia: Implications and Policy Options for Pakistan: II', *Frontier Post*, 14 May 2007.
7. Asian Development Bank, 'Central Asia: Increasing Gains from Trade Through Regional Cooperation in Trade Policy', prepared for the Regional Economic Cooperation Conference, New Delhi, 18–19 November 2006.
8. *The Kabul Declaration*, Final Draft, 2nd RECC, New Delhi, 1996.
9. S. Frederick Starr, *The New Silk Roads: Transport and Trade in Greater Central Asia*, Monograph, Central Asia Caucasus Institute and Silk Road Studies Program, 2007
10. Keohane, *After Hegemony*, p. 50.
11. James E. Dougherty and Robert L. Pfaltzgraff, Jr., *Contending Theories of International Relations: A Comprehensive Survey*, New York: Longman, 1997, 4th edn., p. 438.
12. 'Afghanistan Investment Opportunities with Regional Significance', Afghanistan Investment Support Agency (AISA), prepared for the Regional Economic Cooperation Conference, New Delhi, 18–19 November 2006.
13. 'A Vision for Regional Cooperation: Progress since the Kabul Conference', Final Draft, Second Regional Economic Cooperation Conference on Afghanistan, New Delhi, 18–19 November 2006.
14. Participating regional countries included the six sharing a border with Afghanistan (China, Iran, Pakistan, Tajikistan, Turkmenistan and Uzbekistan) plus India, Turkey, UAE and Kazakhstan. In addition to the G-8 some key international institutions participated (i.e. UK, US, Japan, Germany, Russia, China, France, Italy, UN, EU, WB, IMF, ADB and the Aga Khan Development Network). Some major regional and subregional bodies also participated.
15. This conference was organized jointly by the AISA and the three apex Indian business chambers (i.e. the Federation of Indian Chamber of Commerce and Industry, the Confederation of Indian Industry and the Associated Chambers of Commerce and Industry of India).
16. *The Kabul Declaration*. Final Draft, 2nd RECC, New Delhi.

17. Halford John Mackinder, 'The Geographical Pivot of History', *The Geographical Journal*, vol. 23, no. 4, April 1904, pp. 421–37.
18. US Department of Energy. Calculated on the basis of *World Oil Balance, 2001–2005*, published by the Energy Information Administration, available at *www.eia.doe.gov/emeu/ipsr/t21.xls*, 3 June 2006.
19. Energy Information Department of the U.S., *Country Analysis Briefing: Caspian Sea*, Department of Energy, USA, 2005, available at *http://eia.doe.gov/emeu/ipsr/t21.xls* 3 June 2006.
20. Atajan Iazmuradov, 'Greater South Asia—America's New Regional Approach To Central And South Asia: How it is Developing and What Prompted it', *Central Asia and the Caucasus*, 40, no. 4, 2006, pp. 79–90.
21. Khan, 'World interest in Central Asia'.
22. Dirty Kestrel, 'From Shanghais to Dutiable', *New Theme on Russian-Indian Affairs* VII, no. 4, July–August 2006.
23. S.F. Starr, 'A Partnership for Central Asia', *Foreign Affairs*, July–August 2005.
24. Ibid., 'A "Greater Central Asia Partnership" for Afghanistan and Its Neighbors', Silk Road Paper, March 2005, pp. 27–34.
25. Iazmuradov, 'Greater South Asia-America's New Regional Approach to Central and South Asia'.
26. Starr, 'A "Greater Central Asia Partnership" for Afghanistan and Its Neighbors', p. 13.
27. Ibid., p. 36.
28. Iazmuradov, 'Greater South Asia-America's New Regional Approach to Central and South Asia'.
29. Keohane, *After Hegemony*.
30. Charles P. Kindleberger, *The World in Depression 1929-1939*, London: Penguin, 1973, p. 305.
31. David A. Lake, 'Leadership, Hegemony and the International Economy: Naked Emperor or Tattered Monarch with Potential?', *International Studies Quarterly* 37, pp. 459–89.
32. Marvin G. Weinbaum, 'Afghanistan and its Neighbours: An Even Dangerous Neighbourhood', *United States Institute of Peace (USIP) Special Report* 162, June 2006.
33. Michael Mastanduno, 'Do Relative Gains Matter? America's Response to Japanese Industrial Policy', *International Security* 16, Summer 1991, pp. 73–113.
34. Charles W. Kegley, Jr. and Eugene R. Wittkopf, *World Politics: Trend and Transformation*, New York: St. Martin's Press, 1993, 4th edn., pp. 239–40.
35. Mancur Olson, Jr, *The Logic of Collective Action: Public Goods and the Theory of Groups*, Cambridge: Harvard University Press, 1965.

8

From *Eretz Yisra'el* to *Medinat Yisra'el*

PRIYA SINGH

The term *Eretz Yisra'el Haslemah* (Greater Israel) indicates the Biblical boundaries of the Land of Israel. Though the borders of Greater Israel are not clearly defined, many committed Jews draw such definition from Biblical sources, namely, the Book of Genesis, which describes God's covenant with Abraham:

> On that day, God made a covenant with Abram, saying: 'To your descendants I have given this land, from the river of Egypt as far as the great river the Euphrates. The land of the Kenites, Kenizites, Kadmonites; the Chitties, Perizites, Refaim; the Emorites, Canaanites, Gigashites and Yevusites.' Genesis 15: 18-21[1]

In terms of the above idea, Greater Israel would comprise, roughly, all of modern-day Israel as well as the West Bank, Gaza Strip, Golan Heights, Jordan and Lebanon, much of Syria, Iraq and Kuwait, as well as parts of Saudi Arabia, Egypt and Turkey.[2] In other words, Greater Israel refers to the entire geographical region of Palestine stretching from the Mediterranean Sea to the Jordan River.

In the Biblical sense of the land promised by God as an inheritance to the Jewish people, the 'Land of Israel' was a territory originally known as Canaan, used as either a geographical or a theological term. The term 'Land of Israel' is derived from the two Hebrew words used in the Hebrew Bible: *Eretz*, which means 'land' in English, and *Yisra'el*, which is written as 'Israel', a direct near-romanticized and transliterated proper noun adopted directly by English from Hebrew.[3] The two words used together in this context mean the 'Land of Israel'.

The name 'Israel' derives from the Biblical patriarch Jacob, later known as *Israel*, literally meaning 'struggled with God/he struggles with God'. According to the account in the Book of Genesis, Jacob wrestled with a stranger (in later tradition said to be an angel) at a river ford and won through perseverance. God then changed Jacob's name to *Israel* signifying that he had deliberated with God and won as he had wrestled and won with men. Jacob's descendents were termed the 'Children of Israel' or 'Israelites' and the land they inherited from Abraham, Isaac and Jacob became known as the *Land of Israel*.[4] The modern State of Israel (*Medinat Yisrael*) derived and based its name on the earlier usages and applications of 'Israel' in Jewish history.[5]

As mentioned earlier, according to the Bible, particularly the book of Genesis, the 'Land of Israel' was promised as an everlasting possession to the descendents of the Jewish patriarchs Abraham, Isaac and Jacob by God, making it the Promised Land.

THE IDEA OF GREATER ISRAEL: SOURCES, INTERPRETATIONS AND CONTRADICTIONS

Varied Sources

A plethora of questions and doubts arise over the origin of the term Greater Israel. What are its sources? And how valid are they? According to Daniel Pipes,[6] the notion of Greater Israel has four main sources.

First, and by far the most important, are several passages in the Jewish Bible, which point to Israeli domination of the Middle East. The Tanakh (or the Hebrew Bible) contains several descriptions of the borders of the land. These descriptions encompass a region which extends from the 'River of Egypt' to the Euphrates. Areas known to be included are the modern State of Israel, the West Bank (Judea and Samaria), the Gaza Strip and parts of modern-day Syria and Lebanon. The Biblically described region also encompasses the Sinai Peninsula, which is widely believed to include the route of the Hebrew Exodus from Egypt. The land allocated east of the Jordan River in Numbers 34:1–15 includes most of Jordan.

Genesis 15:18–21 describes what is referred to in Jewish tradition as *Gevulot Ha-aretz* (Borders of the Land) regarded as the full text of the land promised to Abraham. In describing God's covenant with Abraham, Genesis 15:18 reads: 'To your descendants I give this land from the River of Egypt to the Great River, the river Euphrates'. Numbers 34:1–15 describes the land allocated to the Israelite tribes after the Exodus. The tribes of Reuben, Gad and half of Manasseh received the land east of the Jordan as explained in Numbers 34:14–15. Numbers 34:1–13 provides a detailed description of the borders of the land allocated to the remaining tribes. The region is called the 'Land of Cannan' (Eretz Kna'an) in Numbers 34:2 and the borders are known in Jewish tradition as the 'borders for those coming out of Egypt'. The English expression 'Promised Land' can denote either the land promised to Abraham in Genesis or the land of Canaan, although the latter meaning is more common.

Ezekiel 47:13–20 provides a post-exilic definition of the borders. It describes the 'Land of Israel', which, according to Ezekiel's prophecy, is a repeat of the 'Promised Land' with tribal allocations for the Israelites to return to after their captivity (The Book of Ezekiel can be dated from the Bobylonian captivity after the fall of Jerusalem in 597 and 586 BC by Nebuchadnezzar). The borders of the land described by the text in Ezekiel stretch from the northern border of modern Lebanon eastwards (the way of Hethlon) to Zedad and Hazar-enan in modern Syria; south by south-west to the area of Basra on the Syrian border (area of Hauran in Ezekiel); the West Bank and a strip of western Jordan down to the Gulf of Aqaba near Ezion-geber; either the entire Sinai peninsula or from Eilat/Taba on the Gulf of Aqaba via Kadesh-barnea to the Brook of Egypt; the Gaza Strip and all the land in between. In Deuteronomy 11:24, Moses announces to the Jews that 'Every place where you set the soles of your feet shall be yours. Your borders shall run from the wilderness to the Lebanon and from the River, the river Euphrates, to the western sea.'

Second, in the words of Daniel Pipes,[7] some Western observers and experts expected modern Israel to recapitulate the ancient state's borders; the British ambassador in Istanbul, for example, predicted as early as 1910 that 'The domination of Egypt, the land of the Pharaohs, who forced the Jews to build the Pyramids, is part of the future heritage of Israel.'

Third, early Zionist leaders referred to an Israeli intent to rule large territories. Around 1900, Theodor Herzl and Isidore Bodenheimer routinely referred to the Jewish settlement in 'Palestine and Syria', as did organizations like the Jewish National Fund and the Zionist Congress. In 1898, Herzl planned to ask the Ottoman Sultan for a territory stretching from the Egyptian frontier to the Euphrates.[8] Four years later he spoke of settling Jews in Mesopotamia.

Finally, later Zionist figures/leaders were also quoted making ambitious claims. Vladimir Jabotinsky, the founder of Revisionist Zionism, was quoted in 1935 as stating that 'We want a Jewish empire.'[9] According to Hafiz al-Asad, on his visit to the Golan Heights, soon after its capture by Israeli troops in 1967, Moshe Dayan announced that 'the past generation established Israel within its 1948 borders;

we have established Israel within the 1967 borders; and you have to establish a Greater Israel from the Nile to the Euphrates'.[10] Whatever the specifics, the Arabs were in consensus that Dayan spurred a new round of Israeli expansionist fervour. Prime Minister Menachem Begin was later quoted as supposedly saying that the Bible predicts that the Israeli State will eventually include portions of Iraq, Syria, Turkey, Saudi Arabia, Egypt, Sudan, Lebanon, Jordan and Kuwait.[11]

Multiple Interpretations

A brief review of the sources arouse several questions in one's mind, such as how valid are these arguments, and how accurate are these quotes? In Pipes opinion,

> The second and third sources—statements by European Christians and early Zionists—clearly have only limited importance. External predictions can hardly serve as authoritative sources for the Zionist movement. Territorial musings before the Balfour Declaration of 1918 were uttered when the Zionist movement was still embryonic; in any case, Herzl did not in fact request the Nile-to-Euphrates region from the Ottoman king or anyone else. As for the bellicose statements attributed to Jabotinsky, Begin, and Dayan; they cannot be verified and as such are not included as authentic sources.[12]

The Biblical passages are a more complex matter. Therefore, certain considerations have to be taken into account to understand what they connote: There are, however, several points of debate: The border with Egypt is given as the *Nachal Mitzrayim* (Brook of Egypt) in Numbers and Deuteronomy, as well as in Ezekiel. The traditional Jewish understanding of the term is that it refers to the Nile, more precisely the Pelusian branch of the Nile Delta, according to Yehuda Halevi,[13] a view supported by Egyptian and Assyrian texts. Later commentators identified it with the Wadi al-Arish, and the Besor has also been suggested in recent times. Genesis, however, gives the border with Egypt as *Nahar Miztrayim*. This is generally understood to be the Nile, 'nahar' denoting a large river. If different from *Nachal Mitzrayim*, the Genesis verse includes a larger area of land westwards. A minority interpret *Nahar Mitzrayim* together with *Nachal Mitzrayim* as a wadi as well. In fact, scholars like Daniel Pipes argue that

> the 'River of Egypt', according to a number of commentators, refers not to the Nile, but to Wadi al-Arish on the north coast of the Sinai Peninsula. The lack of parallel between the two formulations, 'the Great River, the river Euphrates' and 'the River of Egypt' seems to corroborate this interpretation. In any case, the principle Jewish commentaries on this text, notably that of Rashi, identifies [*sic*]

the River of Egypt with Wadi Al-Arish. These commentaries, it bears noting, have for centuries accompanied the Biblical text itself in published editions of the Bible, and thus predisposed Zionists to understand 'the River of Egypt' along these lines.[14]

The precise southern and eastern borders of the land of Israel are also the subjects of debate. Only the Red Sea and Euphrates are mentioned, which can be understood to mean that the whole Arabian Peninsula is included as well. More reticent interpretations take the southern border to be a line from the mouth of the Euphrates to Eilat or a line of latitude from the mouth of the Gulf of Eilat. Still another view is that the Euphrates forms only a northern border and that the southern and eastern borders extend from Eilat to an undetermined point on the Euphrates.

Another point of debate for some religious scholars is the consistent reference to the inclusion of 'the Land of Hittites' within the borders. Some view the Hittites as one of the tribes that had settled in Canaan and were conquered by Joshua, while others refer to a greater empire which encompassed most of central Turkey.[15] Moreover, the rules of Biblical exegesis hold that specific laws always take precedence over general laws. Accordingly, the detailed, and geographically far more constrained, delineation of *Eretz Yisrael* (the Land of Israel) in Numbers 34:1–12 ('It shall then turn from the south up to the ascent of Akrabbim and pass by Zim, and its southern limit shall be Kadesh-barnea . . .') and Ezekiel 47:13–20, supplant the much vaguer ones in Genesis and Deuteronomy. For this reason, it is argued that Jewish tradition has long viewed the Genesis statement as non-operational.[16] Furthermore, it is contented that in the Biblical account, Abraham's 'descendants' include not just the Jews through Isaac, but also their 'cousins', the Arabs, through Ishmael—in which case the covenant was long ago amply fulfilled.

In fact, to assess the contemporary importance of the Biblical injunctions, a number of points need to be kept in mind: To begin with, it is contended that Greater Israel is an inexact translation of *Eretz Yisrael Hashlemah*, Hebrew for 'the Integral Land of Israel'. The English term implies a geographical expansion not present in the original. Early Zionists considered a wide range of lands for Jewish colonization, including Cyprus, Sinai, Mesopotamia, East Africa and Argentina. In addition, the Soviet regime made Birobidzhan, a distant region of Siberia, into its version of a Jewish homeland. Therefore, these territories should be understood as alternatives to, not extensions of, Palestine.[17]

For decades the Zionist debate[18] centred on what emphasis Jewish control over the whole of *Eretz Yisrael* should have. Labour Zionists thought this less important than other objectives (such as establishing a sovereign Jewish state) but Revisionist Zionists made it their first priority. In nearly all cases, it bears noting, the Revisionists lost out to their Labour rivals.

Several contemporary Israeli political analysts[19] argue that the Israeli government has not adopted the Bible as a policy document. In their opinion, secularists inspired by nationalist and socialist goals, and not religious ones, founded Israel. In keeping with this line of thought they further contend that it is preposterous to assume that passages dating from three millennia ago would guide the actions of a modern democratic polity.

While Revisionist Zionists did claim Jordan and parts of Lebanon and Syria as a part of *Eretz Yisra'el* during the Mandatory Period, no Zionist ever laid claim to or sought to control Egypt, Sudan or Iraq, much less Mecca and the Persian Gulf. The notion of *Eretz Yisra'el* subsequently shrank, to the point that today it includes just the territory of Mandatary Palestine. As proof, it can be observed that the Revisionists in recent decades have viewed the Sinai, the Gaza Strip, the Golan Heights and southern Lebanon in strategic terms only, and not in historic ones. This confirms that they now view these areas as outside *Eretz Yisra'el*. No Israeli political party today (not even Meir Kahane's Kach) aspires to Israeli rule over all *Eretz Yisra'el*; rather, the Revisionists' only demand now is that Israel not give up any part of *Eretz Yisra'el* already under its control.[20]

Realists, in order to validate their argument, point to the fact that the Israelis did have a chance to choose their ideal borders in June 1967, and they stopped far short of the Nile and the Euphrates. Had they had plans to expand to those rivers, they could have done so with virtual impunity at that time. In addition, Israel thrice won part or all of the Sinai Peninsula (in the 1948–9, 1956 and 1967 wars) and thrice returned the captured territories to Egypt. How can this fact be reconciled with the supposed plans of wanting to rule from the Nile to the Euphrates?[21] Thus, according to this school of thought, the whole idea of a Greater Israel from the Nile to the Euphrates has to be dismissed as groundless fantasy. Yet, leading politicians from the major Arab/Islamic states of the Middle East (with the important exception of Turkey) have over the years expressed themselves on the subject of Greater Israel from a different angle.

King 'Abd al-'Aziz ibn Sa'ud of Saudi Arabia (who ruled between 1902 and 1953) is regarded to be the first important politician to have firmly believed in Greater Israel. He expected a Zionist invasion of his kingdom, as he confided to a retired British diplomat in October 1937: 'the Jews contemplate as their final aim not only the seizure of all Palestine but the land south of it as far as Medina. Eastward also they hope some day to extend to the Persian Gulf.' Why as far as Medina, the second holiest city of Islam? The Saudi king recalled the Jewish presence in that city during the Prophet Muhammad's lifetime; and he assumed they wanted to return to what he called 'their old stronghold'.[22]

Gamal Abdel Nasser of Egypt[23] also argued along the same lines. He contended that the Israelis sought a Greater Israel to include the whole central Middle East and thereby to turn the Arabs into 'a horde of refugees'. The Israelis would never give up this aspiration: 'Even if they do not expect to realise their talk today or tomorrow about an Israeli state or a Kingdom of Israel from the Nile to the Euphrates, they will persevere in this goal until they find an opportunity [to attain it].' It seems that at times he agreed with the Saudi king and declared that 'the Jews intend to conquer Mecca and Medina', or that 'they planned to annihilate all Arabs'. Abdel Nasser's aide, Hasan Sabri al-Khuli,[24] toed the same line and portrayed Greater Israel as a way to implement 'Zionist aspirations for world domination'. In fact, even as recently as the 1990s, an editorial in the Egyptian *Al-Akhbar* held that the immigration of Soviet Jews to Israel would lead to the expulsion of Palestinians from the disputed territories of the West Bank and Gaza Strip—'an important step toward fulfilling the old dream of Greater Israel, stretching from the Nile to the Euphrates'.[25]

The Libyans visualized the concept of Greater Israel as the quest for dominating water sources in the region, from the Euphrates to the Nile. 'Jews covet the Nile and Euphrates Rivers', Mu'ammar al-Qaddafi asserted, 'to control Arab waters', and 'are ready to settle millions of Jews in the Arab countries. Controlling the sources of these waters would take the Israelis from Turkey to Central Africa.'[26] President Qaddafi in fact conjured up the greatest expanse of the concept of Greater Israel: 'The Israelis have said their home is from ocean to ocean, from the Indian Ocean to the straits of Bab al-Mandib, straits of Hormuz, the Red Sea . . . to the Atlantic Ocean together with the straits of Gibraltar and the Mediterranean.'

After 1985, Hafiz al-Asad[27] of Syria often raised the Greater Israel theme, presenting it as an imminent danger and calling on the Arabs to mobilize 'to prevent the establishment of Greater Israel. Asad even portrayed the attainment of Greater Israel as a Jewish religious duty and accused the Israelis of talking mildly to deceive world opinion'. 'The Syrians brought Greater Israel into their diplomacy, too. In January 1992, during the peace process negotiations, the Syrian delegation displayed a map of Greater Israel and claimed it represented the Jewish state's territorial goals.'[28]

Since the Islamic Revolution of 1979 till date, Iran has over and over again strongly emphasized the threat of Greater Israel, often in connection with accusations of Jewish plans to control the world.[29] A 1985 Tehran reprint of *The Protocols of the Elders of Zion* included a map, the 'Dream of Zionism', which purports to show Greater Israel's ideal boundaries. It showed within this Israel the whole of inhabited Egypt, Saudi Arabia down to Medina, all of Syria, Iraq, and Kuwait, the oil-producing region of Iran, and a good-sized slice of Turkey. The Iranians often refer to Israel as a 'tribe' which 'considers its geographical boundaries' to extend from the Nile to the Euphrates. A 1990 newspaper report warned that, because of Greater Israel, 'six Arab countries around Palestine will be destroyed, or their inhabitants will be reduced to refugees'.[30] Former President Rafsanjani noted the emigration of 'millions of Jews from all over the world' (foremost from the USSR, but also from Argentina and other countries), and interpreted this in terms of a Greater Israel 'from the Euphrates River to the Nile River'. Included in this vast area, he speculated, would be the north of Saudi Arabia and a large section of the Red Sea coast. The Zionists hoped to settle 10 to 12 million people, Jews and others, to make Israel 'a mighty and invincible state'. Rafsanjani portrayed the last major advance towards this goal taking place in 1967, with the border zone of Lebanon being brought under Israeli control providing the finishing touch.[31] President Ahmadinejad's Iran continues to harp on the threat posed by 'Greater Israel'.

Arabs in other states, not always government officials, have occasionally echoed these sentiments. In fact, just weeks before the Iraqi invasion, a Kuwaiti newspaper[32] accused the Zionist movement of planning to reach the Nile River, which it termed 'the southern border of the Torah's Israel'. In Jordan, Sultan al-Hattab,[33] editor of the newspaper *Sawt ash-Sha'b* wrote, 'Greater Israel means Jordan, Syria, and Iraq as an immediate target and the entire Arab homeland as Israel's *Lebensraum*.' The Israelis are said to see Lebanon as a no-man's-land and intend to annex it up to the Wadi at-Tim, north of Sidon.

In fact, the fear of Greater Israel is widespread on the Arab street. When tens of thousands of Palestinians participated in May 1990 in a 'march of return' (a walk to Jordan's border with Israel), they inevitably chanted slogans against Greater Israel.[34] These fears are also echoed by scholars like Muhsin D. Yusuf, a historian at Birzeit

University who concluded in an essay in 1991 that Jerusalem had territorial ambitions to a Greater Israel stretching from Sudan to Kuwait.[35]

The idea has even spread outside the Middle East. Patrick Seale,[36] a British journalist of considerable reputation, had flatly asserted, on several occasions, that 'some nationalist Israelis (especially those in the Herut Party) dream of the Jewish state extending 'from the Nile to the Euphrates'. Foreign Minister Claude Cheysson of France, in 1983, called the division of Lebanon between Greater Syria and Greater Israel 'our nightmare'.[37] On the other hand, Palestinians living in Israel have almost always exhibited a degree of caution, at least in public, about endorsing the notion of Greater Israel. As, for example, 'Abd al-Wahhab ad-Darwasha,[38] a former leading Israeli Arab politician, sidestepped a question from an Arab journalist asking him if most Israelis supported a Nile-to-Euphrates Greater Israel, referring instead to Israel's lack of constitution and the disagreement about Israel's final borders.

Emerging Contradictions

Analysis of the various opinions on the concept of Greater Israel does reveal certain contradictions in the Greater Israel argument. To begin with, the borders keep changing; moreover, the same speaker might offer different borders. As, for example, in late April 1990, the late Yasser Arafat announced that the Zionists aspired to (among other territories) the whole of Lebanon, three-quarters of Iraq and most of Sinai. Less than two weeks later, his Greater Israel included just two-thirds of Iraq and no part of Lebanon or Sinai.[39] In March 1989, President Asad[40] defined a conventional Greater Israel as extending from the Nile to the Euphrates. A month later (12 April 1990), Radio Damascus reduced this to a country merely 'double the size of the Zionist entity'. However, years ago, Prime Minister 'Abd ar-Ra'uf al-Kasm had told a Turkish audience that the Israelis intend to occupy everything 'from the sources of the Nile [in Ethiopia and Uganda] to the sources of the Euphrates [in central Anatolia] . . . Greater Israel includes Turkey, Iran, and Africa'. And in 1992, Asad declared that Israel 'wants to extend wherever there are Jews.' Which is his greater Israel?[41]

Israeli political commentators also argue[42] that there are contradictions amongst the Arabs themselves about their future under Israeli rule. Sometimes they see themselves as dominated and exploited, sometimes expelled so that Greater Israel becomes a place 'where only Jews can live'. Sometimes they foresee a single giant Jewish polity. At other times they expect today's Arab states to be replaced by 'illegitimate cardboard entities' which would eventually accept the existence of Israel. Moreover, Israeli politicians have often raised the question: 'Do Arabs really believe what they say about Greater Israel?' Yitzhak Shamir,[43] former Prime Minister of Israel, thought not, telling an interviewer in 1989 that Hafiz al-Asad knew this talk to be 'sheer nonsense'.

Foreign reporters who have encountered the Greater Israel mentality understand it to be genuine. An examination of the Syrian case reveals, as *The Wall Street Journal*[44] had reported, that 'Just as Israelis fear Damascus's old dream of a "Greater Syria", encompassing Israel, Syrians believe that Tel Aviv craves an "Eretz Israel" stretching from the Nile to the Euphrates.' Indeed, Mamdu Adwan,[45] a leading Syrian poet, used almost these exact words in asserting that 'We are as afraid of Greater Israel as they are of Greater Syria.' According to Larry Cohler,[46] an American journalist, Adwan is not alone: 'most Syrians support these huge outlays [on the military] out of a genuine fear of Greater Israel.'

The belief in Israel's plan to expand from the Nile to Euphrates, and maybe beyond, makes the Jewish state's very existence a threat to the entire Middle East and increases the already substantial paranoia in the Middle East to still higher levels. Greater Israel means the Arabs cannot live in peace with Israel. The Greater Israel myth also justifies anti-Israel behaviour as a defensive act. The Greater Israel calumny bounces back to harm the Arabs too: by exciting Arab hatred of Israel, it persuades many Israelis to hold on to the territories they won in 1967 and not take a chance on peace treaties.

Nearly every polity's rhetoric contains statements of geographic grandeur which practical experience renders non-operational. It serves no one, and as the establishment of the State of Israel revealed, the political reality demanded different sensibilities.

THE TERRITORIAL-POLITICAL AXIS: *ERETZ YISRA'EL* VERSUS *MEDINAT ISRAEL*

During the British Mandate of Palestine, Eretz Yisra'el was part of the official name of the territory, when written in Hebrew. The official name was also minted on the Mandate coins. Some in the government of the British Mandate of Palestine wanted the name to be Palestina while the Yishuv wanted *Eretz Yisra'el*. A compromise was eventually reached, and consequently, in twentieth-century political usage, the term 'land of Israel' usually denotes only those parts of the land that came under the British Mandate, i.e. the land actually controlled by the State of Israel, the West Bank, and the Gaza Strip and sometimes also Transjordan (now the Kingdom of Jordan).

In fact, the declaration of the establishment of the State of Israel commences by drawing a direct line from Biblical times to the present:

> The Land of Israel was the birthplace of the Jewish people. Here their spiritual, religious and political identity was shaped. Here they first attained statehood, created cultural values of national and universal significance and gave to the world the eternal Book of Books.
>
> After being forcibly exiled from their land, the people kept faith with it throughout their Dispersion and never ceased to pray and hope for their return to it and for the restoration in it of their political freedom.
>
> Impelled by this historic and traditional attachment, Jews strove in every successive generation to re-establish themselves in their ancient homeland. In recent decades they returned in their masses. Pioneers, ma'apilim [(Hebrew)—immigrants coming to Eretz-Israel in defiance of restrictive legislation] and defenders, they made deserts bloom, revived the Hebrew language, built villages and towns, and created a thriving community controlling its own economy and culture, loving peace but knowing how to defend itself, bringing the blessings of progress to all the country's inhabitants, and aspiring towards independent nationhood.
>
> On the 29th November, 1947, the United Nations General Assembly passed a resolution calling for the establishment of a Jewish State in Eretz-Israel; the General Assembly required the inhabitants of Eretz-Israel to take such steps as were necessary on their part for the implementation of that resolution. This recognition by the United Nations of the right of the Jewish people to establish their State is irrevocable.[47]

As one attempts to review what has been outlined so far regarding the origins of Israel, one can come to the conclusion that the questions of what Israel shall be, where it should be founded, and which territory it shall comprise prompted discussions within the Zionist movement from the outset. However, in view of the almost simultaneous tasks of building a state and building a 'nation', Israel's core integrating elements were left ambiguous—such as 'Jewish ness', and 'the Jewish State'. Over the years, however, and often triggered by specific developments, these ambiguities gave rise to partly incompatible concepts of Israel's identity. At present, Israeli society and politics are characterized by certain fault lines, which cut across each other. One such fault line is the perceived division between the 'Land of Israel' and the 'State of Israel'.

Reflecting the traditional divisions within the Zionist movement, this axis invokes two concepts, namely, *Eretz Yisra'el*, i.e. the Biblical 'Land of Israel', and *Medinat Israel*, i.e. the Jewish and democratic State of Israel. While the concept of *Medinat Israel* dominated the first decades of statehood in accordance with the aspirations of Labour Zionism, the 1967 conquest of the land that was part of 'biblical Israel' provided a material basis for the ascent of the concept of *Eretz Yisra'el*.[48] Expressing the perception of rightful Jewish claims on 'biblical land', the construction of Jewish settlements in the conquered territories intensified after the 1977 elections, which ended the dominance of the Labour Party.[49] Yet, as the first *Intifada* made disturbingly visible, Israel's *de facto* rule over the Palestinian population created a dilemma of democracy *versus* Jewish majority in the long run.[50] With the beginning of the Oslo peace process and the option of territorial compromise, the rift between supporters of *Eretz Yisra'el* and *Medinat Israel* deepened to an unprecedented degree culminating in a dramatic climax in the form of the assassination of Prime Minister Rabin in November 1995.

As stressed earlier in the essay, the concept of *Eretz Yisra'el* emphasizes the bond between the 'biblical territory' and the Jewish people. According to its secular version, as represented by the Likud party and some ultra-nationalist parties in Israeli politics, Jewish sovereignty over the 'biblical territory' is essential for Israel's Jewish *national* character. The *religious* version of *Eretz Yisra'el* interprets Jewish sovereignty over the territories as the divinely inspired 'Return to the Promised Land'. Defended mainly by the National-Religious Party (NRP) in Israeli politics, this orientation opposes the relinquishing of territories on religious grounds.[51] Conversely, the concept of *Medinat Yisra'el*, as promoted mainly by the Labour Party, is compatible with territorial compromise, as it prefers maintaining a Jewish majority without infringing on democratic principles.[52] Differing from this pragmatic position, some supporters of *Medinat Yisra'el* (e.g. factions of *Meretz* or Israel's peace movement) also condemn Israel's occupation of the territories on mainly *ethical* grounds.

It is also important to highlight that besides the territorial dimension that separates what is commonly termed Israel's political Right from the Left, this axis also invokes two different sets of values. Presupposing the endless persecution of Jews and the permanence of the Arab–Israeli conflict, the narrative of *Eretz Israel* evolves around the principle of 'no choice', and entailing quite a gloomy perception of Israel's place in the region, 'security' becomes a supreme value.[53] In addition, *Eretz Israel* is basically a nationalist concept, which, by definition, promotes particularism and a collectivist concept of state identity. In its religious version, this feature is even more pronounced, as the theme of the 'chosen people' conveys.[54] Conversely, the concept of *Medinat Yisra'el* considers universalistic democratic values as more important than national-religious considerations appertaining to territory, although it still assumes that the State shall first serve the interests of the Jewish collective.[55] It is important to note, however, that there are also religious Jewish Israelis who adhere to these principles, represented, for instance, by the small Meimad party in Israeli politics.[56] Another orientation of *Medinat Yisra'el* lays a stronger emphasis on individualist and liberal principles, and considers secularism, democracy and equality of all Israeli citizens as supreme values. Mainly promoted by the political 'Left', this orientation is often anchored in a humanistic interpretation of the Jewish religion, and still supports the idea of a Jewish majority and the principle of Jewish immigration.[57]

ISRAEL AS A STATE IN THE LAND OF ISRAEL: ITS IMPLICATIONS

The present State of Israel, with or without the territories occupied as a result of the Six-Day War, does not encompass the entire land of Israel, what Arieh Eliav, noted for his willingness to cede the territories occupied by Israel in 1967 to a Palestinian state, has referred to as 'the land of the twelve tribes'.[58] Recognizing this does not imply or suggest espousing irredentism. The historical evidence reveals that even in the heyday of Jewish national existence in the land, it was more common than not for the land to be divided among several polities. Only the Davidic and Hasmonean empires briefly succeeded in bringing the whole of *Eretz Yisra'el* under a single Jewish government, at a price which few Israelis today would wish to pay. Thus, although re-establishing Jewish national existence in the land could be viewed as a proper exercise of the Jewish people's religious and historical rights, complete redemption of the land may well be, in traditional religious terms, 'forcing the end', that is to say, attempting more than can be achieved through human agency alone.[59]

That the State of Israel embraces less than the Land of Israel has several important implications.[60] First, there is a difference between the religious commitment to the land and loyalty to the state; the two are not identical. It is expected of a Jew to love *Eretz Yisra'el* in its entirety, beyond the boundaries of the State of Israel. From a religious perspective, a good Jew must be committed to the State for what it is but should not make that commitment monistic: it is part of one's multiple commitment to the land, the people, the Torah and God. This further reduces the tendency to view the State as an end in itself. Many secular Jews have emphasized, love of state as equivalent of love for the country. Religious Jews have not had that problem to the same extent, though some have also been susceptible to it.

In other words, a point of view within Jewish thought[61] espouses accepting and recognizing the fact that *Eretz Yisra'el* must presently be shared with another people does not require Jews to give up their love for it. In their opinion, perhaps the day will come when peace will permit the settlement of Jews in all parts of the land, even outside the territories embraced by the State of Israel.

THE FUTURE OF ERETZ YISRA'EL AS A VALUE CONCEPT[62]

From a totally different and rather interesting viewpoint, *Eretz Yisra'el* may be seen as this complex of value concepts which deals with the land itself, its ownership, control and use. It is obvious that Israel and Zionism have reached a crossroads with regard to *Eretz Yisra'el.* After the turnabout in 1967, when it seemed that the 1947–9 partition of the land west of the Jordan was repealed as a result of the Six-Day War, Israel now finds itself going back to a repartition. Unlike the earlier partition, which was based upon those parts of the land where the Zionist movement had established its settlements, after 1967, the Zionists succeeded in settling in all parts of the land west of the Jordan. The issue of repartition and the subsequent de-settling of the settlements in the West Bank occupies centre stage in the Israel–Palestine conflict and is likely to continue to do so in the near future and perhaps even beyond.

Moving along this line of thought, even more than that, the outlines of Israel's peace with the Palestinians suggest that simple repartition will not occur, that there will be a certain amount of federalization along confederal lines, in ways which resemble the developments in many other parts of the world and this will be integral to the success of a peaceful solution. At the very least, joint authorities for Israel and the Palestinians will handle strong economic interconnections and the handling of many tasks ranging from dealing with environmental problems to promoting tourism. Thus, if Israel gives up primary control, it does not necessarily mean that the Israelis will not be able to maintain a strong relationship backed by a degree of secondary status throughout the historic land of the twelve tribes (in the words of Arieh Eliav[63]) or historic *Eretz Yisra'el.*

However, in this case, the Jewish value of *Eretz Yisra'el* publicly expressed, actually stands in the way of its achievement by frightening its neighbours and awakening in them fears that the Israelis are still pursuing goals that they should have abandoned in the very act of implementing the peace process. Still, while Israeli Jews may accept a smaller territory for *Medinat Yisra'el*, '*Eretz Yisra'el*' will remain a matter of special concern for them. Confederal ties with their Palestinian neighbours may make it possible for Israelis to satisfactorily give expression to this value in ways other than the political for the benefit of all the entities.

On the other hand, *Eretz Yisra'el* may also be understood as a value concept concerned with use of the land. In other words, viewing the land as having a special sanctity, Jews and Zionists should lead to a more respectful and caring attitude towards it and make possible better land use. Just as in the pre-state days (*Yishuv*), this value led to a policy of land acquisition which emphasized common national ownership by the Keren Kayemet LeYisrael in the name of the Jewish people, land use may acquire an ecological dimension in the name of the Jewish people, which would otherwise be absent were the matter to be left entirely to market forces. This could, in fact, turn out to be one of the greatest contributions that Jewish values would make to the coming generation of Israelis.

CONCLUSION

In the process of exploring the journey of evolution from *Eretz* to *Medinat Yisra'el*, this essay arrives at the conclusion that in contemporary mainstream Israeli discourse, no prominent Zionist or Israeli intellectual or political figure openly advocates pursuing such borders as envisaged in the concept of '*Eretz Yisra'el*'. Yet, even today, the term 'Greater Israel' in Israeli political life refers at least to parts of the West Bank, the Golan Heights and the Gaza Strip. In the opinion of scholars like Ian Lustick and Daniel Pipes,[64] the three major usages of the term are (1) the views of right wing groups in Israel for whom the State of Israel (*Medinat Yisra'el*) is *Eretz Yisra'el*, (2) the opinion of far-right Jewish Mandate groups, such as Betar and Irgun Zvai-Leumi who regard Greater Israel as the pre-1923 Mandatory Palestine, i.e. both the historical region of Palestine and what was later Transjordan, and (3) according to a group of Arab nationalists, the idea of Greater Israel refers to a Zionist plan to extend the borders of Israel to the region from the Nile to the Euphrates in keeping with the Kingdom of David as mentioned in the verse from the Bible—the book of Genesis—which describes God's covenant with Abraham, wherein the Land of Israel was promised as an everlasting possession to the descendants of the Jewish patriarchs Abraham, Isaac and Jacob, making it the Promised Land. In reality, *Eretz Yisra'el* Haslemah (Greater Israel) continues to be a dream which could not be realized primarily for two reasons. First, contrary to the expectations of the early Zionists, most of the world's Jews did not join their brethren to live in Israel—there are more Jews in the US than in Israel, even today. Secondly, the Palestinian population has grown far more rapidly and the Palestinians have proved far more willing to fight than many on the Israeli right had anticipated and as the two *intifadas* have in fact revealed. In other words, many Israelis argue that unless they yield territory, they will have to choose between a Jewish State or a democratic one; they will not be able to have both.

NOTES

1. For all Biblical quotes mentioned in the article, see *Christians, Zionism and Palestine: A Selection of Articles and Statements on the Religious and Political aspects of the Palestine Problem*, Lebanon: The Institute for Palestine Studies, 1970.
2. See Israel Finkelstein and Niel Asher Silberman, *The Bible Unearthed: Archaeology's New Vision of Ancient Israel and the Origin of its Sacred Text*, Free Press, 2002.
3. See 'Jewish History', available at *http://www.jewishhistory.org.il.*
4. Ibid.
5. Ibid.
6. Article by Daniel Pipes, available at *http://www.danielpipes.org.*
7. Ibid.
8. For greater details on Zionist Statements, see Assa'd Razzouq, *Greater Israel: A Study in Zionist Thought*, Beirut: Palestine Liberation Organisation Research Center, 1970.
9. Ibid.
10. For quotes by Arab and Israeli Leaders, see 'History of Israel and Palestine and the Arab-Israeli Conflict', available at *http://www.mideastweb.org/briefhistory.htm*).
11. Ibid.
12. Essay by Daniel Pipes, available at *http://www.danielpipes.org.*
13. See 'Jewish History'.
14. Essay by Daniel Pipes, available at *http://www.danielpipes.org.*
15. See 'Jewish History'.
16. Ibid.
17. H.H. Ben-Sasson, *A History of the Jewish People*, Harvard: Harvard University Press, 1976.
18. Ibid.

19. See Howard M. Sachar, *A History of Israel*, New York: Knopf, 1976; and Rinna Samuel, *A History of Israel: The Birth, Growth and Development of Today's Jewish State*, London: Weidenfeld and Nicolson, 1989.
20. Ibid.
21. Ibid.
22. All quotes of Arab leaders, irrespective of the various journals and newspapers mentioned have been sourced from the following site: *http://www.mideastweb.org/briefhistory.htm*).
23. Ibid.
24. Ibid.
25. Ibid.
26. Ibid.
27. Ibid.
28. Ibid.
29. Ibid.
30. Ibid.
31. Ibid.
32. Ibid.
33. Ibid.
34. *Haaretz Daily*, 24 May 1990, available at *http://www.haaretz.com.*
35. Muhsin Yusuf, 'The Zionists and the Process of Defining Borders', *Journal of South Asian and Middle Eastern Studies*, no. 15, 1991.
36. Patrick Seale, quoted in *Al Majalla*, 23 July 1982, available at *http://www.almajalla.htm.*
37. Reuters, 7 February 1983. Source: *http://www.reuters.com.*
38. *Haaretz Daily*, 7 September 1990.
39. *The Jerusalem Post*, available at *http://www.jpost.com.*
40. Essay by Daniel Pipes, available at *http://www.danielpipes.org.*
41. Ibid.
42. *The Jerusalem Post.*
43. Article by Daniel Pipes, available at *http://www.danielpipes.org.*
44. *The Wall Street Journal*, 27 September 1990, available at *http://www.wsjopinion.com.*
45. Quoted from Larry Cohler, 'Rethinking Syria', available at *http://www.jdispatch.com.*
46. Ibid.
47. Declaration of the Establishment of the State of Israel, Source: Ministry of Foreign Affairs, Government of Israel website: *www.mfa.gov.il.*
48. See Shlomo Avineri, *The Making of Modern Zionism: The Intellectual Origins of the Jewish State*, New York: Basic Books, 1981. See Also Boaz Evron, *Jewish State or Israeli State*? Bloomington: Indiana University Press, 1995.
49. See Shmuel Sandler, *The State of Israel, the Land of Israel: The Statist and Ethnonational Dimensions of Foreign Policy*, London: Greenwood Press, 1993.
50. It is argued that by keeping the territories while enforcing democracy would mean granting equal citizenship rights to the Palestinian population. But in this case, and in view of the higher birth rate of the Palestinians at large, Israel would lose its Jewish majority in the long run. In fact, this is considered to be one of the reasons behind the non-annexation of Gaza and the West Bank into the State of Israel, keeping it as a sort of settler-colony.

51. For details of the policy of the NRP, see the official website of the party (also called Mafdal): *www.hamafdal.org.il.*
52. See *www.mfa.gov.il*, website of the Ministry of Foreign Affairs of the Government of Israel for statements made by leaders of the Labour Party, especially statements issued by Ehud Barak.
53. See Arian Asher, *Security Threatened: Surveying Israeli Opinion on Peace and War*, New York: Cambridge University Press, 1995.
54. See Ilan Peleg, 'The Peace Process and Israel's Political Culture', in *The Role of Domestic Politics in Israeli Peace-Making,* ed. Alan Dowty et al., Jerusalem: The Leonard Davis Institute for International Relations, The Hebrew University of Jerusalem, 1997.
55. The granting of formal citizen's rights to Israel's non-Jewish minority is considered as sufficient condition for defining Israel as a democracy.
56. See *Meimad* party platform: *www.meimad.org.il.*
57. See *Meretz* party platform: *www.meretz.org.il.*
58. Arieh Eliav, *Land of the Heart*, Philadelphia: Jewish Publication Society of America, 1974.
59. Daniel J. Elazar, 'An Answer to the New Anti-Zionists: The Rights of the Jewish People to a Sovereign State in Their Historic Homeland', available at *http://www.jcpa.org.*
60. Ibid.
61. Ibid.
62. See Daniel J. Elazar, *Kinship and Consent: The Jewish Political Tradition and its Contemporary Uses*, Ramat Gan, Philadelphia, London and Montreal: Turtledove, 1981. See also by the same author, *Israel: Building a New Society*, Bloomington, Indiana University Press, 1986.
63. Arieh, *Land of the Heart.*
64. See Lustick Ian, *For the Lord and the Land: The range of disagreement within Jewish Fundamentalism*, Online edition of this book is available at *http://www.sas.upenn.edu/penncip/lustick/index.html.* Also see article by Daniel Pipes, available at *http://www.danielpipes.org.*

9

Twenty Years After: Can SAARC Deliver?

SHANTANU CHAKRABARTI

BACKGROUND: REGIONAL COOPERATION AND SOUTH ASIA

It has become almost a ritual to begin any discussion on the South Asian Association on Regional Cooperation (SAARC) by stressing upon the poor impact this organization has had in enhancing the regional cooperation agenda. The SAARC, as an organization, in fact has had such bad press right since its inception in 1985. During the 1980s, for instance, *The Economist* had once described it as 'The Unmagnificent Seven'! More academic analyses have pointed out several factors which have been responsible for the poor functioning of the organization, ranging from strategic and political regional rivalry to lack of available economic complementarities. In this connection, the SAARC has also been unfavourably compared to the more successful regional organization in South-East Asia, namely, the Association of South East Asian Nations (ASEAN), and has been found wanting in all respects. While determining whether any particular regional organization has succeeded or not, one, however, must remember the fact that the process of regionalization is a dynamic and heterogeneous one, much dependent upon local specificities. According to one analyst: 'Regions are not so much measurable building blocs of the international order as spatially defined cultural, economic, and political constructions whose nature and functions are transformed over time.'[1]

It is also important to remember that any progress of regional cooperation cannot only involve the process of economic integration. It must also involve greater political commitment and interaction at the government level, as well as the proliferation of greater interaction and people to people contacts within the civil society networks in the region.

Thus, the region of South Asia cannot simply pick and choose any successful model of regionalism and try to implement it in its own area because, without having any links with indigenous processes and dynamics, such experimentations are sure to fail. The only option, however, difficult it may seem, is to develop its own model of regional organization. The rest of this chapter will try to analyse this process, which has been going on for over twenty-two years now.

REGIONAL DYNAMICS AND HINDRANCES TO REGIONAL COOPERATION

All recent talks on the viability of the SAARC as an economic organization should not make one oblivious of the fact that the organization was born out of a process of political commitment or as an input of a regional confidence-building measure (CBM). Depending upon one's outlook, the birth of the organization has been attributed to either the regional desirability to have a localized South-South cooperative venture, or, more sceptically, as a strategic attempt by Bangladesh to organize a bloc of India's neighbours. The region of South Asia has also been characterized as a region with a long history as a coherent political, economic and even administrative unity. All the countries belonging to this region and the erstwhile parts of the Indian subcontinent are geographically compact. South Asia also constitutes a coherent environmental region with a conjoint ecological cycle and common river, ocean and mountain systems. The region also enjoys an extremely rich common historical tradition and legacy as well as cultural and socio-economic commonalities.

Such legacies, however, failed to generate momentum for substantial cooperative links among the South Asian countries that became independent during the post-1945 period. A combination of historical problems along with the problems of new dimensions arising from the factors related to the partition vitiated the prospects for regional cooperation during the early years.[2] During the initial decades, the South Asian countries were also busy with the process of nation-building, which was a difficult task given the individual domestic turmoil and conflicts with their intra-regional linkages, set within the adversarial global paradigm created by Cold War politics. The linkages between the South Asian countries and the West, determined by the 'Centre-Periphery' paradigm during the colonial period, were again further reinforced through the import of credit and technology from the Western countries during the early periods of development leading to what has been characterized by Raul Prebisch[3] as the 'dependency syndrome'. Thus, there was little scope for enhancing economic transactions between the countries in the region. Moreover, given the asymmetrical geopolitical structure in the region, with the greater prominence of India and her central regional location, it was but natural for her neighbouring countries to harbour suspicion of her alleged or real 'hegemonic' designs in the region. The nature of the state-building process and domestic politics was also divergent in different regional countries. Countries like India and Sri Lanka, for instance, have been able to establish and continue with democratic state structures, at least in a formal sense although the state structure even in these two countries has been affected by the long civil war in Sri Lanka and the rising sectarian (both communal and caste-related) violence in India. Among the other countries, Pakistan, has witnessed a see-saw battle between long periods of military rule and brief intermittent gaps of democracy. In its period of independent existence for over sixty years, Pakistan has experienced more than twenty-five years of military rule. Even during the period of democratically elected governments, the Pakistani army did manage to retain its formidable grasp over the state structure and Pakistan's economy, which perhaps explains the relative ease with which General Pervez Musharraf could complete the latest coup and transfer of power in 1999 and why he has been largely successful in controlling all recent civilian opposition and civil society-led outbursts against him. Bangladesh's emergence as a democratic country in 1972 also proved to be relatively short-lived with the establishment and continuation of army rule between 1975–90. The restoration of democracy after a long period of civilian struggle had generated new hopes. The continuous violent nature of opposition politics in the country, which includes mob violence, frequent strikes and acrimonious exchanges, has, however, severely hampered the functioning of democracy in the country. Very recently, a military backed non-political caretaker government has once again come to power in Bangladesh and has been involved in the process of stripping the two major political formations of all power in the name of cleaning up the entire political system. Democracy was restored in Nepal in 1990, though the frequent collapse of governments, the rising influence of Maoist guerrilla groups and problems with the constitutional monarchy have contributed in making the democratic set-up very fragile. The continuing political tension in the country as a result of disagreements and mistrust between the Maoists and the political parties raises little hope for the prospects of a successful democratic regime in the immediate future. In Bhutan, despite certain reforms introduced under the initiative of the monarchy to convert the monarchy into a constitutional one and the proposal to introduce a democratic regime in 2008, *Drukpa* elitism still continues to be the dominant governing trend in the country. The island nation of Maldives has a party-less republican form of government with the current president (Mamoon Abdul Gayoom) ruling since 11 November 1978, as both the head of the state and head of government. Afghanistan, which has recently joined the SAARC as its eighth member, continues to suffer from utter destabilization due to the civil war in spite of a democratic regime under President Hamid Karzai tenuously holding onto power with the backing of the US-led coalition force. All the South Asian countries also continue to suffer from the struggle for socio-economic mobilization, both at the intra-elite level as well at the mass level which often gets manifested through ethnic divides, religious and sectarian differences, inter-caste and community rivalry, etc. All these have resulted in violence re-emerging as the main characterizing feature in state-society relations in South Asia.[4]

Apart from the post-colonial state becoming more violent, the way in which subordinate ethnic groups and social classes relate to each other and negotiate with the state has come to be characterized by a recurrent propensity to use collective violence as a means of articulating their demands. Needless to say, given the long shared legacy of the region, such divisions are most often reflected across the state boundaries, which then affects regional relations. To an extent, this has given rise to the tendency in the South Asian ruling circles to interfere and sometimes encourage sectarian conflicts or violence in neighbouring countries. Pakistan's help to the militant organizations operating in the Indian state of Jammu & Kashmir and to the militants operating in the Indian state of Punjab has been well documented. India too has, time and again, officially complained to Bangladesh, Nepal and Bhutan about shelter and facilities being given in these countries to the separatist militants operating in the north-eastern states of India and of the Inter Services Intelligence (ISI)-operated training camps being allowed to be run there. On the other hand, Indian support proved to be crucial during the struggle for independence in East Pakistan and the subsequent emergence of Bangladesh as an independent state in 1972. Similarly, it has been alleged that the Indian secret service (RAW: Research & Analysis Wing) sends clandestine help to the separatist groups in the province of Sindh in Pakistan. During the early 1980s, the Indian government also provided arms and training facilities to the Tamil Tigers, belonging to the Liberation Tigers of Tamil Eelam (LTTE), fighting for a separate state in Sri Lanka. Thus, a general sense of insecurity has prevailed in the region, which has hampered the development of regional cooperation. The Cold War global paradigm, and the involvement of the two Super Powers as well as China, has also been an important determinant in influencing inter-state relations in South Asia.

One fundamental factor that has contributed substantially to regional hostilities are the existing differences between India and her neighbours over respective security and strategic perspectives. India, in fact, has consistently endeavoured since its independence to keep at bay foreign powers from this region, and to establish the principle of bilateral resolution of problems between the countries of this region without inviting foreign intervention. In this sense, India could be regarded as a 'status-quoist' power, trying to maintain the already established patterns of South Asian relationships. Other South Asian states, particularly Pakistan, have sought to deny this pre-eminence to India and limit its regional role either by attempting to subvert the existing patterns of South Asian relationships through the establishment of greater links between the South Asian countries, bypassing India, or by encouraging multilateral regional interaction in place of one-to-one bilateral relations with India. Another method, which has proved to be more successful, has been to invite external players into regional geopolitics. To that extent, India's South Asian neighbours (particularly Pakistan) could be designated as irredentist powers. Pakistan, for instance, became a strategic ally of the USA by becoming a member of the South Asian Treaty Organisation (SEATO) and Central Treaty Organisation (CENTO) in the 1950s. It also became a close ally of China following the War of 1971–2 and the liberation of Bangladesh. China's relations with India's neighbours, like Bangladesh, Myanmar and Nepal, have also been a source of concern for many Indian strategists. India, in turn, in spite of retaining its official position as the leading 'Non-Aligned' country, became an important strategic ally of the USSR, especially since the signing of the Treaty of 1971. For instance, during the 1980s India was placed among the USSR's top ten non-Communist Third World trade partners, second to the Middle East in Soviet arms transfers, and received large amounts of Soviet development assistance.[5]

POST-COLD WAR REGIONAL STRATEGIC IMPERATIVES

The post-Cold War global developments and paradigmatic shifts have also had their impact upon the South Asian region. In fact, such changes have posed before the region both opportunities and challenges. The end of the Cold War has also provided fresh incentives to regionalism by ending global rivalries and by putting more emphasis on economic development and liberalization so that economic considerations are now playing a decisive role in defining the parameters of regional groupings beyond strategic and geographical boundaries.

A second development in post-Cold War strategic thinking has been the increasing concern for emerging non-state oriented threats, or security problems, particularly the rising menace of global terrorism, having the potential of creating conflict-oriented situations in South Asia. The collapse of the Soviet power and the subsequent reorientation of its foreign policy resulted in her [the USSR's] disengagement from the region in the late 1980s and early 1990s. Soviet disengagement, in turn, should have logically led to the lowering of the US strategic and military presence in the region, particularly in terms of providing assistance to Pakistan. On closer inspection, however, it would seem that external influences have increased through the reorientation of global focus upon the alleged 'hot zones' or, in other words, the conflict prone regions of the world like the Middle East, North-East Asia, the Balkans and South Asia. There has also been a renewed global focus on South Asia, especially since the nuclear tests conducted by India and Pakistan in 1998, which were regarded as adding a nuclear dimension to the potentially dangerous Indo–Pakistan bilateral conflict and affecting the Clinton administration's plan of creating a stable nuclear structure through the enforcement of the Nuclear Proliferation Treaty (NPT), the Comprehensive Test Ban Treaty (CTBT) and the Fissile Material Cut Off Treaty (FMCT). A wave of sanctions were imposed immediately after the tests upon both countries and payments of loans and grants were stopped by the US, the Western world, Japan, as well as international organizations like the International Monetary Fund (IMF) and the World Bank. The sanctions, though they severely affected Pakistan's economy, did not, however, have the same severe effects on the Indian economy. Moreover, the Clinton administration itself had to adopt a soft approach towards India for commercial reasons, and towards Pakistan for fear of its total disintegration. India also adopted better damage-limiting measures through continuous engagement with the US authorities (several rounds of talks between External Affairs Minister Jaswant Singh and Deputy Secretary of State Strobe Talbot were crucial in this connection). In return, there is now greater acceptance of India's regional aspirations and concerns on the part of the US administration. As a part of this new policy, there has also been greater recognition of regional disputes like Kashmir as a bilateral issue which should be solved through peaceful negotiations. For instance, it has been alleged that US pressure played a major role in limiting the Kargil conflict to a specific area and also acted as a catalyst behind the Pakistani establishment's decision to withdraw troops and Mujahideen fighters from some of the occupied peaks during the height of the Kargil war.

Better recognition of India's regional aspirations has become more evident during the term of President George W Bush. There is talk in strategic circles of a new 'strategic partnership' between the US and India, especially over issues like free trade, Islamic terrorism and other issues of mutual interests. The Bush administration has also been more accommodative on South Asian proliferation. In the aftermath of the terrorist attacks in the US on 11 September 2001, President Bush also waived the post-Pokhran II sanctions imposed on India and Pakistan as a part of the US strategy to build-up a global alliance against terrorism. The ongoing bilateral negotiations over the treaty on Indo–US cooperation in civilian nuclear technology since 2006 is another example of this growing proximity.

Such efforts to forge new ties with the South Asian countries in recent times have not been limited to the US alone. Russia, for instance, is once again showing eagerness to develop fresh ties in the region as a strategic measure *vis-à-vis* the US and the West. It has sought to revive its old ties with India by signing a treaty in 1993 and another one on 3 October 2000, which declares the establishment of a new bilateral 'strategic partnership', which includes military cooperation.[6] There are ongoing talks within strategic circles about the possibility of forging a new 'Strategic Triangle', comprising Russia, China and India, which could pose a challenge to the US-dictated 'unipolar global strategy'. This would, however, be difficult to achieve, given the nature of Chinese engagement in the region already, which includes close military cooperation with Pakistan, building of bases in the Bay of Bengal region, including Myanmar, and long-term border disputes with India.

External influences thus continue to affect the pattern of regional relations even during the post-Cold War years. It must, however, be remembered that the establishment of any sort of a 'strategic partnership' with any external power would have the potential for increasing regional tensions. This would be particularly relevant for the Indian strategists and decision-makers. For instance, one scholar has cautioned for instance that, 'A US sponsored thesis like the "Clash of Civilizations" advocated by Samuel Huntington threatens to demonise the Islamic world and plots an insidious role for India as a counterweight'.[7]

This, in turn, would certainly lead to further deterioration of India's relations with its neighbours. Moreover, overt security ties between India and the US would certainly lead to the enhancement of strategic cooperation between Pakistan and China. A further increase in arms build-up in other countries of the South Asian region also cannot be ruled out. Such developments are bound to effect intra-regional and internal conflicts, the chief sources of post-Cold War insecurity, as the past experiences would suggest. Thus, the basic purpose of achieving better security through such strategic tie-ups would be defeated. There is, therefore, little alternative to developing better ties between the South Asian countries in the context of globalization as well as for the purpose of ensuring better regional security and stability.

The post-Cold War years have indeed witnessed a significant shift in India's policy in South Asia. India's bilateral relations with several of her neighbours have, in fact, shown signs of improvement during this period. According to the Indian analyst, C. Raja Mohan, for instance, one of the most significant developments in the subcontinent during the 1990s has been the sea change in India's policy towards its smaller neighbours. Relations with Bangladesh, for instance, improved with the repatriation of the Chakma refugees, transfer of the Tin Bigha corridor, and the signing of the 1996 agreement on the sharing of the Ganga waters. Relations with Sri Lanka have also improved with the withdrawal of the Indian Peace Keeping Force (IPKF) from Sri Lanka and the gradual disengagement of India from direct intervention in Sri Lankan affairs over the Tamil question. The Indo–Lanka Free Trade Treaty of 1998 also has the potential for substantially enhancing the level of bilateral trade. India's relations with Nepal, Bhutan and the Maldives have also witnessed an upswing during this period. Indo–Pakistan relations, however, continue to remain the most important problem factor in the region. In fact, relations between the two countries have been subject to a roller coaster ride in the recent years, worsening during the beginning of the 1990s and reaching a crisis point as a result of the 1998 nuclear tests carried out by both countries. The Kargil crisis and the army coup in Pakistan once again frustrated hopes of salvaging ties rekindled by the Lahore bus diplomacy and the Lahore declaration in 1999. From 2001 and onwards, official-level talks, however, have been re-established between the two countries, which have become overt nuclear powers since the tests in 1998. A large number of confidence building measures (CBMs) have also been undertaken by both countries in recent years, though relations are yet to reach a stabilizing point.

India has also taken substantial initiatives in increasing the level of multilateral interaction with particular emphasis on functional cooperation in the region. Efforts, for instance, have been made in the 1990s to increasingly involve the prime regional organization SAARC in enhancing regional economic cooperation and development.

Though such changes in foreign policy were becoming evident during the tenure of Prime Minister Narasimha Rao in the early 1990s, the first clear articulation of India's changing regional policy, however, came from I.K. Gujral in his capacity as external affairs minister and later as prime minister of the country. During his speech at Chatham House, London, on 23 September 1996, Gujral specified a set of five principles which were to guide the conduct of foreign relations of India with its immediate neighbours. This policy has since come to be characterized by Indian analysts and strategists as the 'Gujral Doctrine'. The five principles of the Gujral Doctrine are that first, with neighbours like Bangladesh, Bhutan, Maldives, Nepal and Sri Lanka, India will not ask for reciprocity but gives and accommodates what it can in good faith and trust; second, no South Asian country should allow its territory to be used against the interest of another country of the region; third, no country should interfere in the internal affairs of another; fourth, all South Asian countries must respect each other's territorial integrity and sovereignty; and, finally, they should settle their disputes through peaceful bilateral negotiations.[8] According to Gujral, these five principles, if scrupulously adhered to, would achieve a fundamental recasting of South Asia's regional relationships, including the difficult relationship between India and Pakistan. Further, the implementation of these principles would generate a climate of close and mutually benign cooperation in the region, where the weight and size of India is regarded positively and as an asset by these countries. A consensus in fact seems to be developing among the Indian political and decision-making community about the constructive regional engagement policy. It has been argued, for instance, that

> Beyond the Gujral doctrine, successor governments from both the right and left are likely to continue pursuing policies towards a more cooperative and less conflict prone South Asian region. The real politic of the South Asian state system, in particular, the economic imperative; will prompt a re-evaluation of the conflict prone policies of the past.[9]

It would thus be most fruitful for India to continue to allot more importance to regional policy involving 'constructive engagement'. In this connection, one could refer to analyst Riefqi Muna's suggestion for greater cooperation among the Asian countries involving the Security Sector Reforms (SSR) which include both traditional and non-traditional security issues, which would seek to give an ideological basis of cooperation.[10] Cooperation among the South Asian countries regarding the SSR can also be envisaged.

The changing geopolitical realities have been reflected in the latest rounds of the thirteenth and the fourteenth SAARC summits held in Dhaka and New Delhi respectively, involving attempts to broad base the organization. Afghanistan, for instance, was formally inducted as the eighth member of the SAARC in 2007. Countries like China, Japan, South Korea, USA and the European Union (EU) have been accorded observer status in the organization.

REGIONAL ECONOMIC COOPERATION

The level of intra-regional economic cooperation continues to be very low. The creation of South Asia Preferential Trade Arrangement (SAPTA) in the 1990s and the coming into operation of the South Asian Free Trade Arrangement (SAFTA) in 2006, as well as the successful bilateral initiatives, like, for instance, the Indo–Sri Lanka Free Trade Agreement (FTA), have not made any remarkable change in the picture. The quantum of trade deals among SAARC countries remains limited to around 4.5 per cent of the total trade flows worth around 135 billion dollars per annum. As against that, inter-country trade deals among countries in the European Union account for 55 per cent of the total trade[11] and intra-ASEAN trade is over 20 per cent. Tables 9.1 and 9.2 give a detailed break-up of intra-regional trade during the period 1991-2000.

Poor regional official trade has generated a flourishing illegal trade in South Asia, which proves, quite ironically, the existence of immense prospects of enhancing the level of commercial activities. It has been pointed out that high tariff and non-tariff barriers, distorted domestic trade policies, poor infrastructure and financial facilities, etc., have all led to the burgeoning illegal trade in the region.[12]

The SAFTA, created in 2006, is thought to have the potential for improving regional economic integration provided the participants accept the provisions in true faith and do not try to circumvent the requirements through other means. In order to make it easier for the smaller member countries, the former foreign secretary of

TABLE 9.1: INTRA-REGIONAL TRADE IN SOUTH ASIA (1991–2000): EXPORTS

(*value in $ million*)

From/To	Bangladesh	Bhutan	India	Maldives	Nepal	Pakistan	Sri Lanka	SAARC	World	SAARC per cent
SAARC										
1991	431	2	100	18	89	115	259	1,014	27,852	3.64
1992	496	3	173	19	75	114	359	1,239	30,686	4.03
1993	542	6	103	16	82	120	324	1,193	33,229	3.59
1994	649	8	107	27	102	121	421	1,435	37,787	3.79
1995	1,129	13	132	27	120	139	461	2,021	45,841	4.40
1996	960	11	172	70	165	215	553	2,146	49,483	4.33
1997	759	9	206	33	154	265	581	2,007	50,651	3.96
1998	1,162	14	450	37	352	198	651	2,864	54,097	5.29
1999	1,052	21	340	38	351	181	697	2,680	57,317	4.67
2000	1,015	15	344	134	398	232	659	2,797	65,500	4.27

Source: IMF Direction of Trade Statistics, Yearbooks: 1998, 2000, 2001.

TABLE 9.2: INTRA-REGIONAL TRADE IN SOUTH ASIA (1991–2000): IMPORTS

(value in $ million)

To/from	Bangladesh	Bhutan	India	Maldives	Nepal	Pakistan	Sri Lanka	SAARC	World	SAARC per cent
SAARC										
1991	60	5	549	10	23	191	62	900	35,084	2.56
1992	75	7	737	9	51	304	66	1,249	40,474	3.08
1993	66	8	889	11	20	193	78	1,265	39,517	3.20
1994	82	12	1,060	15	16	223	94	1,502	44,275	3.39
1995	131	22	1,693	17	33	231	115	2,242	58,318	3.84
1996	108	22	2,290	14	55	203	109	2,801	61,996	4.51
1997	93	15	1,941	16	88	134	120	2,407	65,310	3.68
1998	108	26	2,410	18	167	231	118	3,078	67,504	4.55
1999	95	35	2,297	19	172	299	126	3,043	72,421	4.20
2000	98	23	2,306	32	186	235	208	3,088	78,482	3.93

Source: IMF Direction of Trade Statistics Yearbooks: 1998, 2000, 2001.

India, Muchkund Dubey, has suggested that some monetary help be provided to them; otherwise it would be a 'race to the bottom' as the participants would be adding more and more items in the negative list of trades ultimately defeating the purpose of the SAFTA itself, to liberalize regional trade.[13]

Regional complementarities, it has been suggested, could also increase once the regional trade regime gets liberalized. The addition of service items, which was suggested during the 13th summit, could further boost the level of regional trade. The share of services in global exports, for instance, has grown from 15 per cent to nearly 25 per cent over the last two decades.[14] There is great potential for developing trade in services among the SAARC countries also, which could benefit all the member countries including the less developed ones.

One must, however, be cautious and admit that progress in the future is likely to be tardy. According to the rosiest estimates, there will be about 10 per cent growth in intra-regional trade within the next 10 years, even if all the necessary arrangements have been implemented. In this connection, when one considers the fact that even with over 20 per cent intra-regional trade, some analysts suggest the necessity of the ASEAN to forge greater intra-Asian linkages, it is but natural to become sceptical about the economic potential of the SAARC. Second, recently, concerns have also been raised about the viability of the FTAs. Jagdish Bhagwati,[15] for instance, has written about the 'spaghetti bowl' syndrome created by the regional FTAs through its criss-crossing networks of rules and regulations hampering free trade rather than helping it. In this context, the viability of the SAFTA in improving regional trade still remains in doubt.

NON-GOVERNMENT COOPERATIVE INITIATIVES

The previous two sections have indicated that the prospects of functional cooperation in the region will continue to be hampered in the prevailing atmosphere of distrust and regional tensions. Thus, the first step towards strengthening regional cooperation must be through peace and conflict resolution initiatives. The Peace Studies analyst and activist, John Lederach, once wrote that there are three approaches to peace building: (a) the top-level approach is constructed around high-level leaders and intermediaries; (b) The middle-range approach is constructed around authoritative figures that do not officially represent any party to the conflict but are generally highly respected as individuals or are formally engaged in the fields of education, health, agriculture, business or humanitarian organizations as insider-partials in the way explained above; and (c) the grass-roots approach is constructed around people who are involved in local communities, members of indigenous NGOs, health officials and refugee camp leaders.[16] Lederach has also highlighted the fact that the Conflict Resolution Theory has been lacking a systematized approach towards middle-level actors, whom he sees as providing a strategic, valuable link between the top and grass-root levels, in favour of external intervention oriented at the top-level. In this connection he has also stressed the importance of 'empowerment' of grass-roots and middle level organizations. The civil society initiatives in South Asia have also remained largely confined to the top and middle levels, mainly resting upon elite initiatives and regional and international think-tanks. The growth of people-to-people initiatives and grass-roots organizations, though not absent, has continued to remain weak in the region.[17]

So analysis of all three approaches—the political/state-level approach, the economic approach and the non-government initiatives—would seem to indicate that the SAARC has not been accorded top-level priority in the regional circles by any country. In this connection, the next section tries to find out whether the organization can ensure its own viability by adopting some new approaches.

ENSURING THE VIABILITY OF SAARC THROUGH ALTERNATIVE APPROACHES

It is becoming increasingly clear that the SAARC in its present form is not destined to survive, let alone flourish, for long. This has led to a churning process within the organization in recent times, to broad base its agenda and functioning. A new initiative which, in this connection, was introduced as a part of the SAARC process in the 1990s was the 'sub-regional approach' to enhance economic cooperation.[18] The first of such initiatives was taken by Nepal in December 1996 when it presented an approach paper in the SAARC Council of Ministers meeting on the feasibility of sub-regional cooperation between Nepal, Bhutan, Bangladesh and India in the form of growth polygons, which were identified as 'localised economic cooperation zones where countries with different economic sizes, socio-cultural patterns and political systems have sought to integrate parts of their territories for mutual gains'. During the 9th summit, the foreign secretaries of the four countries also met separately to examine the feasibility of such a quadrilateral grouping.

The proposal had initially generated a controversy as 'outsiders' like Pakistan and Sri Lanka criticized such an arrangement as a violation of the spirit of the SAARC Charter, which stipulates collective action. The controversy, however, seemed to have been settled with all the SAARC countries agreeing to encourage the development of specific projects involving three or more members, as per the SAARC Charter provisions included in the Articles V1 and X of the Charter.[19] The proposal for a Quadrilateral Growth Initiative comprising India (the component states in the north-east and West Bengal), Nepal, Bhutan and Bangladesh, thus, has come under the SAARC framework.

The proliferation of economic ties on an inter-regional basis has also become a necessity in the age of geo-economics. Recent attempts by India and some other South Asian countries to forge closer ties with the 'growth areas' of South-East Asia, south-west China and the Indian Ocean rim countries must be understood in the context of such global movements. India's relations with the ASEAN countries, in fact, have substantially improved since the early 1990s though the commercial ties are yet to reach the desired level. Such efforts till now, however, have involved bilateral ventures, lacking regional coordination. The formation of two new associations, the Indian Ocean Rim-Association for Regional Cooperation (IOR-ARC) and the Bangladesh–India–Myanmar–Sri Lanka–Thailand–Economic Co-operation (BIMST-EC) formed in 1997 (recently regrouped as the 'Bay of Bengal Initiative for Multi-Sectoral Technical and Economic Cooperation' with the inclusion of new members like Nepal and Bhutan since 2004), also holds tremendous potential for the SAARC regional grouping to enhance regional cooperation, especially in prioritized areas like trade and investment, technology, transportation and communication, energy, tourism and fisheries. Attempts are also underway to increase economic interaction between the Indian north-eastern region and the south-western region of China.[20]

On closer inspection, this trend to develop further links with the South-East Asian region and the south-west part of China seems to hark back to the ancient economic and cultural linkages that interconnected the Asian continent from very early times. According to Fernard Braudel, the Far East world economy consisted of three gigantic world-economies: Islam, overlooking the Indian Ocean from the Red Sea and the Persian Gulf, and controlling the endless chain of deserts stretching across Asia from Arabia to China; India, whose influence extended throughout the Indian Ocean, both east and west of Cape Comorin; and China, at once a great territorial power—striking deep into the heart of Asia—and a maritime force, controlling the seas and countries bordering the Pacific. Braudel, in this connection, also challenged the contention of 'peddling trade' in Asia and argued in favour of this trade being carried through more sophisticated capitalist networks.[21] The concept of subregional cooperation in this region, to a large extent, involves modern attempts to integrate the same regions. Thus, even if the SAARC does not survive in its present form, it would not be an end to the process of regional cooperation but a process of rekindling of efforts into different, more open channels.

CONCLUSION

Having completed twenty-two years of existence, the organization of SAARC, like a young adult, currently faces an identity crisis. For all these years, in trying to fulfil both the role of a regional CBM exercise as well as that of a facilitator of regional economic cooperation, the organization failed to achieve either objective. Global changes and the commensurate regional shifts in recent times have also affected the functioning of the SAARC, which had, till recently, been given up as a moribund organization. A new trend to revitalize the organization as a viable economic group mainly focuses on a 'Look East' policy with attempts to forge closer linkages between South Asia and the South-East Asian regions. This should not, however, lead to the neglect of the South Asian region itself. It may be suggested that the organization should continue with its task of greater political engagement in the region, which had been one of its original objectives, along with its attempts to emerge as a key facilitator in forging intra-Asian economic networks.

NOTES

1. Raimo Vayrynen, 'Post Hegemonic and Post Socialist Regionalism: A Comparison for East Asia and Central Europe', Joan B. Kroc Institute for International Peace Studies, August 1997. Source: URL: *http://www.ciaonet.org/wps/var01.html* (accessed on 24th May 2001).
2. V.P. Dutt, *India's Foreign Policy*, New Delhi: Vikas, 1984, p. 13.
3. Paul, Probisch, *The Economic Development of Latin America and its Principal Problems*, New York: United Nations Organizations, 1950.
4. Jayadeva Uyangoda, 'Militarization, Violent State, Violent Soceity: Sri Lanka', in *Internal Conflicts in South Asia*, ed. Kumar Rupesinghe and Khawar Mumtaz, London: PRIO & Sage, 1996, p. 118.
5. Linda Racioppi, *Societ Policy Towards South Asia Since 1970*, Cambridge: Cambridge University Press, 1994, p. 1.
6. Alexander Salitsky, 'China, India, Russia', *World Affairs* 5, no. 1 (January–March 2001).

7. Rita Manchanda, 'India', in *Security in South Asia: Comprehensive and Co-operative*, ed. Dipankar Banerjee, New Delhi: Manas, 1999, p. 31.
8. Padmaja Murthy, 'The Gujral Doctrine and Beyond', *Strategic Analysis* XXIII, no. 4, July 1999. Source: *url: http://www.idsa-india.org* (accessed on 7 March 2000).
9. Manchanda, 'India', p. 31.
10. Riefqi Muna, 'Landscape of Regional Coopration: Its Meaning for a Security Sector Reform Network in Asia,' *Journal of Security Sector Management* 1, no. 3, 2003.
11. 'Making SAFTA Effective', *The New Nation*, Dhaka, 3 July 2006.
12. For illegal trade in South Asia see, Nisha Taneja, 'Informal trade in the SAARC Region', Working Paper no. 47, New Delhi: Indian Council for Research on International Economic Relations (March 1999).
13. Bishal Rai, 'Greater Integration in Need', *Kuensal*, Bhutan, 11 September 2006.
14. Shiv Raj Bhatt, 'Services Under SAFTA: How to Make it Work for South Asia?' http//:www.NepalNews.com (accessed on 6 September 2006).
15. See for instance, Ross Garnaut and Jagdish Bhagwati, 'Say No to This Free Deal', The Australian, 11 July 2003 (Source: *http://www.cfr.org/publication/6116/say_no_to_this_free_trade_dela.htrml?breadcrumb = %2Fbios%2F1735%2Fjagdish_n_bhagwati%3Fpage%3D3*) accessed on 7 September 2007).
16. John Paul Lederach, *Building Peace: Sustainable Reconciliation in Divided Societies*, Washington: USIP Press, 1997, pp. 46-50.
17. For details on non-government civil society-led initiatives towards cooperation in South Asia, see Sundeep Waslekar, 'Track-Two Diplomacy in South Asia', *ACDIS Occasional Paper*, International Center for Peace Initiatives Bombay & Research of the Program in Arms Control, Disarmament, and International Security, University of Illinois at Urbana-Champaign, 2nd edn., October 1995; Aqil S. Shah, 'Non-Official Dialogue Between India And Pakistan: Prospects and Problems', *ACDIS Occasional Paper*, Program in Arms Control, Disarmament, and International Security, University of Illinois at Urbana-Champaign, and Quaid-e-Azam University Islamabad, Pakistan, August 1997; Shantanu Chakrabarti, 'Relevance of Track II Diplomacy in South Asia', in *International Studies* 40, no. 3, 2003.
18. Sangeeta Thapliyal, 'Potential for Cooperation in South Asia: The Need For a Sub-regional Approach', in *South Asian Survey* 6, no. 1, January–June 1999.
19. Tenth SAARC Summit Declaration, 1998.
20. For details regarding the potential see, Jayanta Kumar Ray and Prabir De, 'Bilateral Cooperation between India and China: Issues and Ways Forward', paper presented at the International Workshop on Facilitation of Trade and Transport Cooperation between India and China, Kolkata, India, 27–8 November 2003; Gurudas Das, 'Sino-Indian Border Trade for Frontier Development: The Case of India's Northeast and China's Southwest', paper presented in the International Workshop on Facilitation of Trade and Transport Cooperation between India and China, Kolkata, India, 27–8 November 2003.
21. Fernard Braudel, *The Perspective of the World, Civilization and Capitalism 15th-18th Century*, vol. III, USA: Fontana Press, 1985, p. 486.

10

Religious Connections between Bengal and Contiguous Ethnicities: Forging an Inter-Regional Arena[1]

SWARUPA GUPTA

INTRODUCTION

> For what boundaries can be marked, when we are dealing not with plants and animals, relief and climate, but men, whom no barriers or frontiers can stop? . . . We should imagine a hundred frontiers, not one, some political, some economic, and some cultural.[2]

Across historical eras, the drawing and redrawing of boundaries between empires, countries, and more recently, modern nation states, have attempted to divide, reorganize and even imagine people/populations into existence. They have sought to emblematize and demarcate identities, through a legitimation of the limitedness of the nation[3] and of regions within it. Identities, however, do not always remain compressed into the framework of neat boundaries. The ways in which identities strive to transcend boundaries can take different forms. In contemporary India, divisive struggles, and scrambles for ethnic homelands stem from separatist tendencies, reflecting legacies of colonial strategies of compartmentalizing communities and separating regions through boundaries.[4] By contrast, the Bengali literati's discourse on nationhood during the late colonial period, drawing on the inclusive idea of a shared social universe (symbolized by *samaj*/ social collectivity)[5] flowed beyond regional/sub-regional boundaries to approximate wider unities. The notion of a nation conceptualized in such terms contextually erased boundaries and dissolved geographical dichotomies. This occurred through a complex and multilayered process of connecting diverse places and people within and beyond Bengal via specific ideological bridges. This essay focuses on one such ideological site: religious interconnections, which went into the complex remaking of the region by connecting it to places beyond it. The specific ways in which religion was deployed as part of a wider process of re-imagining unities within a harmonious social order constituted the unique focus of Bengal's imagination of 'geographies of religion' which have been seen as operating within ideological frameworks investigating historical geographies of religious identities, belongings and communities.[6] The deployment of religious unities in an imaginary readjustment of boundaries in eastern India fed into a framework having a wider applicability, as it was extended to approximate larger unities. While the inclusive connotation embedded in the idea and practice of Hindu religion has been a key element in the envisioning of a subcontinental civilizational unity,[7] the specific trajectories of the deployment of religious interconnections in a regional (Bengali) discourse to approximate wider unities through an imaginary geography entwined in a meaningful nexus between history, religion and ethnic identity, have remained relatively unexplored. This essay concentrates on filling this analytic void by focusing on how the Bengali literati excavated historical lineages and ancient bonds to forge modern religious linkages, memorializing locales and conjoining them through the symbolism of sites, shrines and synergies of pilgrimage and religious movements to forge a cultural constellation encompassing eastern India. These thematic explorations are contextualized within theoretical-analytic frames interrelating place, space, subregion and trans-region.

BEYOND COLONIAL BOUNDARIES

The discourse on a common inter-regional space based on religious interconnections between Bengal and her neighbours subtly transmuted and moved beyond colonial understandings of religion as a sociological key to objectify indigenous populations and situate them within the fixity of censuses and enumerative frames. By underscoring the application of religion as an inclusive force, this essay aims to show how identities remained fluid despite objectification and sociological crystallization. The use of religion as a sociological key to fix and freeze communities, groups and sects was evident from the beginning of the all-India census operations (1871). Indians were counted, ranked and classified by caste, tribe and ethno-religious community.[8] Imperial strategies of segregation—administrative and cartographic divisions, and demarcations—were also related to convictions that certain areas needed to be bounded-off from others on the basis of distinct social systems and religious customs and practices. L.S.S.

O'Malley's clear-cut segregation of Bengal from Bihar and Orissa demonstrated this point.[9] These convictions, underlying the logic of creating and maintaining boundaries, were subtly transmuted in the delineation of an eastern Indian cultural constellation by the Bengali literati, in which disparate units/sites/regions were woven together by the sinews of religion.

The prioritization of religion as an ideological platform for reworking fusions was closely related to the fact that Bengal had a distinct socio-religious tradition that blended diverse currents. This regional religious tradition was different from the high culture of Vedic Hinduism. Unlike Orissa, where a central cult (Jagannath)[10] constructed a pivotal regional religious tradition, Bengal 'lacked a dominant symbol supported by the regional state'.[11] In this variegated religious culture in Bengal, a semblance of unity developed under the aegis of Brahmanism in the early medieval period. But the element of fusion remained. From the nineteenth century, when a turn towards a history of culture and attachment pivoted around *samaj* gathered momentum in the literati's cultural construction of the nation, religion formed a significant element as the very notion of *samaj* was grounded in *dharma* (religion as faith as well as practice, implying righteous life and conduct). The adherence to *dharma* formed a chief criterion for inclusion into a wider *samajik* universe. In the deployment of *samaj* to forge unity among fragments, populist religious strands were accommodated and internalized into a flexible Hindu-Brahmanical framework. The language of inclusion was, however, not a simple hegemonic imposition of a religious metanarrative to facilitate the inclusion of people and places within and beyond Bengal. The recognition of plural religious elements facilitated more multilayered groundings of identity, interrogating, and at times, contesting the ideology of hierarchy. In such constructions, regional religious traditions intertwined with wider identities which were projected beyond the region, negotiating and mediating trans-regional particularisms within a flexible rubric of unity. This underpinned a wider process of reworking a cultural continuum of South Asia, redefining the relationship between the region and the nation or between local and pan-Indian levels.

ANCIENT BONDS AND MODERN UNITIES

History, harnessed to the agenda of revisiting the issue of territoriality via a reappraisal of religious linkages, was transformed into a vibrant and vivid meeting place between the past and the present. The rhythms and trajectories of the commingling of faiths in the past were sought to be captured with a view to annexing such unities to the present, and reorienting and situating them within the contexts and dynamics of interactions between 'new' religious creeds (such as Brahmoism from the 1830s) and the older Hindu Brahmanism in Bengal and the contiguous areas. The intersection of the past and present in the commingling of faiths was related to two main exploratory arenas in the literati's discourse: (1) the religio-cultural assimilation in dynastic contexts, emphasizing the 'Hinduization' of 'alien' kings of neighbouring regions; and (2) the idea of a common religio-cultural unity epitomized in the concept of Pancha Gour (five Bengals or Gours). Both these arenas reflected an interpenetration of the domains of culture/religion and polity, thereby demonstrating that in late colonial Bengal, religion was problematized and approached as a concept entwined in, rather than disentangled from political processes. Illuminating this linkage between polity and culture in a discourse on unity (marking a shift from perspectives that de-link culture from politics),[12] this section concentrates on the various dimensions and trajectories of reorienting ancient bonds to forge modern unities.

During the 1880s, the literati delved into an archive of ancient history to highlight how different faiths, religious streams and sub-streams had commingled. The historical landscape was revivified by highlighting symbols of such interblending—caves, temples and shrines—which poignantly immemorialized the significance of religious links in recreating unities in the present (late-colonial period). An essay called 'Urishyar Itihas' printed in the well-known periodical *Bharati* in 1882, underlined this significance: 'Three miles west of Bhubaneswar are the ancient caves of Khandagiri and Udaygiri. They are symbols and repositories of ancient local history. As they have been built by Buddhist, Jain and Hindu devotees, they are emblems of the commingling of religious currents.'[13] The convictions underlying this quotation are clear. The trajectory of unity between the different strands of Hinduism was far more significant to the literati than distinguishing Brahmanical Hinduism from 'deviant' creeds such as Buddhism and Jainism. Such past instances of commingling of faiths were regarded as antecedents of nineteenth-century interactions between relatively 'new' religious creeds such as Brahmoism and older religious traditions, especially the predominant Hindu Brahmanism of the 'orthodox' variety. The rational note of Brahmoism interacting with traditional Hindu Brahmanism endowed the latter with an assimilative nature, resonating with the note of unity immanent in ideas about religious comminglings in the past. The contextualization of the theme of an overarching Hindu religious unity in a discourse relating Bengal to her neighbours meant that such harmonies were explored and debated with a view to linking regions via a reconsideration of religious parallelisms between Bengal and her neighbours. Bengal, as a site witnessing the historic interblending of contrasting currents such as late-Aryanization, Hindu Brahmanism, Buddhist and even tribal religious lineages,[14] constituted an alter-arena, overlapping with similar sites of religious intermixture (Udaygiri and Khandagiri) as in Orissa.

The commingling of religious faiths was related to the theme of religio-cultural assimilation in dynastic contexts. The historicization of the Hinduizations of 'alien' kings, as well as the tracing of parallels in the religious faiths of the kings of Bengal and those in the neighbouring areas (such as Orissa) were geared towards a reworking of religious affinities between Bengal and her neighbours. The Hinduization of the Ahoms of Assam was especially glorified. In 1654, Chutamla, an Ahom king, ascended the throne. Deeply influenced by Niranjan Gosai, a Hindu saint, he became a convert to Hinduism and adopted the Hindu name of Jayadhvaj Sinha.[15] The Bengali literati viewed the Hinduization of the Buddhist Ahoms and their adoption of Hindu names as an extension of (Bengali) Hindu cultural influence, metamorphosing kings of alien origin and changing popular lifestyles. Hinduization continued to an increased degree during the reign of Rudrasinha, a disciple of a Vaishnava saint of Santipur.[16] What is interesting is that the laxity of Ahom Hinduism, referred to in colonial sources, was glossed over by the literati in their attempt to claim a Hindu heritage for Assam and orient it to their agenda of a wider identity embracing Bengal and her neighbours. They elided accounts of non-Hindu practices and customs which lingered among the Ahoms:

> Though converted to Hinduism the Ahoms found the restrictions of their new religion irksome; and their *gosains* . . . allowed their new disciples a considerable degree of latitude. Rudra Singh, though he had been publicly admitted to the church by the Auniati *gosain*, feasted his followers on buffaloes and pigs on the occasion of his father's funeral; while not only buffaloes but even cows found a place in the menu of his coronation banquet. . . . Before taking any decisive step [conversion to Hinduism]—it was the practice to refer, not only to the Brahmans and Ganaks, but also to the old Ahom priests, the Deodhais and Bailongs.[17]

As in Assam, the impact of Hindu *dharma* in Cachar was explored within the contexts of dynastic history, tracing and highlighting longer lineages of Hinduization and relating them to specific practices emanating from the ideological nucleus of religious assimilation. Upendrachandra Guha wrote:

> There is a general belief that the impact of Hindu *dharma* in Cachar was felt especially after King Krishnachandra accepted the Hindu faith. But this had actually happened much earlier, when Cachari kings, accompanied by many *jatis*,[18] went on pilgrimages. . . . A conch shell dating back to 1671, with an engraving of Vishnu proves that King Bidarpa was a devotee of this deity. . . . King Krishnachandra who worshipped the goddess Kali begot two sons after observing some Hindu rites.[19]

Yoking dynastic history to the forging of religious linkages moved beyond instances of the Hinduization of alien kings in places like Assam and Cachar, and highlighted parallelisms between Bengal and traditionally Hindu regions such as Orissa (for example, the Kesaris of Orissa had been Saivas,[20] and the Ganga kings of Orissa[21] were supposed to have migrated there from south-west Bengal). Dynastic history in such cases became a site for glorifying the commingling of diverse religious strands within Hinduism. King Guhasimha of Orissa, despite being a Buddhist, was deeply attracted to mainstream Hinduism.[22] Similarly in the sixteenth century, King Prataprudra, though initially attached to Buddhism, became a Vaishnava under Chaitanya's influence.[23] According to Kailashchandra Sinha, during the reign of a Buddhist king of the Daladbangshiya dynasty, there was a religious synergy of Buddhism, Jainism and mainstream Hinduism in Orissa.[24] The amalgamation of Hinduism with its variant creeds, such as Buddhism, set against a historical/dynastic backdrop, acquired seminal significance in the construction of a wider religious identity underpinning an imaginary geography.

The connection between ancient bonds and modern unities inhered in a framework which prioritized the element of process, which, of course, was not simple, unfragmented or continuous. For the literati, the engrossing point was how, despite tumultuous transformations and fragmentations, some ideas and traditions had continued, symbolizing and, to an extent, eternalizing religious, social and cultural connections. One such conceptual site/tradition as mentioned earlier, was the ancient idea of Pancha Gour. It signified the collectivity of five Gours (Bengals) in history, highlighting religious and cultural connections between them. The late colonial prioritization of the commingling of faiths in the past and the modern-day interactions between the different strands of Hinduism were reworked and contextualized within the idealized unity of Pancha Gour, envisioned as the fountainhead of a synergetic culture encompassing the whole of eastern India. This idea had political significance too. The five Gours were Sarasvat, Kanyakubja, Gauda, Utkala and Mithila.[25] Many kings of Bengal and Magadha were rulers of Pancha Gour (Panchagouresvar). On the basis of this, writers such as S.N. Bhadra concluded that during the ascendancy of Pataliputra and Gour, Utkal and Magadha were included within a common realm.[26] What was especially underlined, however, was the cultural significance of Pancha Gour. Oriya culture was incorporated as an integral element in ideas about a Bengali–Oriya identity. Ideas about a composite culture epitomized in Pancha Gour had a continuing impact on later social historians of Bengal. S.N. Bhadra's glorification of Pancha Gour in a tract dealing with the history of eastern India (*Uttar-Purba Bharat*) were echoed by Dineshchandra Sen who referred to a common religious and social exchange between Bengalis and Oriyas for generations, as written in *kulajigranthas* or books on ancestry.[27]

PLACE-MAKING, SITES, SHRINES AND SPATIAL SYNERGIES

A religious geography, glimpsed and conceptualized through a relationship between ancient and modern unities, drew on a paradigm of religion, place-making and cultural unity. It highlighted specific sites and sacred places as symbols of unity. A late colonial tract entitled *Tirthadarshan* aligned an ancient religious geography (through glorification of particular sites and temples) to a modern remapping of Bengal and contiguous regions such as Orissa through the narrative of pilgrimage. The pilgrim's prism focused on dynastic history to knit together religion and a trans-regional geography:

> Ananga Bhimdeb, the fifth king of the Ganga dynasty [in Orissa] was a very able king. He measured the land and demarcated it for purposes of revenue collection. The northern limit of his realm was Hugli [in modern Bengal], and the southern limit was marked by the river Godavari. He built many temples, ten bridges, forty lakes and 152 bathing *ghats*, and brought 450 Vaidik Brahmans from Jajpur to Puri . . . he built the famous Jagannath temple in 1194 . . . his descendant Narasimhadeb built the famous Surya temple at Konarak on the shores of the Bay of Bengal . . . [the tradition continued] during the reign of Purushottamdeb who extended his [religio-political] control to Kanchipur. In Krishna district, he established/founded a village. *Till now* [down to the present] this village exists and is known as Purushottampattan. It is twenty miles distant from Vijaywada. In Ganjam district also he established a town called Purushottampur. These places are similar to those in Utkal [Orissa proper] where some villages act as symbols of his immortal name.[28]

The above narrative linked specific sites immemorialized by religion (such as Puri in Orissa proper) to Hugli (in Bengal), Kanchipur,

Ganjam and the Krishna district (in the south) within a religious geography which spanned the past and the present.

The symbolism of sacred sites was strengthened by the related trajectory of temple-building, seen as mirroring religious parallelism between regions. Similarities between methods of construction, and presiding deities of temples in Bengal, Assam and Orissa, and the celebration of identical/similar festivals within their precincts were seen as significant elements metamorphosing dynastic alien-ness, blending local legends, myths and multiple overlapping traditions (not always Brahmanical) to conjoin sites across the borders of the region/province. The emphasis on the relatedness of famous temples built by traditionally (and originally) Hindu kings such as the Kesaris of Orissa to those built by non-Hindu (but Hinduized) Ahoms of Assam showed how the literati negotiated the foreign origin of 'Hinduised' kings and traditionally zoned off non-Aryan/non-Hindu tracts (in Assam) through the symbolism of temple worship. 'Just as during the heyday of the Kesaris, the famous Shib temple of Bhubanesvar was built. . . . Rudrasimha, the Hinduised Ahom king, built the famous Rudresvar temple at Guwahati.'[29] Temples were expressions of a composite culture celebrating a common religious glory[30] in places as diverse and distant as Puri (in Orissa) and Guwahati (in Assam). The literati highlighted the similarities between holy shrines and temples in different neighbouring areas: Puri in Orissa and Kamakhya in Assam were both called 'Nilachal' and the methods of construction of the Kamakhya, Shibsagar and Puri temples were identical.[31] The celebration of Hindu festivals in the temples of neighbouring areas brought them culturally closer to Bengal. 'In Uma mandir on the river Brahmaputra, Shib ratri festival is celebrated with elan.'[32] The Shiv temple built by Raja Madhab Das in Sylhet was, according to Monomohan Dasgupta, an enduring emblem of Hindu dynastic and religious linkages across borders.[33] Down to 1905, the creation of boundaries ostensibly for administrative convenience was predominant in official circles. Monomohan Dasgupta's inclusion of Sylhet in an imaginary religious geography (in 1903) erased the 1874 boundary separating Assam and Sylhet from Bengal. The symbolism of temples drew a religious map which extended from Assam in the east to central Orissa in the south, thus turning from the fixity and divisiveness of colonial boundaries and creating an expanding and dynamic cartographic line in flux.

In this religious remapping, the dynamics of place-making through emphases on specific sites (villages and towns), dynastic-religious genealogies of their nomenclature, and parallelisms and symbolisms of temples involved a transition from place, and its transformation into space. Many recent scholars of the humanities and social sciences interested in 'place' define it in opposition to 'space'. Whereas space is abstract, homogeneous, unmarked and neutral, place is concrete, particular and differentiated. Anne Feldhaus, looking beyond such traditional hierarchical distinctions, has focused on 'place' as embodying a multitude of complex cultural and religious meanings contained in a given area.[34] In my understanding of the Bengali literati's discourse on place-making by forging religious linkages, I relate space and place in a way which endows both with a positive connotative content. The particularization and deification of specific places did not constitute a sharp, contrasting foil offsetting 'negative', 'unmarked', 'neutral' space. While Feldhaus prioritizes place-making, I highlight a place-space connectivity and continuum. Place-making, as seen in the literati's discourse, endowed space with an emotive and ideological content, transforming it from a 'vaporized, transcendent vision' to an arena of real, lived experience, which was the 'very foundation and container of religious experience'. It was therefore a 'fundamental, . . . a priori dimension of social action',[35] and its continuity and limits depended more on the 'cognitive domain of mental processes', rather than on 'physical structure'.[36]

NETWORKS OF PILGRIMAGE

This lived-in religious space was animated by networks of pilgrimage. The symbolism and actuality of pilgrimages linked a pre-colonial sacred geography to late colonial experiential realities. Through a conscious interplay with ideas about inclusive social and cultural unities, which gathered momentum in Bengal from the beginning of the nineteenth century, pilgrimage became the metaphor and symbol of a broader intellectual and cultural quest.[37] The significance of pilgrimage was strengthened during the eighteenth and nineteenth centuries through an interaction between ideological and material factors. The development and proliferation of travel networks, railways, and the employment connections of Bengalis in the contiguous areas expedited religious peregrinations, connecting specific communities to larger worlds, as well as the local to the wider community. The general aim of pilgrimage, worship of Gods and ancestors, interacted with regional specificities, which made way for a wider understanding and use of the symbolism of pilgrimage. The overlapping of religious movements such as Vaishnavism and its populist basis[38] explained the reification of Orissa as a pilgrim-arena with its centre at Puri (traditionally a Vaishnava centre). The interaction between the populist ideological thrust of Vaishnavism and notions about the opening out of the *samaj* via the idea and practice of pilgrimage was reflected in strong convictions about pilgrim sites such as Puri acting as the forum for the meeting of many *jatis*. As Jogendranath Ray wrote, 'Before *doljatra*, many Bengalis, Hindustanis, Marwaris, Punjabis, Dravids, and Marathis went to sea for religious bath and rites of purification.'[39]

The synergetic significance of pilgrimage was highlighted within the dual, interrelated contexts of the past and the present. Connecting history, legend and modern-day actual locations of pilgrim-sites, Goshtha Behari Dhar glorified temples and shrines in Orissa renowned for pilgrimages:

> In Orissa, in Lake Bindu is the Jagati temple with the idol of Chadrasekhar Deb Jiu. Near it is the Srimandir of Bhubanesvar Jiu, built by Bisvakarma during the reign of the Kesari king Lolatendu. According to legend, the Kesari king asked for a boon and was blessed by Bhubanesvar.[40]

In a similar vein, Rajendralal Mitra asserted that neighbouring rulers such as King Kalyanmanik of Tripura went on pilgrimages to Orissa.[41] The glorification of pilgrimages in Orissa by renowned aristocratic and professionally qualified intellectuals (such as Rajendralal Mitra) having connections with the colonial government[42] as well as by less well-known individuals (Goshtha Behari Dhar) represents an intersection of viewpoints among the different sections of the literati. Such opinion emphasized the religious interconnections between the neighbouring ethnicities (for instance, between Tripura and Orissa), which were then interwoven into a common cultural and religious fabric encompassing the whole of eastern India. In the late colonial period, the dual roles of pilgrim and writer, and interconnections among the literati (for example, between a writer and an acquainted individual who was a pilgrim), facilitated an interplay between belief/text on the one hand, and practice on the other. The private papers of the eminent Brahmo leader and intellectual Shibnath Shastri offer insights into the experiential reality of pilgrimage. His acquaintance, the well-known Sri Bhagirathi Rao, lived in Cuttack and Puri as a pilgrim.[43]

The literati's contextualization of pilgrimage in past and present scenarios points to the fact that there existed in India (before the colonial advent) frameworks facilitating participation in larger structures of identity/unity. Bengal's reification of the region and areas beyond it through the thread of pilgrimage across eras enlivened the links between the pre-colonial past/pasts and the colonial present. Pilgrimage, based on linkages between regions, provided notions of religious community long before the British entered the scene, reinforcing the larger moral community of the civilization.[44] The forging of an eastern Indian arena through pilgrimage was actually part of a wider process of the unfolding of the idea of India, glimpsed and reified through interconnections via clusters of pilgrimage centres. Thus the literati situated the importance of pilgrim centres in Orissa within a more extended nexus of pilgrim sites spanning parts of north and central India. Just as Orissa was the site of many famous pilgrim centres, north and central India had historic pilgrimage centres such as Mathura, Vrindavan and Varanasi. The eastern Indian pilgrims' land extending from Kamakhya and the Brahmaputra Valley in Assam to Puri, Cuttack and Bhubaneswar in Orissa was part of a wider subcontinental domain of the divine. The moving boundaries of pilgrim-geography apprehending the idea of India drew on the notion of an expanding *samaj*,[45] creating the basis for a larger national identification.[46] The process involving the flow of movement across the boundary of a local community points to the significance of pilgrimage as a public sphere, not à la Western lines (as the channels of expression differed from those in Europe), but conditioned through historical specificities of the pre-colonial and colonial situations. The positioning of pilgrimage at the crossroads of history/tradition and modernity as a conceptual and experiential domain transcending local community boundaries goes against the tendency to see the public sphere in sharp contradistinction to a *gemeinschaftlich* local community underpinned by the polarity between modernity and tradition.[47]

RELIGIOUS MOVEMENTS ACROSS BORDERS

The forging of an inter-regional religious spatiality was further reinforced by ideological overlap, human flow and place-making through the thread of common religious movements in Bengal and contiguous regions. The literati's emphasis on consonance between the regional and trans-regional forms and manifestations of a common religious movement such as Vaishnavism formed an integral part of conceptualizations of a social-cum-cultural collectivity encompassing Bengal and the neighbouring areas. This section problematizes how the tracing of concentric perimeters of religious unity emanating from the nucleus of Nabadvip in Bengal, actual interactions and flows of devotees across borders, and connections between the main

Vaishnava centres played a pivotal role in interrelating place-making, history and experiential socio-religious norms and practices.

Significantly, the origin, causal factors, spread and specific features of Vaishnavism in regional and trans-regional contexts were contextualized within the twin reference frames of historical synchronicity and ideological connections/similarities:

> In the 11th century Assam was completely under the sway of Buddhism, which continued until the advent of Sankardeb. During the same era, Buddhism was prevalent in Orissa,—who can say that this had not resulted in a similarity of religious temper and milieu in the two areas? ... Chaitanya and Sankardeb were contemporaries, and both believed in Krishna and Hari, neither accepted divisions among *jatis*. Like Chaitanya, Sankar was regarded as a reincarnation by his followers.[48]

A common ideological lineage activated and underscored through an excavation of history, exploring common formative factors moulding religious sensibilities thus sought to create a connected space integrating Bengal, Orissa and Assam. This was strengthened by the paradigm of place-making, delving into the dynamics of the origins of particular place names in these connected regions, and vivifying place through actual travels of the leaders of the Vaishnava movement. Linking Orissa to Assam through such interconnecting threads, the literati underlined Sankardeb's residence in Puri for a long time before preaching Mahapurushiya *dharma* in Assam. 'It seems that many Oriya followers of Sankar went to Assam with him. . . . In Sankar's native district, Nagaon, there are two villages known by Oriya names, and his Oriya disciples stayed there. Many Oriya customs, manners, and modes of worship were inducted into the religious movement pioneered in Assam.'[49] Simultaneities between historicizations of ideological influences, and dynastic accounts recording the conversions of kings (of contiguous regions) to Vaishnavism closely conjoined to place-making (through naming), drew on the related trajectory of royal pilgrimage, often suggesting unities beyond eastern India. The pilgrimage of King Gobinda Manikya of Tripura to Vrindavan and Mathura[50] connected an eastern Indian inter-regional religious arena to a wider Vaishnava India.

The specific ways of deployment of the influence of common religious movements such as Vaishnavism to fit different contiguous regions into a connected spatial framework varied subtly in specific cases of integration (of particular sites and subregions). While place-naming and travels of leaders played crucial roles in connecting Assam, Orissa and Bengal (as seen above), the drawing in of Manipur and Sylhet underlined the trajectory of the inter-blending of Vaishnavism into other streams of Hinduism. The crucial point here is, however, that whatever the particular mode of integration, a connection was argued on the basis of the common religious matrix of Vaishnavism, which, significantly, was not seen as something deviant from mainstream Brahmanical or other forms of Hinduism. Monomohan Dasgupta traced the spread of Vaishnavism from Bengal to Sylhet, and from there to Manipur. The famous Vaishnava pundit Advaitananda, the son of Kuber Tarkapanchanan (chief courtier at the royal court of Laur), went to Shantipur and spread the Vaishnava faith.[51] Connecting the story of the spread of Vaishnavism in Sylhet to the dynastic histories of Manipur, recording the origin and impact of Vaishnavism in Manipur, he wrote, 'In 1715, during the Manipuri king Pamheiba's rule, Manipuris were converted by Adhikari of Sylhet to the Vaishnava *dharma*.'[52] This Vaishnava stream, according to Monomohan, spread and blended into other religious streams such as Saiva and Sakta in Manipur. At the same time, living links with Nabadvip[53] in Bengal fostered trans-regional and trans-border connections.

CONCLUSION

This essay has sought to demonstrate how specific thematic trajectories emanating from the nucleus of religion were interwoven into the delineation of an imaginary geography in eastern India. By illuminating the links between this discourse on religious unity and a wider unity underpinned by the inclusive concept of *samaj*, which apprehended a pan-Indian unity, it has shown how religion operated as an integrative factor in larger conceptual settings of unity. Further, by historicizing religious links[54] between Bengal and her neighbours, and contextualizing them within the twin referential frames of culture and political processes, it has sought to rescue religion from an 'inner' domain, delinked from an outer 'public' sphere. By highlighting the literati's emphasis on linkages between past and present religious interconnections, the essay has sought to show that unities forged through religion moved away from essentialist, primordialist models, which relegate religion to ur-traditional worlds. The deployment of religion in the literati's discourse, emphasizing expansion of 'inner' bonds to include larger populations (seen as operating within a longer historical tradition) reveals how indigenous ideas about unity cannot be understood in terms of iconic oppositions of inner/outer or traditional/modern.

Against this theoretical setting, the essay has shown that the interregional place-world[55] imagined through religion reflected a remaking of the idea of region by expanding boundaries. The existence of a multi-stranded religio-cultural heritage connecting with the fact that Bengal did not have a strong, separatist regional distinctiveness, facilitated the remaking of the region and its expansion to include other parts of eastern India, and even beyond. The transformation of lived-in places to shared space in Bengal and the contiguous areas, reifying and connecting the region to areas beyond it through the use of religious narrative, practices and ideas was subtly different from discourses on the same theme elsewhere in India. In Maharashtra, the discourse on a geography of religion highlighted origins of rivers, pilgrim sites and routes of religious processions to interweave sets of holy places which were the same as holy places in other parts of India. In Anne Feldhaus's theoretical framework, this inclusive vein, however, veers towards an idea of the region underpinned by contrast and otherness:

> A set of places that are connected to one another and that . . . contrast with some other set of places . . . an area with a distinct identity and significance for people who live in it and for others who think and care about it.[56]

Bengal's religious geography had more fluid boundaries. In fact, its construction was part of a wider process of imagining a utopic socio-cosmic universe, which ideologically approximated the idea of an Indian *samaj*. The interconnection between religion-as-idea and social praxis, and its location in larger settings of ethnicity and inclusive ideas about a social universe made for an anti-separatist spatio-religious imagination. Such imaginings prioritized what Henri Lefebvre has designated as the notion of space as a social product, based on social production of meanings,[57] and contextualized it within a wider agenda of imagining the nation. The ideological odyssey for religious interconnections between Bengal and her neighbours underpinned by the overarching idea of *dharma* and cultural Aryanness, implied that the remaking of the region (via religious links) was not a static but dynamic process, which could open up a regional or eastern Indian (trans-regional) *samaj* to include other Indians and other places within India which resonated with or adhered to the norms of cultural Aryanism (acceptance of the epics and *puranas*, connections with Sanskrit and belief in a supreme Godhead) or followed the trajectory of *dharma*.

The construction of an imaginary geography has been studied here in the context of an internal (Bengali Hindu literati's) discourse framed within a Hindu religious lineage. Notions of assimilative unities were rethought within the framework of a valorized Hindu–Aryan–Bengali identity (late-nineteenth-century tracts equated 'Aryan' and 'Hindu' in many contexts).[58] The dynamics of unity in the discourse operated at two main levels: (1) inclusion of non-Hindu areas or pockets such as Ahom Assam through religious and cultural metamorphosis (Hinduization); and (2) links between Hindu areas (such as between Hindu Bengal and Hindu Orissa) by highlighting interconnection between the various currents within Hinduism. There could have been a third level—extension of the language of inclusiveness to non-Hindu communal 'others' such as Muslim. This remained elided in the literati's discourse. The question of inclusion of communal 'others' such as Muslim (in neighbouring regions) did not form a central concern, though the rhetoric of religious interconnection did not oppositionally arraign 'Hindu' and 'Muslim' in all contexts.

Despite this limitation, the imaginary geography transcending regional boundaries cannot be simplistically called a religious utopia. The contextual glossing over of internal fragmentations and the elision of the Muslim element reflected the fact that the discourse was framed, in certain respects, within parameters of a utopic unity. But the worlds of utopia and reality converged at a complex interactive level. Actualities of travel, pilgrimage, and place-making endowed the utopia with everyday living meanings, affirming the relevance of Keith Basso's famous remark: 'We are, in a sense, the place worlds we imagine.'[59] Moreover the geography of religion in eastern India was not a segregated world floating in the vacuum of a delinked religious ethos in isolation from other material, sociological, social and cultural factors. The framework of religious geography enmeshed with larger and more meaningful constellations of social, cultural and material connections.

NOTES

1. The expression 'inter-regional arena' is used here to denote a terrain connecting generalities (trans-region) and specificities of particular regions. It offers an entry-point for understanding the ways in which an imaginary geography based on religious connections was shaped in eastern India.
2. Fernand Braudel, *The Mediterranean and the Mediterranean World in the Age of Philip II*, vol. 1, Berkeley, 1995, pp. 168–70, quoted in Sugata Bose, *A Hundred Horizons*, Delhi: Permanent Black, 2006, p. 4.
3. Benedict Anderson has remarked that the nation is imagined as limited, because it has finite, if elastic, boundaries beyond which lie other nations. See Benedict Anderson, *Imagined Communities: Reflections on the Origin and Spread of Nationalism*, London: Verso, 1983, p. 7. The concept of territory is crucial in nationalism

and for the production of the nation state. A nation state, as Peter van der Veer writes, is a spatial unity lying between borders that it must defend. However, despite this emphasis on the bounded-ness of the national territory, nationalism transcends local boundaries. See Peter van der Veer, *Religious Nationalism: Hindus and Muslims in India*, Delhi: Oxford University Press, 1996, p. 106.

The ways in which boundaries are crossed vary across countries and are conditioned by specific historical and socio-cultural settings. This essay sees how regional boundaries were shifted and expanded imaginatively in a discourse prioritizing religious interconnections between Bengal and the contiguous areas, situating this within an interrelated dynamic of rethinking Indian unity.

4. A striking example of such division is the partition of Bengal in 1905, ostensibly for administrative convenience, but really to weaken the nationalist movement, which was gathering momentum.
5. For details relating to ideas about the nation as a cultural entity historically rooted in the evolution of *samaj*, see Swarupa Gupta, 'Notions of Nationhood in Bengal: Perspectives on *Samaj*, 1867–1905', *Modern Asian Studies* 40, no. 2, 2006, pp. 273–302; and '*Samaj*, *Jati* and *Desh*: Reflections on Nationhood in Late Colonial Bengal', *Studies in History* 23, no. 2, 2007, pp. 177–203.
6. See, for instance, Catherine Brace, Adrian Bailey and David Harvey, 'Religion, Place and Space: A Framework for Investigating Historical Geographies of Religious Identities and Communities', in *Progress in Human Geography* 30, no. 1, 2006, pp. 28–43.
7. Wilhelm Halbfass has emphasized that the Hindu system has the flexibility to assimilate 'others' albeit at a subordinate level. This forms the basis of a 'traditional Indian xenology', which has been seen as functioning in ancient Indian society, where different communities are integrated into the social system of the Aryans to maintain the cosmic order. See Christophe Jaffrelot, 'The Idea of the Hindu Race in the Writings of Hindu Nationalist Ideologues in the 1920s and 1930s: A Concept Between Two Cultures', in Peter Robb (ed.), *The Concept of Race in South Asia*, Delhi: Oxford University Press, 1995, pp. 327–8.
8. Barrier (1981); Cohn (1987); Dirks (1989), mentioned in Susan Bayly, *Caste, Society and Politics in India from the Eighteenth Century to the Modern Age*, Cambridge: Cambridge University Press, 1999, p. 99.
9. L.S.S. O'Malley, *The Census of India, 1911*, vol. V, *Bengal, Bihar and Orissa*, Calcutta: Bangal Secretariat Press, 1913, pp. 2–4.
10. Anncharlott Eschmann, Hermann Kulke and Gaya Charan Tripathi (eds.), *The Cult of Jagannath and the Regional Tradition of Orissa*, Delhi: Manohar, 1978, p. xiii, mentioned in Kunal Chakrabarti, *Religious Process: The Puranas and the Making of a Regional Tradition*, Delhi: Oxford University Press, 2001, p. 2.
11. Chakrabarti, *Religious Process*, p. 2.
12. Theoretical perspectives influenced by the Saidian model de-link culture from nationhood, counterpoise community and fragmentation to the modern political nation state. See Partha Chatterjee, *The Nation and its Fragments: Colonial and Postcolonial Histories* in *The Partha Chatterjee Omnibus*, Delhi: Oxford University Press, 1999, p. 112.
13. Kailashchandra Sinha, 'Urishyar Itiḥas', *Bharati*, Jyoishtha 1882, pp. 50–1.
14. The late Aryanization of Bengal has been emphasized by scholars such as Niharranjan Ray. See Ray, *Bangalir Itihas, Adi Parba*, vol. I, Calcutta, 1949,

rpt. 1980, pp. 277–80, 296–306. Traditionally regarded as a zone outside, and beyond the pale of core areas of Aryan culture (such as central north India or Madhyadesa), Bengal's indigenous animistic, tribal cults and religious practices formed a counterfoil to as well as an integrated strand in the late-Aryan cultural lineage. To such currents were added strong Buddhist influences which gathered momentum under the Pala kings. It was only during the Sena period that Brahmanical Hinduism became a major current and dominant force in the religious tradition and social reordering of Bengal.

15. S.N. Bhadra, *Uttar Purba Bharat*, Dacca, 1911, pp. 20–1.
16. Ibid., p. 21.
17. B.C. Allen, *Assam District Gazetteers, Kamrup*, vol. 4, Allahabad, 1905, p. 50.
18. The term *jati*, etymologically meaning birth, became multifunctional from the 1850s and encompassed a range of connotations including caste, tribe, race and nation. In the quotation cited here, *jatis* referred to diverse caste and/or ethnic groups.
19. Upendranath Guha, *Cacharer Itibritta*, Dacca, 1911, p. 136.
20. The Kesari kings of Orissa were Saivas. Foremost among them was Jajati Kesari who brought Brahmans from Jajpur to Puri.
21. Rajkrishna Mukhopadhyay, *Banglar Itihas*, Calcutta, 1877, p. 27; Lalmohan Vidyanidhi, *Sambandhanirnoy*, part I, 4th edn., Calcutta, pp. 179–88; and Mahimchandra Gupta, *Goure Brahman*, Calcutta, 1900, p. 238.
22. Ibid., p. 55.
23. Baradaprasad Basu, *Tirthadarshan, UrishyarItihas,* Calcutta, 1891–4, p. 50.
24. Sinha, 'Urishyar Itihas', pp. 49–51.
25. Promode Lal Paul, *The Early History of Eastern India*, Delhi: Sharada Prakashan, 1990, p. 133.
26. Bhadra, *Uttar Purba Bharat*, p. 25.
27. Dineshchandra Sen, *Brihat Banga*, Calcutta, 1935, 'Introduction', p. 2.
28. Basu, *Trithadarshan*, p. 5. Emphasis added.
29. S.N. Bhadra, *Uttar Praba Bharat*, Dacca, 1911, p. 21.
30. Basu, pp. 1–2.
31. Article in *Bharati*, Magh 1878, p. 456.
32. Mahimchandra Gupta, 'Kamakhya', *Pradeep* 3, no. 1 (Poush 1899), p. 54.
33. Monomohan Dasgupta, *Srihatter Itihas*, Calcutta:, 1903, p. 9.
34. Anne Feldhaus, *Connected Places: Region, Pilgrimage and Geographical Imagination in Maharashtra*, New York: Palgrave Macmillan, 2003.
35. K.N. Chaudhuri, quoted in Bose, *A Hundred Horizons*, p. 5.
36. Bose, *A Hundred Horizons*, p. 5.
37. Ibid., p. 203. While Bose has pointed out how pilgrimage became part of a wider intellectual and cultural quest in the context of an interregional arena of the Indian Ocean, tracing the journeys of Indians to various parts of South-East Asia, this chapter focuses on the significance of pilgrimages within India.
38. Ramakanta Chakrabarty has pointed to the mass base of Vaishnavism as a sociological system, highlighting the conversion of tribals in Mymensingh and the low castes of northern Mymensingh, Barisal and Rangpore. See Ramakanta Chakrabarty, *Vaishnavism in Bengal: 1486-1900*, Calcutta: Sanskrit Pustak Bhandar, 1985, pp. 327–9.
39. Jogendranath Ray, *Utkaler Panchatirtha*, Calcutta, 1906, p. 62.
40. Goshtha Behari Dhar, *Tirthadarshan Kahini* or *Bharatbarshiya Tirtha Samuher Mahatmya Prokash*, Calcutta, 1914, pp. 49–51.

41. Rajendralal Mitra (ed.), *Rahashya Sandarbha*, vol. 42, part 4, p. 154.
42. Rajendralal Mitra, deeply influenced by an inherited tradition of Sanskritic learning, was closely associated with the Asiatic Society.
43. Letter from Shibnath Shastri to the Bhagirathi Rao's grandson, written in 1897, in *Private Papers of Shibnath Shastri*.
44. Gananath Obeyesekere, 'The Buddhist Pantheon in Ceylon and its Extensions', in Manning Nash (ed.), *Anthropological Studies in Theravada Budhhism*, pp. 1–26, mentioned in Peter van der Veer, *Religious Nationalism: Hindus and Muslims in India*, Delhi: Oxford University Press, 1996, p. 120.
45. *Samaj*, deployed in late-colonial Bengal as a model for inclusion and harmonies, made way for the interflowing of arenas of the self and the other (regional self and trans-regional others, and caste/sub-caste/class/communal otherness), rather than antagonisms. The redefinition of pilgrimage as a site of unity drawing on this idea of *samaj* was rather different from Peter van der Veer's model of pilgrimage and religious arena as a site of antagonism between the self and the other, where unity is achieved at the price of violence, through a dominance of the self over a tyrannized or 'demonized' other. See Peter van der Veer, *Religious Nationalism*, p. 123.
46. David Mandelbaum has argued that pilgrimage acts to create national identification. Acting as a traditional basis for larger national identification, it helps in imagining a divine entity of India as a single religious setting, to which all inhabitants belong. Mandelbaum, *Society in India*, Berkeley and Los Angeles: University of California Press, p. 401, mentioned in van der Veer, *Religious Nationalism*, p. 120.
47. Peter van der Veer has critiqued the tendency to see the spheres of the nation and that of the local community as mutually exclusive and opposite in nature. See van der Veer, *Religious Nationalism*, p. 107. Interpretations of colonial nationalisms influenced by Saidian perspectives de-linking culture from politics counterpoise community and fragmentation to the modern political nation state, and see nationalism as a political and modern phenomenon. Veer points out that nationalism cannot be neatly fitted into this modernization scheme, and the limits of the 'traditional' and 'parochial' community were crossed by participations in larger identifications before the colonial advent.
48. Essay in *Bharati*, Magh 1878, p. 456. Interestingly, this essay glossed over the fact that some aspects of the Vaishnava theology and ritual in Sankardeb's philosophy differed from Gaudiya Vaishnava concepts. Chakrabarty, *Vaishnavism in Bengal*, p. 280.
49. Ibid., pp. 457–8.
50. Dineshchandra Sen, *Brihat Banga*, vol. 2, Calcutta, 1935, pp. 1035–6.
51. Dasgupta, *Srihatter Itihas*, pp. 13–14.
52. Ibid., p. 8.
53. Manipuri Vaishnavas had a high regard for Chaitanya and hundreds of them visited Nabadvip every year, attending the festival held to commemorate Chaitanya's birth. Chakrabarty, *Vaishnavism in Bengal*, p. 280.
54. This element of historicization can be related to perspectives of what has been called 'historical geography' intersecting with human or cultural geography (which often prioritizes language and religion). It implied the study of geographies of the past to see how a place or region changed through time, and how the people created a religio-cultural landscape whose boundaries were conditioned historically.

55. Keith Basso has analysed the various dimensions of place-worlds founded on senses of place. See Keith H. Basso and Stephen Feld (eds.), *Senses of Place*, Santa Fe, NM: School of American Research Press, 1996.
56. Feldhaus, *Connected Places*, p. 5.
57. Henri Lefebvre, trans. N. Donaldson-Smith, *The Production of Space*, Oxford: Basil Blackwell, 1974.
58. This was done by writers such as S.N. Bhadra. See Bhadra, *Uttar Purba Bharat*, pp. 2-3. Whether 'Aryan' actually meant 'Hindu' is debatable. This point has been discussed, among others, by G. Flood. See G. Flood, *An Introduction to Hinduism*, Cambridge: Cambridge University Press, 1996, p. 23.
59. Basso, in Basso and Feld, *Senses of Place*, p. 1.

11

Revisiting the Ethnic-Enclave Paradox in North-East India's Economy

RAKHEE BHATTACHARYA

CORE-PERIPHERY MAPPING

Geographers have adopted and applied the established practice of core-periphery mapping to understand and analyse the geographical context of a nation. In the political-economic perspective of regional development, G. Myrdal[1] was the pioneer in conceptualizing this core-periphery mapping in a most appropriate manner to distinguish between the advanced and backward regions. In a simplistic manner, one can identify the industrialized countries/regions as the core, and the backward countries/regions as the periphery. Development thinkers have argued and shown that over time the core has continued to develop and industrialize itself by drawing resources from the periphery, leaving the latter without the means or the resources to progress. It soon became apparent that the development gap between the most and the least economically prosperous countries widened instead of narrowing over time. This theory, which is commonly known as the 'dependency theory' developed by Raul Prebisch in the 1950s,[2] derives from the hypothesis that colonialism is responsible for the outflow of resources from the less developed but resourceful periphery to the more developed and industrialized core. Looked at from this perspective, India's north-east can be understood in the context of the periphery within the core context of the rest of India. Despite the fact that it is the reservoir of the country's immense natural resources—like 37 per cent of India's river water, 20 per cent of its hydrocarbon potential, huge reserves of limestone and dolomite and low-ash high-sulphur coal—the region remains hopelessly impoverished and underdeveloped. Assam itself 'produces more than

50 per cent of India's natural oil and gas; 58 per cent of India's and 30 per cent of the world's tea; 60 per cent of India's plywood; and about 30 per cent of India's jute.'[3] But sadly despite such huge reserves the region could never attain a self-sustaining economy.

UNDERSTANDING COLONIAL INTEREST

Development thinkers have found a common historical cause for such a peripheral structure of north-east India. They are of the view that the British government systematically attempted to isolate this region from the rest of India and the neighbouring countries, though the pre-British scenario was quite different. S. Baruah[4] has shown clearly that along with ethnic and cultural affinities, that pre-British economic links through trade existed, and expanded, between north-east India and Tibet, Bhutan, Burma and Indo–China; the region even had a southern trail of the historic silk routes. But with the advent of the British into this region, barriers began to be erected and introduced in these important traditional economic links with neighbours. The British, for their own strategic interests, disrupted these economic ties to a significant extent, which, according to Baruah[5] is 'colonialism's most enduring negative legacy'. The British intervention and subsequent occupation and control of this region changed the course of the economic as well as political history of north-east India. Even within the region, the usual trade transactions and intercourse between the hills and plains people across this frontier were severely disrupted due to the introduction of the Inner Line Regulation of 1873 by the British in the name of preserving indigenous cultures in tribal, areas and also to protect the plains villages from tribal raids. It was at this time that the word 'tribal' was first used and emphasized by British ethnographers to systematically alienate these people from the rest of India, so much so that even today this region remains caught up in the time warp, of a so-called 'tribal identity' as against the concept of a modern Indian identity, or a twenty-first century identity—in other words, a flat world identity of people with the benefits of modern education, technology and profession. This so-called 'tribal identity' has become so deep-rooted that people are not hesitant to receive the benefits that are being extended in the name of welfare and upliftment of the 'tribal people' of India. This, according to J.B. Ganguly,[6] 'has been the most crucial factor in the differences between the tribal communities in north-east India, excluding those of Tripura and Assam plains, and those in other parts of India in respect to the preservation of indigenous social and cultural institutions and practices and economic power of maintaining indigenous system of community or other forms of ownership and command over land and other productive resources.'

For the British rulers, however, north-east India became and remained only a periphery to supply lifeblood to the core and to act as a rich storehouse for raw materials, which were eventually extracted by them and exported outside the region to develop the core. The British knew the economic worth and surplus revenue-yielding potential of this periphery. The economic worth of this region together with the vast tracts of uncultivable and uninhabited lands caught the fancy of the British who used them in the most productive and profitable way for generating economic surplus and not for recycling it back into the region for developing it economically. Amalendu Guha[7] has brought in another significant dimension in the colonial interest in turning 'Assam into an agricultural estate of tea drinking Britons and to transform local traditional institutions in such a manner as to suit the colonial pattern of exploitation.' The creation of the huge tea industry by British in Assam is another important aspect, which served as an oasis of modernization amidst the ethno-traditional economic set-up and which actually created another core-periphery paradigm within the state itself. The modern tea sector, established by the British, was never successful in extending its economic benefits to the rest of the traditional sectors; as a result, eventually a dual economy had to evolve within the state. In the words of H.K. Nath,[8] 'these investments could not establish any link between the modern and the traditional sectors through important linkage effects in capital, labor and commodity markets. With these missing links the dual economy that emerged, instead of projecting the economy in a path of long run growth, gave rise to an economic enclave that remained backward for years to come.' An almost irreparable imbalance and a paradox thus emerged due to colonial economic exploitation in this region, and these paradoxes bequeathed a legacy of insurmountable complexities and problems which would continue to afflict the region for decades to come, and which are yet to be resolved.

The massive tea industry created by the colonialist British became an 'enclave economy' confined to a small region; it was 'inserted in a community for reasons that have nothing to do with the community's demands or needs and has no immediate, significant and permanent positive impact on its standard of living'.[9] H.K. Nath explains the reasons why the magnificent economic gains from the tea sector could not permeate through the entire region:

The discovery of tea in the Brahmaputra valley in the very beginning of the British administration was a prelude to the presence of the British capital in the following years and the subsequent evolution of a modern sector, which crucially hinged on the growth of tea plantation. However the growth of the modern sector did not bring opulence and welfare to the people of this region. By the end of the 19th century the economy of Assam had developed all the characteristics of a dual economy with huge investments pouring into the modern sector and the traditional sector having been left out of this development process. Notwithstanding the role of the imperialist designs, there had been deeper economic reasons as to why there were no spillovers in the traditional sector. The peculiar socio-economic conditions of the region at that time came in the way of a process of dynamic interactions between the two sectors. Consequently the traditional sector remained an enclave in the years to come.[10]

OTHER ECONOMIC CONSEQUENCES

Colonial investment in tea plantations had begun by 1871, and more than 300,000 acres of wasteland was converted to tea plantations in Assam. Since tea was a land-based and labour-intensive industry, more and more skilled migrant labourers were brought in since the local people were not considered adequately skilled for this task. In this process a sizeable number of the helpless, poor indigenous villagers of this region were marginalized economically and eventually uprooted. The rising tea plantations also led to a serious destruction of the forest wealth in Assam. Tea planters were responsible for a colossal waste of timber, as they had to turn timber into charcoal for use as fuel in the tea factories. Keya Dasgupta[11] says that about 1,000 trees were used annually for this purpose alone in each tea garden without planting a single tree to replace them. Along with the tea industry, a typical imperialistic set-up had also started working in the region under British command, to deplete the region systematically of its other natural resources like oil, coal, and other forest resources. Because Assam was the first Indian state where oil was discovered in the British period, it definitely played an important role in the development of India's energy sector. One of the main reasons for the resentment of the people of Assam is justifiably that despite the state's huge reserves of oil which had contributed enormously to India's vertical economic prosperity, the state remained neglected, its wealth only contributed to accentuate its regional economic disparity *vis-à-vis* the rest of India. To the British, the north-east frontier was solely a reservoir of natural resources to be milked. In the words of P.S. Dutta[12] 'Colonial interest provided a common political map to the culturally related, but frequently independent people of India.

They played with the internal geography again and again and grouped and regrouped the territories and the people according to their own interest of cost minimization in the administration and profit maximization in economic ventures.' The inevitable result of such continued deprivation and exploitation was that when the country attained independence at the cost of partition, the north-east became an economic burden for free India. Partition, the price of independence, had worked to the disadvantage of the north-east in more than one way: by blocking the free legal mercantile trades between the north-east states and the then East Pakistan, later to become Bangladesh. The perishable raw agricultural materials, which were easily exported to this nearest territory, had now to follow a winding route to reach the Indian markets through the Sole corridor of roadway connectivity, i.e. Siliguri, a small town of North Bengal from north-east India to rest of the country, which is commonly termed as the chicken neck of Siliguri. In fact, this became a distant dream for most of the traders in this impoverished region without a viable, market-friendly infrastructure like roads. In the words of S. Khanna,

> However, partition and independence ended whatever remained of this intercourse. The partition transformed the region at the crossroad of emerging Asia, into a landlocked outpost of a large continental economy. The huge landmass comprising the seven states (Assam, Arunachal, Manipur, Meghalaya, Mizoram, Nagaland and Tripura), approximately 225,000 sq. km., was now cut off from its hinterland by the creation of East Pakistan. Linked by [a] 37 km. wide Siliguri corridor with the rest of India, it soon lost its natural advantage as its integration with the economy in the south and the west was disrupted by trade and industrial policies pursued by independent India.[13]

The course of history that had pathetically stymied the region's economy also disrupted the means of livelihood of its population and increased its isolation from the rest of the country. Over time, and more dangerously, it turned the mindset of a simple people from one of trust to one filled with distrust, grievances, alienation and despair. This despair would ultimately threaten and destroy the social fabric of harmony between the different communities that had lived in this region peacefully the decades, eventually leading to the emergence of scores of ethnic insurgent groups each separately clamouring for sovereignty of certain territories inhabited by its people. This would also turn this region into one with an increasingly isolated ethnoculture and with an unsustainable political economy.

POST-COLONIAL PROBLEMS

To understand the immediate post-independent north-east scenario, S. Khanna explains:

> In the first two decades of planned development, the region was transformed from being a potential outpost for trade with neighbouring countries emerging from colonial rule and war, into a small captive market for the produce of the Indian hinterland. Its exports of tea and forest produce, though an important source of export earnings initially for India, soon lost their importance as Indian exports diversified towards manufactures. Its petroleum, whether in crude form or processed, ultimately found its way to the major markets in the north and western states of India.[14]

The region, therefore, never got the opportunity to shake off its peripheral status and integrate into the process of the modernization of independent India. Though in post-independent India continual border skirmishes with neighbours like China, Myanmar and Bangladesh, especially the disastrous 1962 war with China, had increased its strategic significance, the economic possibilities were never explored to increase the wealth and well-being of the people of the region. The perverted import substitution policies of industrialization that the Congress governments followed after Independence, turning the country into a closed economy with disastrous consequences, had further deprived the region of the advantage of the pre-existing trade links with the natural markets in the neighbouring countries just across the border by preventing access to them. Finished products were poured into the north-east market from distant regions in India where they were manufactured and these became costly due to their transportation over an almost non-existent transport network in the north-east. The same products could easily have been procured from across the borders from neighbouring countries at a much lower cost. The shortsightedness of the Indian policy makers' vision only succeeded in multiplying the isolation in the region, adding to its peripheral backwardness.

GEOGRAPHICAL HINDRANCE

Even today 'inaccessibility' is a term used very frequently in relation to the inherent geographical disadvantages of the entire north-eastern region. The disruption of roads and rail and communication links, migration of channels, erosion of land and flooding of human habitat and valuable cultivable land are endemic across the entire Brahmaputra Valley, sole negotiable corridor of the region with the rest of the country (and also with the rest of the region). Except for the Brahmaputra Valley, which represents recent alluvial rocks, the rest of the region represents Archaean rocks. The peculiar topography of this region had also posed natural hurdles and created intra- and inter-regional barriers to better connectivity and communication. J.B. Ganguly[15] has clearly categorized the region into two broad physical divisions, viz., the hills and mountains of different heights and the plains or river valleys. The proportions of the hills in the different territorial units vary from 54.34 per cent in Assam to 92 per cent in Manipur. Narrow, flat valleys lie between the hill ranges and mountains of the contemporary states of Arunachal Pradesh (north-eastern frontier hills), Meghalaya (Khasi, Jaintia and Garo hills), Mizoram (Mizo hills) and Nagaland (Naga hills) which together make up nearly 100 per cent of the hill areas of the region. The Brahmaputra Valley is an alluvial plain, about 450 miles (725 km) in length, with an average breadth of about 50 miles (80.4 km), lying almost east and west in its lower portion, but in its upper half tending somewhat to the north-east. The valley covers an area of approximately 55,000 sq. km. The Barak Valley or the Cachar plains, approximately 3,000 sq. miles, consists of alluvial level stretches except where broken up by isolated hillocks and low ranges of hills, which project from the surrounding mountains. The chief river is the Barak, which is between 100 and 200 yards in width and in places over 70 ft. deep. Despite some differences in land formation and climate, these plains closely follow the broad pattern of the upper Brahmaputra Valley. The turbulent Brahmaputra River cuts across the region vertically, dividing it into two unapproachable halves during the prolonged monsoon season with recurring floods and consequent landslides from the surrounding hills. North-east India is also an earthquake-prone zone. The recorded history of earthquakes indicates heavy damage to property and loss of life, with severe economic collapses from the series of massive earthquakes in 1869, 1875, 1882, 1897 and 1918. Therefore, like the heavy rainfall resulting in recurring floods in the river valleys, earthquakes are also a great cause of destruction which have changed the economic history of this region many times. The natural geographical barriers have been equally responsible in turning this region into a periphery for the core of 'mainland' India; if ever there was a possibility of developing better connectivity, Partition destroyed it completely.

The narrow stretch of passage, which is just 50 km. wide, popularly known as chicken neck through North Bengal's Siliguri corridor, is the only surface point into the region from the rest of India. Tripura, a small strip of land, has hardly any land passage to move across or out of the region. Some states share large borders with other neighbouring nations rather than with other Indian states, and about 98 per cent of the geographical boundaries of the states in this region are shared with China, Bhutan, Myanmar and Bangladesh. Sixty-five per cent of the total land area of 2,54,979 sq. km. (without Sikkim) in this region is under dense forest cover. Due to such a difficult geographical terrain and a high incidence of natural disasters, communication, the key to all development and modernization, has always remained undeveloped in this region. The natural geographical barriers, as well as the barriers of communication, increased the physical isolation of the region, and the same isolation may also have turned north-east India into a somewhat homogeneous identity, despite the multiplicity of ethnicities and races and tribal groups in this region and despite the frequent internecine fights between many of these groups. But the fact remains that geographical inaccessibility and isolation have significantly contributed to the economic backwardness of the region and its isolation from the rest of the country.

Geography no less than history has shaped and evolved the methods for sustenance of the people and their modes of production through primitive and ethnic practices. The primitive and unscientific shifting cultivation (popularly known as Jhum Cultivation) still remains one of the most widely used methods of cultivation in the hill states of the region. Ethnic handloom and handicraft industries are another distinctive aspect of north-east India, which could be used to generate income for the people. But since resources could not be mobilized optimally within the region, the economic surplus, linkages and marketability that could have flowed from these rich and traditional sectors could not be exploited to greater advantage and, by and large, the entire region still survives primarily as an agrarian economy, unsustainable by the current practices in the long run.

BACKUP: CENTRAL ASSISTANCE

The regional governments failed miserably to address the problems in an effective manner—in respect of training and skill development among their populace so as to usher in some restructuring of their subsistence economy and modernizing it, or by developing the physical infrastructure and local markets, or by providing political stability, which alone could have ensured economic growth, the basic job of any government. In the absence of these prerequisites, the half-hearted policy initiatives of the Government of India and its various experimentations to correct the inherent imbalances and inequities of the region, have also failed to deliver. The government's developmental expenditure was misdirected, unproductive and inadequate, and was further beset with problems of sub-optimal utilization and leakages which again failed to improve the mobility between the region and the rest of India by breaking the age-old geographical barriers. The regional economies continued to remain simple and agrarian, plagued with high deficits and almost entirely dependent on the rest of the country even for many of its basic needs. The status of 'special category states' enabled these states to obtain liberal Central assistance and loans on soft terms, their development plans being almost entirely financed by the Centre on the basis of 90 per cent grant and 10 per cent loan. The development-funding pattern for the special category states accorded them preferential treatment and further discouraged self-sufficiency, since the development plans failed to create enough economic opportunities with their misplaced priorities and lack of infrastructure. Thus, these states have been surviving, in an inappropriate economic environment largely on Central assistance. The role of their political economies to improve things and make the region economically competitive has remained minimal, and the dependence on outside assistance continues to increase. '[The] Center pumped in disproportionate sums of money into the new state without trying to build up an infrastructure for proper dispersal and utilization of such funds. The benefits did not percolate to the masses but instead helped to create a class of people who developed strong stakes in the Indian market.'[16] The region had a low tax-generating capacity and low tax-base scope; the governments failed to create opportunities to generate additional revenue within the region by the proper targeting and utilization of the plan funds on the one hand, and by falling back increasingly on Central assistance on the other, ultimately getting caught in the vicious circle of low development, low tax base and low revenue earning, each reinforcing the other.

Tables 11.1 and 11.2 depict the degree of dependence of the north-eastern special category states, as compared to the other special category states, as well as the other small but non-special category states of the country during the 14 years from 1993–4 to 2006–7. This time period has been chosen firstly because the 1990s marked the ushering in of far-reaching reforms in the Indian economy, and secondly, because compared to the 1980s, the 1990s marked a better period of peace and stability for the north-eastern states. In the 1980s insurgency and underground militancy were at their peak in the region and government expenditures to deal with such unrest and violence were very high.

TABLE 11.1 RATIO OF GROSS TRANSFERS OF RESOURCES FROM THE CENTRE TO AGGREGATE STATE DISBURSEMENT (%)

States	1993–4	1994–5	1995–6	1996–7	1997–8	1998–9	1999-2000
Special Category States							
Assam	62.86	62.83	68.40	75.28	74.35	67.69	55.90
Arunachal Pradesh	84.38	80.10	87.53	87.59	84.58	90.24	86.81
Manipur	94.90	80.18	79.05	75.74	81.16	87.90	59.68
Meghalaya	77.68	80.56	73.38	80.79	74.36	73.59	66.52
Mizoram	93.35	87.70	84.90	79.54	80.55	81.35	81.40
Nagaland	76.45	65.83	72.59	76.21	77.64	78.50	82.65
Sikkim	74.60	36.02	31.61	27.71	27.51	27.44	30.98
Tripura	78.25	80.64	89.27	83.79	78.92	82.33	76.41
Jammu & Kashmir	77.72	86.32	86.54	91.30	85.21	72.42	76.90
Himachal Pradesh	73.04	58.81	63.03	67.20	63.36	48.01	54.89
Non-Special Category States							
Delhi	16.56	25.08	27.38	30.06	33.15	27.49	26.97
Goa	33.87	36.22	21.77	24.40	19.78	18.28	11.37
All States	43.06	39.70	39.22	40.43	41.82	38.90	30.69

Source: Estimated from CMIE data and Finance & Accounts of CAG Reports of the respective years for the respective states.

TABLE 11.2 RATIO OF GROSS TRANSFERS OF RESOURCES FROM THE CENTRE TO AGGREGATE STATE DISBURSEMENT (%)

States	2000–1	2001–2	2002–3	2003–4	2004–5	2005–6	2006–7
Special Category States							
Assam	53.63	55.36	59.94	48.22	44.89	54.06	53.38
Arunachal Pradesh	74.17	70.38	77.90	70.49	69.40	72.64	74.17
Manipur	86.26	75.58	103.39	78.83	100.76	79.62	80.56
Meghalaya	68.24	67.34	74.79	66.34	63.34	73.94	81.04
Mizoram	63.15	66.68	70.73	61.74	80.06	76.01	80.86
Nagaland	75.98	77.75	90.75	78.76	81.48	80.23	83.40
Sikkim	27.95	33.31	32.55	51.87	39.91	40.85	43.41
Tripura	70.23	69.25	66.35	67.63	75.66	72.16	72.31
Jammu & Kashmir	62.26	74.20	68.62	83.36	72.51	71.12	75.45
Himachal Pradesh	44.40	51.22	41.41	86.74	37.41	51.59	52.40
Non-Special Category States							
Goa	14.41	11.74	19.18	10.33	30.90	33.45	27.97
All States	30.96	31.79	30.81	26.93	28.59	28.93	33.59

Source: Estimated from CMIE data, Finance & Accounts of CAG Reports of respective years for respective states.

The gross transfers of Central resources to aggregate state disbursement over the last 14 years ranged from 62 to 95 per cent in 1993–4; in 2006–7, this ranged from 55 to 82 per cent except for Sikkim where it was only 43 per cent. Thus no structural change is visible here. In 2002–3, one can see that this ratio was abnormally high in some states, like Manipur (103.39 per cent) and Nagaland (90.75 per cent). Among these states, only Himachal Pradesh, Sikkim and Assam remained the least dependent on Central assistance. For the other small and non-special category states, this ratio was, however, less than only 35 per cent. Self-sustainability for the north-eastern states is distant dream and shall remain so for a long time to come. This empirical evidence, once again, shows that even in the contemporary scenario, the core of 'shinning India' has left the periphery of 'north-east India' way behind in terms of economic reforms, modernization and globalization.

DEVELOPMENT STRATEGY: LOOK EAST POLICY AND REGIONAL TIES

The colossal gap in development cannot be sustained any longer without seriously damaging the country's national development strategy and this thought has forced the policy makers to realize that a thorough restructuring of the development strategy of north-east India is an urgent necessity. The lopsided development of the region had engendered an unstable and unsafe society where a sizeable number of youths had turned to militancy due to the lack of economic opportunities. The problem became even more complex due to unchecked illegal infiltration and export of terrorism from across the border and threats of illegal intrusion by some countries, as reported in 2006 in the media. The time has indeed come to think for an alternative strategy which could provide a solution to this complex scenario. Fast and visible economic development is the need of the hour, and this alone can give confidence to north-east India to assume a new identity, not in the ethno-traditional perspective but in a modern-economic sense. This resurgence is now being attempted by opening the long-forgotten, pre-British economic and trade ties and routes with the north-east's neighbours along with a fresh initiative with India's 'Look East Policy'. Since 1991, India has adopted a policy of radical restructuring, by dismantling trade barriers, abolishing import licences, attracting foreign investment in many sectors of the economy, and promoting the Preferential Trade Arrangements (PTAs) with the neighbouring countries through bilateral trade agreements.

At the same time, India's astonishing growth story is increasingly attracting the attention of its eastern and south-eastern neighbours and engaging them in a blending of economic ties with India, like the South Asia Growth Quadrangle (SAGQ), the South Asian Sub-region for Economic Cooperation (SASEC), the Bangladesh–India–Myanmar–Sri Lanka–Thailand–Economic Cooperation (BIMSTEC), the South Asian Free Trade Area (SAFTA), etc. These initiatives are providing an economic stimulus to the north-east which had remained neglected for decades. Numerous economic possibilities and prospects are gradually opening up for this region through such economic cooperation and ties. Given that this small cluster of states share more than 90 per cent of its borders with its neighbours like Bangladesh, Bhutan, Myanmar and China, policy makers are right to assume that India's 'Look East Policy' can very well make way for a gainful economic integration with its neighbours by extending transnational trade and other investment and market connectivity with north-east India. The region is also strategically positioned to take advantage of the opportunities by exploring the ASEAN market and diversifying its economic base. With these potentials, 'development' has become the *mantra* for this region, and only now is one seeing the long-awaited thrust towards investments in physical infrastructure, connectivity and other developmental needs to make north-east India a 'happening zone' and a corridor for regional integration with India's south-eastern neighbours. India is seriously beginning to focus its attention on this 'unnoticed periphery' and to integrate it into the 'core paradigm' of 'contacts and connectivity between India and South-East Asia'.

THREATS OF ENCLAVING THE NORTH-EAST AGAIN?

The orthodox thinkers are still apprehensive that this new vision for north-east India may again give rise to new conflicts between this 'modern enclave economy' and its 'traditional ethnic economy'. This sudden restructuring of the development strategy for north-east India from 'New Delhi' is again building suspicion and causing them to think that this initiative may not go hand in hand with the region's internal ethno-political-economic dynamics, and that this may again lead to another form of 'enclave economy' catering to its eastern economic tigers like Thailand. According to this group of orthodox thinkers, ushering development and modernization in north-east India from outside through investments, trade and expanding markets may not yet be appropriate to create an ambiance for economic freedom and prosperity for its people, and a strong resistance may yet attempt to prevent economic growth through this route. They also think that it is equally important to preserve the existing traditionalism and ethnic identity of the region. Further, one needs to keep in mind that the trade linkages that had existed in the pre-British period were primarily for trading indigenous products. Today, the reopening and revival of the trade routes may simply turn the north-east into a potential market for dumping consumer durables and the indigenous products might not get a fair deal. Similarly, if the neighbouring tigers make investments in this region, an inflow of entrepreneurs and skilled migrant labourers may again capture the north-east economy, marginalizing the local population. They argue that it is essential for any development strategy for the region to be carefully blended with the internal dynamics of the region to prevent the possibility of repeating the colonial blunder, along with an inclusive and endogenous growth model.

LINKAGE BETWEEN MODERNITY AND ETHNICITY

It needs to be remembered that today the threat of another enclave economy in north-east India is minimal. Unlike the British rulers, this is an initiative of free India, where the region is no longer perceived as a 'peripheral storehouse of resources' but as a 'future core economic hub' from the points of view of both regional economic integration with South-East Asia and the Indian economy as a whole. This is the development strategy of the country, which is today unleashing the innate strength, innovation and resourcefulness of its people, for so long marginalized, and the effect of an unshackled economy is being seen every day across the length and breadth of India. The north-east will be either an active and eager player in this economic march or perish through increasing militancy and backwardness—there is no third alternative. This initiative is to cater to the needs of local employment, entrepreneurship and the creation of local opportunities, and this cannot be compared with the pre-Independence days, when skilled labourers were brought in from outside and profits were taken out, leaving the region increasingly impoverished. Today the fruits of development are unlikely to flow entirely out of the north-east, thanks to the region's strong base of an educated, aware and politically conscious civil society and growing skilled human resources, who is eager to play its role in the nation's economic adventure and move up the economic ladder. Thus, this initiative from New Delhi of opening up the economic connectivity with the bordering nations cannot really pose any threat to the regional economy; on the contrary, this move is essential to dispel once and for all the oft-repeated notion of an 'isolated north-east India'. It is time to realize that the ethnic and tribal essence that north-east India has so long preserved can just as well be an asset for economic returns and mobilization. The geographical barriers of hilly terrains and virgin forests and rivers that had so long hindered economic development can be gainfully turned into an astounding potential for tourism with the creation of an appropriate physical infrastructure and connectivity. This initiative of economic resurgence may finally be the long-awaited means to make the north-east truly independent in the economic sense and transform its 'ethno-stagnant peripheral structure' to an 'ethno-dynamic core economic hub'. The modern economic dynamics not only adds value to the aggregate economic gains but also helps to spread these gains to those who have so far remained marginalized. The region needs both ethnicity and modernity, which are actually complementary to each other, for its development. An inflow of modern economic ideas and knowledge along with its existing ethnic structure can also create a greater social network for the region as a whole.[17]

To bridge the link between the modern and ethnic economic sectors of this region, the participation and initiative of the people of north-east India in this regional economic integration is imperative. The economic success of north-east India depends to a great extent upon the local people whose capability and competence alone should be enough to face the challenge of any enclave economy. The experience of 60 years has utterly failed to reduce the economic dependence of north-east India, let alone make it a viable economic entity. There is no harm in trying a new initiative to revamp the region through market forces and to rejuvenate the confidence and competence of its people. Despite the ominous prophecies of the prophets of doom, let the north-east rediscover its lost linkages with its neighbours, for who can say it will not once again become the crossroads for Asian integration in the near future, a possibility which was stymied and throttled by the British enclaves.

NOTES

1. G. Myrdal, *Economic Theory and Underdeveloped Regions*, London: Duckworth, 1957.
2. Used by Vincent Ferraro, 'Dependency Theory: An Introduction', cited in 1996, available from *http://www.mtholyoke.edu/acad/intrel/depend.htm.*

3. A.K. Das, *Assam's Agony: A Socio-Economic and Political Analysis*, Delhi: Lancers Publishers, 1982.
4. S. Baruah, 'Between South and Southeast Asia Northeast India and Look East Policy', Ceniseas Paper 4, Guwahati, 2004.
5. Ibid.
6. J.B. Ganguly, *An Economic History of Northeast India: 1826 to 1947*, Delhi: Akanksha Publishing House, 2006.
7. Amalendu Guha, *Planter Raj to Swaraj: Freedom Struggle and Electoral Politics in Assam, 1826-1947*, Delhi: Peoples Publishing House, 1988.
8. H.K. Nath, 'The Rise of an Enclave Economy', cited in 1999, available from *http://www.shsu.edu/~eco_hkn/nath_enclave.pdf.*
9. Juan J. Llach, Gonzalo Biggs and Donald Rhatigan, 'Independent Investigation Mechanism. Termoeléctrica del Golfo Project. Tamuín, San Luis de Potosí, Mexico', used in Document of the Inter-American Development Bank (2004), 'Enclave Projects: What Are They and What Can Be Done?' cited in 2003, available from *http://www.iadb.org/sds/doc/EnclaveProjectsEN.pdf.*
10. Nath, op. cit.
11. Keya Dasgupta, 'Plantation Economy and Land Tenure System in Brahmaputra Valley, 1839–1914', *Economic and Political Weekly* 18, no. 20, 1983.
12. P.S. Dutta, *Autonomy Movement in Assam*, Delhi: Omsons Publications, 1993.
13. S. Khanna, 'Economic Opportunities or Continuing Stagnation?', cited in 2005, available at Manipur Online: *http://www.manipuronline.com/Economy/November 2005/stagnationoropportuny18_1.htm.*
14. Khanna, op. cit.
15. Ganguly, op. cit.
16. U. Mishra, *The Periphery Strikes Back: Challenges to the Nation-State in Assam and Nagaland*, Shimla: Indian Institute of Advanced Studies, 2000.
17. A. Greve and J.W. Salaff, 'Social Network Approach to Understand the Ethnic Economy: A Theoretical Discourse', cited in 2003, available from *http://www.chass.utoronto.ca/~salaff/Greve&Salaff-enclave-ntw.pdf.*

Essays

12

Do Educational Institutes Always Generate Positive Externalities?

DEBORSHI BRAHMACHARI

INTRODUCTION

Regional imbalances have always been one of the major hurdles in the development of developing countries and India is no exception. This is because the country is now experiencing the initial phase of development. North-eastern India in particular has always been like a leakage in the Indian development process, sucking in the fruits of development. Political turmoil and social unrest resulting from insurgency and autonomy movements, have further weakened the north-eastern economy. The north-eastern region of India is situated between longitude 21.57°N and 29.30°N and longitude 89.46°E and 97.30°E. The region comprises of eight states, viz., Assam, Arunachal Pradesh, Manipur, Meghalaya, Mizoram, Nagaland, Sikkim and Tripura. It accounts for 7.81 per cent of the total land area of the country. Hilly ranges forming part of the great Himalayan mountains guard the northern border of the region. The region embraces a total area of 255,000 sq km, of which 70 per cent is hilly terrain. It has a considerably large international boundary with China in the north, Bangladesh in the south-west, Bhutan in the north-west and Burma in the east. The McMahon Line separates the region from Tibet.[1]

One of the main reasons why the north-eastern region is suffering from a sense of being 'left out' is that British rule came to these parts very late and in an ineffective manner. Most of the north-east was never strongly integrated with British India politically, socially and economically. The careless exploitation of mineral resources to meet the commercial demands of the rest of India and the link of the plantation industry with foreign capital with the consequent poor multiplier effect on income and employment, also added to this malaise. In spite of the policy of reservations and other measures of protection meant for the tribal and other disadvantaged groups, the spillover of the benefits takes so long that any attempt at development inevitably generates inequality not only between the tribal and non-tribal or between the hills and plains but also between the advanced and backward groups of the tribals themselves. The north-eastern region is also characterized by all sorts of dualisms—social, technological and regional. The rural–urban dualism is reinforced by the tribal–non-tribal dualism and the hills–plains divide. Moreover, the technological approach and agricultural techniques are also different within the north-east. There are differences in social customs and attitudes between the indigenous and imported social systems. So no uniform policy is applicable to all parts of the region.

Both inter-state and intra-state disparities are prominent in this region. One such prominent disparity can be seen within the state of Assam. The present state of Assam is comprised of three physical divisions, namely, the Brahmaputra Valley, the Barak Valley and the Hill range. The Brahmaputra Valley, which forms the northern part, is the largest in size, comprising 71.7 per cent of the total geographical area of the state. On the other hand, the Barak Valley region, which forms the southern part, is comparatively smaller in size. The two valleys derived their names from the respective main rivers, the Brahmaputra and the Barak flowing east to west in the valleys. The Barak and Brahmaputra valleys are geographically, socially, economically, culturally and linguistically different from each other.[2]

The Barak Valley region is situated between longitude 92°15' E and 93°15' and latitude 24° 8' and 25° 8'N covering an area of 6,922 sq km. The valley constitutes 8.9 per cent of the geographical area of the state but it contains only 11.22 per cent of the population as per the 2001 census. The region shares its border with the north-Cachar hills district and the state of Meghalaya in the north; the state of Manipur in the east; the state of Mizoram in the south and the state of Tripura and the Sylhet district of Bangladesh in the west. Administratively, the region at present is comprised of three districts, namely, the Cachar, the Karimganj and the Hailakandi. The Cachar is the largest and the Hailakandi the smallest district with total geographical areas of 3,786 sq km and 1,327 sq km respectively. Karimganj district has an area of 1,809 sq km as per the 2001 census. The district headquarters of Cachar, Karimganj and Hailakandi are Silchar, Karimganj and Hailakandi respectively.

The population density is higher in the Barak Valley than in the Brahmaputra Valley or Assam and even India as a whole. The density of the population of the Barak Valley, according to the 2001 census, is 448 per sq km, while the respective figures for Assam and India as a whole are 340 and 324. The 2001 census reports reveal that the sex ratio in terms of females per thousand males in Karimganj district is 945, while it is 944 for Cachar district and 933 for Hailakandi district. The average for the Barak Valley as a whole stood at 941 females per thousand males in the 2001 census. On the other hand, for Assam as a whole, the ratio became 932 per thousand males in 2001, while for India it was 933 females per thousand males. Thus, it is evident that the female population in Barak Valley is high as compared to Assam or the country as a whole. As per the 2001 census, the literacy rate for the Barak Valley region stood at 65.16 per cent (72.95 per cent for males and 76.81 per cent for females); for Assam as a whole it was 64.28 per cent (71.93 per cent for males and 56.03 per cent for females), and for all India it was 65.38 per cent (75.85 per cent for males and 54.16 per cent for females).

The region has a long tradition of poor economic infrastructure, given the fact that most of the developmental activities carried out were inefficient. The marginal efficiency of developmental projects has been low.[3]

In the light of this background, the Government of India aimed at setting up some Central educational institutes which would educate and train manpower for development of the Barak Valley and the state of Assam, and to pay special attention to the improvement of the social and economic conditions and welfare of the people of that region; including their intellectual, academic and cultural development.[4]

Given the fact that educational growth centres are targeted at the region with the aim of developing the socio-economic atmosphere of its peripheral underdeveloped areas. This chapter attempts to assess the efficiency of a particular educational institute in the Barak Valley and its spillover effects on its surrounding underdeveloped areas, thus accessing the ability of education growth centres in developing an underdeveloped areas.

EDUCATIONAL INSTITUTIONS—A TOOL FOR CORRECTING REGIONAL IMBALANCES

Education is the process by which an individual is encouraged and enabled to fully develop his or her potential. Education is viewed as a positive externality by economists. This means education is not an individual consumption; it is an investment in a long-term social benefit. Even illiterates can be benefited by associating themselves with the educated. Social evils, conflicts, superstitions, etc., which hinder the development process can be overcome through this tool. It increases an individual's productive skills as well as a society's welfare.[5]

Amartya Sen defines education as one of the two sources of a person's freedom,[6] health being the other. The five features, which, according to Sen, make education a source of freedom are

1. *Intrinsic importance*: Being educated is an achievement in itself and can help to utilize economic resources for the purpose of production, consumption and exchange.
2. *Instrumental personal roles*: Education helps a person to use an economic activity better, for example, getting a job and thus increasing his/her income (freedom/choices).
3. *Instrumental social roles*: Greater literacy and basic education can facilitate public discussion of social needs and encourage informed collective demand. It provides openness as it brings people in touch with others.
4. *Instrumental process roles*: Schooling can have positive externalities other than education itself. The incidence of child labour, for example, may decrease as students' attendance in schools increases.
5. *Empowerment and distributive roles*: Education increases a group's ability to resist oppression, raise its voice against exploitation, organize politically and to get a fairer deal.[7]

Both monetary and non-monetary benefits are associated with higher education. Table 12.1 gives a better idea of how private and social benefits can be classified into monetary and non-monetary benefits.

Educational Institutions, likewise, are viewed as 'externality generating centres'. Owing to their 'externality generating' ability, they are expected to develop a healthy 'socio-economic and cultural' environment, in and around their surroundings.[8] Further, educational institutes, which are set up on the outskirts of urban areas due to huge space requirements, act as 'growth centres' for economic development in those underdeveloped areas. This phenomenon can be better explained by what G. Myrdal calls 'Circular Causation'.[9] Myrdal in his theory of 'Circular & Cumulative Causation' explains how the developed areas grow at the expense of underdeveloped areas (peripheries), as raw materials, raw human power and capital from the peripheries are directed towards the developed centres (he calls it the backwash effect).

TABLE 12.1 THE PRIVATE AND SOCIAL BENEFITS OF HIGHER EDUCATION

MONETARY BENEFITS	
Private	*Social*
Higher productivity and thus higher net earnings	Higher national productivity.
Better job opportunities	Greater flexibility in labour force.
Higher savings	Higher consumption.
Personal and professional mobility	Less dependency on government.
Higher tax revenues	
NON-MONETARY BENEFITS	
Private	*Social*
Educational enrichment	Social cohesion, appreciation, social diversity and cultural heritage
Better labour conditions	Higher social mobility
Higher personal status	Lower crime rates
Higher job satisfaction	More donations and charity work
Better health and life expectancies	Increased capacity to adapt to new technologies
Improved spending decisions	Higher social/political participation
More hobbies and value of leisure activities	
Personal development	

Sources: B.W.A., Jongbloed and J.J. Vossensteyn, 'Keeping up Performances: An International Survey of Performance-based Funding in Higher Education', *Journal of Higher Education Policy and Management* 23, no. 2, 2001, pp. 127–45; World Bank, *Constructing Knowledge Societies: New Challenges for Tertiary Education*, Washington, D.C., 2002.

Sadly, the 'spread effects' of technical knowhow and finished output from developed areas to peripheries gradually decline at a constant rate with an increase in the spatial distance from the developed area. An underdeveloped area therefore depicts a case of BWE (Backwash Effect) > SPE (spread effect). This implies 'Cumulative Causation' towards poverty and regional imbalance.[10]

The remedy to this problem may be obtained by setting up 'growth centres' in underdeveloped areas themselves, so that the raw material, human power and capital do not move out of these places and the underdeveloped region can use its resources for its own betterment. Educational institutions are one of such 'growth centres', which can 'rebound' the backwash effects and create 'circular causation' of development in backward areas. This is because setting up educational institutes in underdeveloped suburbs will bring with it increased employment opportunities for the indigenous, less privileged people. Educational institutes will also bring along high quality migration in the form of students, teachers and employees from different parts of that country. Markets will grow and there will be an expansion of demand with students, teachers, and employees crowding the place. Most importantly, with education come the positive externalities of education like better health, low criminal rates, low delinquent activities and increased expenditure on education. Education will bring more education. This creates more employment opportunities, exposure, awareness, education, infrastructural development, reach, social upliftment and socio-economic changes leading to a socio-cultural and intellectual revolution.

But the question is does the process run smoothly? Will the adjacent underdeveloped area always gain from the educational institute? Or in other words, *do educational institutes always generate positive externalities?* This paper tries to answer these basic questions.

RATIONALE OF THE STUDY

This study is an attempt to explore the problems and prospects that a periphery area of a non-residential educational institution faces. It is a 'cost-benefit' analysis of what the students and the institution as a whole bring to the area. For this study, the study area was Irongmara, the neighbouring village of Assam University, Silchar.

OBJECTIVE OF THE STUDY

The main objective of the study was to explore whether or not Assam University, Silchar, has been successful in acting as a development centre for Irongmara—a growth centre which has efficiently used indigenous raw materials, raw human power and skills and also, side by side, encouraged human capital (students, teachers and other employees residing in Irongmara) investment (the money they spend here) for the development of the area.

DATA SOURCE, SCOPE AND METHODOLOGY OF THE STUDY

Both primary and secondary data sources have been used. The secondary data sources include:

(a) Gram Panchayat, Irongmara
(b) Post Office, Irongmara
(c) Community Information Centre (CIC), Irongmara
(d) Electoral register
(e) Local people.

Primary data was collected using simple random sampling without replacement. Sample units were chosen from the sample frame rather than population due to time and cost constraints. The sample frame, which is a proper subset of the population, was restricted to those houses that have university students as tenants. This is because the Local-Student Mix could be precisely studied from those samples. Though the total number of houses was around 1,000 (which is the total population), by the end of 2006 there were around 155 houses in group 3 and group 4 of the village (source: Gram Panchayat, Irongmara) where most of the university students lived as tenants. The study team used the electoral register to identify all 155 sample units. So the sample frame was 155, out of which 40 households were randomly selected using tables of random numbers. Information on sample units was collected through a door-to-door sample survey. The study was undertaken in a twofold process. First, the house owners of those 40 households were interviewed. Second, the student tenants of those 40 houses were asked questions following an indirect interview method. The data was analysed using standard statistical and econometric tools.

Limitations: The study was conducted within a span of two months. Lack of time and cost forced a small sample size. The scope of the study was limited to group 3 and group 4 of the village. It is a rudimentary effort to spur re-thinking of, if not a revolution against, the existing stereo-typed educational structure that exerts positive spillover effects with a lesser intensity than negative ones.

PROFILE OF THE STUDY AREA: ASSAM UNIVERSITY, SILCHAR, AND THE VILLAGE OF IRONGMARA

Assam University came into existence through the Assam (Central) University Act, 1989 (Act No. XIII). It was established in 1994. The campus, situated near the village of Irongmara, about 20 km from Silchar, has a total area of 600 acres. Drawing its 120-plus faculty from many disciplines, from all over the country, the university sustains a multidisciplinary approach to higher education. The university has eight schools on major disciplines. They are social sciences, humanities, languages, life sciences, physical sciences, environmental sciences, and information sciences and management studies. There are 27 departments under these eight schools. The university is all set to become a full-fledged residential university in the near future. Assam University is a teaching-cum-affiliating university. All the colleges in the five districts of South Assam, viz., Cachar, Karimganj, Hailakandi, North Cachar Hills and Karbi Anglong, fall within its jurisdiction. As of now there are 50 colleges, which include a medical college, a few law colleges and teachers' training colleges. The main objectives of the university are to disseminate and advance knowledge by providing instructional and research facilities in such branches of learning as it may deem fit; and by the examples of its corporate life to make provisions for integrated courses in the humanities, natural and physical sciences and the social sciences in the educational programme of the university; to take appropriate measures for promoting interdisciplinary studies and research in the university; to educate and train manpower for the development of the state of Assam and to pay special attention to the improvement of the social and economic conditions and welfare of the people of that state.

The university campus, situated at Dargakona adjacent to the village of Irongmara, is fast growing into an urban complex with several amenities and facilities like a post office, telephone exchange, public call offices, bank, police patrol post, water treatment plants, electric substations (a dedicated power line will be opened shortly), students' hostels, staff quarters, shopping complex, guest-house, auditorium and parks among others. Some amenities like an ATM, a health centre and a sports complex will be added. These amenities and facilities were once only a dream for the people of Dargakona and Irongmara. The university has now given them access to many of these facilities.

There are at present three hostels on the university campus, one for boys and two for girls. The maximum accommodation available is for 240 students only. The rest have to stay as tenants in Irongmara and Dargakona. The hostels also offer employment opportunities for the local people. This study is an effort to measure how much of an identity Assam University has given to this unknown, undeveloped and uncared for village.

The village of Irongmara is about 21 km from Silchar. Silchar is the district headquarters of Cachar district of Assam. The town is a doorway to the states of Manipur, Tripura and Mizoram. Access to the town is by rail, road and air. It is connected to Guwahati, the capital of Assam, through National Highway 44.

The village of Irongmara stretches 10 sq km and has a resident population of 10,000 plus (2006). The Irongmara Gram Panchayat has been bifurcated into two, Irongmara Grant and Chotojalenga-I, with 334 and 196 ha of land area respectively. Irongmara Gram Panchayat consists of the following localities: Irongmara Bazar, New Colony, Teletilla, Maltilla, Banglatilla, Hathitilla, Gotitilla, Harintilla, Uportilla, Rajubari, Borjalenga, Murgimara, Dakbangla, Purana Irongmara, Basti No. 6, Harinagar, G.P. Office area and Irongmara Part.

Irongmara is a Hindu-dominated village with the people speaking mainly two languages—Bengali and Hindi. Their caste and creed vary intensely and there is no caste-based discrimination. Very few of them can speak more than one language. Most of the respondents under study are economically weak, although the situation is changing day by day. Female literacy is low. Most of the their parents are illiterate. Most of the respondents' native place is within Assam. A majority of them are third generation residents of the village. Most of the respondents live on agriculture, all of the respondents' mothers are housewives. Mainly rice grown in the study area. Traditional implements are used for cultivation. Fertilizers and insecticides are also used. Most of them have pet animals. The well is the major source of drinking water. The majority of them cook on a *chulha*. They do not have bank accounts or post office accounts and have not taken a loan. Most have a very low consumption pattern and low exposure to mass media. The majority of the people in the study area have not visited places outside Barak Valley. Medical facilities are very poor. Communication is not up to the mark. Only a few respondents subscribe to newspapers and none of them subscribe to magazines. None of them have a telephone at home. Most of the popular *pujas* are performed in the locality/family of the respondents. Less than one-fifth of the respondents participate in the activities of the Gram Panchayat, i.e. community participation and awareness are low. There is an indication of the presence of elitist characteristics in the political system of the village along with pluralism. Women's representation is very low in the political arena and at village functions.

Irongmara, years ago, was a garden under the British government in India. It had a different name then, which is unknown. Historically, there is a difference of opinion about how the name 'Irongmara' actually came about. Some say a tragic incident was the reason behind its present name. The garden owner, an Englishman, had a beautiful daughter named Irine. One day everyone in the garden learnt that 'Irine' 'Mara Geya', that is, Irine had died. Soon the place began to be called 'Irine Mara'. Today's 'Irongmara' is nothing but a distorted version of 'Irine Mara'. Others are of the opinion that there was a type of reptile that lived there in abundance. It was called 'Irong'. They were everywhere, all over the place. When the British came to this place, they killed a lot of 'Irongs'. From that came the name 'Irongmara'. Fifteen to twenty years ago hardly anybody knew about this place. The birth of Assam University worked wonders for the village and the people around and gave it an identity and exposure to the place.

ANALYSIS OF SECONDARY DATA

Ten years back, when the campus of the Assam University near Irongmara had just opened it was very different from what it is today. Strange as it may seem, but even the thought processes have changed—in the way the locals live, the way they interact with the students and the way the students see them (locals). Students from all parts of north-east India brought with them their culture, way of dressing, etc. The local people of Irongmara were in for a 'culture shock'. The simplicity of the place got distorted. Moreover, illiteracy and conservative ideas prevented the locals from coming out of their shell and mixing with the students.

With time the gap started to close. The locals have accepted the students and their ways. Most of them have become very close to the students, helping them in need, playing together and even treating them almost like family. The students who live as tenants in Irongmara have good relations with the landlords, shopkeepers, auto-rickshaw drivers and others. In the process, the locals receive some positive vibes from the educated externality generators and have become polished socioculturally and sound economically. Because students bring in money, the locals intentionally shy away from or are forced to hide the negative externalities, generated by the students in the form of drinking, drugs, smoking, sex and offensive language and dressing. They are almost myopic about the social degradation that the village is experiencing. The students, who were supposed to be the role models for the local illiterates and their next generation, have redefined the definition and image of a student in the eyes of the locals.

The study of secondary data gives a clear indication of the *socio-cultural and economic transformation* that the village of Irongmara has undergone with the setting up of the Assam University, Silchar. Changes were observed mainly on two fronts: economic and sociological.

Table 12.2 gives a comparative idea of the vital statistics of this region at two different time periods, 1991 and 2001. The population increased from 7,111 persons to 8,365 persons, i.e. 1,254 more people were added to the total in that decade at a growth rate of 0.176. This resulted in an increase in the number of households from 740 to 860. Further, the establishment of the Assam University in 1994 led to an increase in the number of households at a rate of 0.162, almost matching the growth rate of the population. The literacy rates of that region speak immensely and explicitly about the establishment of the Assam University in that decade. From a humble 1,422 literate persons, the figure reached 2,258 (0.588) in a single decade. While male literacy increased to 1,189 from 799 (0.488), it is the female literacy that almost doubled to 1,069 from 623 (0.716).

The alarming feature, however, is the rate at which the non-workers have increased during the decade. Due to unavailability of more fragmented data, it was not possible to frame a pre-university establishment (till 1993) and post-university establishment (after 1994) comparison of data relating to non-workers. Nevertheless, a growth rate of 0.358 per cent for non-workers (compared to 0.148 per cent of workers) is indeed alarming. While the total number of workers in the region increased from 2,409 to 2,766 in that decade, the non-workers increased from 1,916 to 2,603. The reason can be attributed primarily to the fact that the establishment of the university, and thus the increased numbers of student tenants, made

TABLE 12.2: VITAL STATISTICS OF IRONGMARA (IN PERSONS)

	1991	2001	Growth rate
1. Population (2 + 3)	7,111	8,365	0.176
2. Male	3,658	4,303	
3. Female	3,453	4,062	
4. Sex Ratio	1,053: 1,000	1,059: 1,000	
5. Decadal variation	17%	15%	
6. Number of households	740	860	0.162
7. Literacy (8 + 9)	1,422	2,258	0.588
8. Male literacy	799	1,189	0.488
9. Female literacy	623	1,069	0.716
10. Total number of non-workers	1,916	2,603	0.358
11. Total workers (12 + 13 + 14)	2,409	2,766	0.148
12. Main workers	1,003	1,199	
13. Marginal workers	913	1,004	
14. Workers in cultivation	493	563	

Sources: Census Reports (1991, 2001), Govt. of India; and Irongmara Gram Panchayat, Gram Panchayat Data, 2001.

the people of Irongmara more 'idle' as they now had an easier way to earn money by renting out their premises to students.

ANALYSIS OF SAMPLE SURVEY: PRIMARY DATA (TABULAR ANALYSIS)

The study of primary data also substantiates the socio-economic transformation Irongmara experienced with the setting up of Assam University, Silchar. Forty student respondents were randomly chosen to answer same questions. The basic findings are listed below:

- Twenty-four of the forty students are very close or close to their landlords. They even share emotions. Students help their landlords and vice versa. Nineteen of these twenty-four students are very close to their landlords; the balance five are just close.
- Sixteen students have a formal relationship with their landlord; they keep their distance.
- Twenty-five students feel that they have some sort of influence on the locals, their attitude, and the way they think, act and behave.
- Fifteen others do not think they have any influence on the locals.
- Thirty-one students feel Assam University is a blessing for Irongmara.
- Three feel Assam University, Silchar, is a curse, socially for Irongmara. They argue that juvenile delinquent activities have increased and this has distorted the simplicity of the place.
- Six students feel Assam University, Silchar, is both a curse and a blessing. It is an economic blessing but a social curse.
- It is important to note the thirty-one students favouring Assam University, Silchar as a blessing took only economic factors into account, while other 9 (6 + 3) who defined it as a social curse included sociocultural factors as well.

TABLE 12.3: RELATIONSHIP OF STUDENTS WITH THEIR LANDLORDS

Very close	19
Close	05
Formal	16
Total	40

Source: Tabulated results of primary survey by author conducted during March/April 2006.

TABLE 12.4: STUDENTS' PERCEPTION OF THEIR INFLUENCE ON LOCAL ATTITUDES

Have some influence	25
Do not have any influence	15
Total	40

Source: Tabulated results of primary survey by author conducted during March/April 2006.

TABLE 12.5: STUDENTS' PERCEPTION OF ASSAM UNIVERSITY, SILCHAR'S, INFLUENCE ON IRONGMARA

Blessing	31
Curse	03
Both	06
Total	40

Source: Tabulated results of primary survey by author conducted during March/April 2006.

The sample survey of the 40 local respondents has some interesting observations as well. The highlights of the survey are listed below:

- All forty of them know the name of Assam University.
- Three of the forty families have family members studying in the Assam University.
- All forty families have students as tenants in their houses.
- All forty of the forty respondents are of the opinion that Assam University is an economic blessing for Irongmara.
- Twenty-two respondents feel that Assam University, Silchar, is a social curse.

Only fourteen of the forty respondents think that the students are not a social hindrance for Irongmara's local people.

- However, almost fourteen out of the forty respondents believe that students are a social blessing for the place.
- Ten of the forty respondents feel that keeping students as tenants generates positive externalities. They find a positive influence in their children's education due to the students' presence.

It is important to note that the Assam University and the Assam University students have organized a number of health camps, awareness campaigns, literacy campaigns and women's empowerment campaign in Irongmara. Besides, students of different streams have worked on different projects relating to Irongmara. A substantial amount of literature about the place is now available and some statistics have been computed to bring the area into focus. The Social Work Department of Assam University, Silchar, is a frontrunner in all sorts of campaigns and studies in and about Irongmara. Associations like the University Students' Association of Irongmara (USAI) and Down to Earth Association (DEA) try to promote socio-cultural and sports-related activities by creating events like USAI SOCIAL WEEK and other health and literacy campaigns. The DEA tries to identify and render service to children with disabilities, provide vocational training for unemployed women and organize workshops on drug abuse and alcoholism in the locality.

So as is evident from the earlier discussions and statements, both positive and negative externalities are being generated by the students living in Irongmara. A macro assessment would show that the negative externalities from the students are more than the positive externalities, when one takes into account social indicators. But one thing is certain: AUS is the economic 'pace-maker' of Irongmara's heart.

TABLE 12.6: ATTITUDE OF LOCALS TOWARDS AUS

Social Blessing	14
Social Curse	26
Total	40

Source: Tabulated results of primary survey by author conducted during March/April 2006.

TABLE 12.7: ARE STUDENTS HELPING THE EDUCATION OF THEIR LANDLORD CHILDREN?

Yes	10
No	26
Does not arise	04
Total	40

Source: Tabulated results of primary survey by author conducted during March/April 2006.

The problem with the study area was the huge sociological constraint that bind any development process and retards it. A 'Big Push' in the social sector through a sociocultural and intellectual

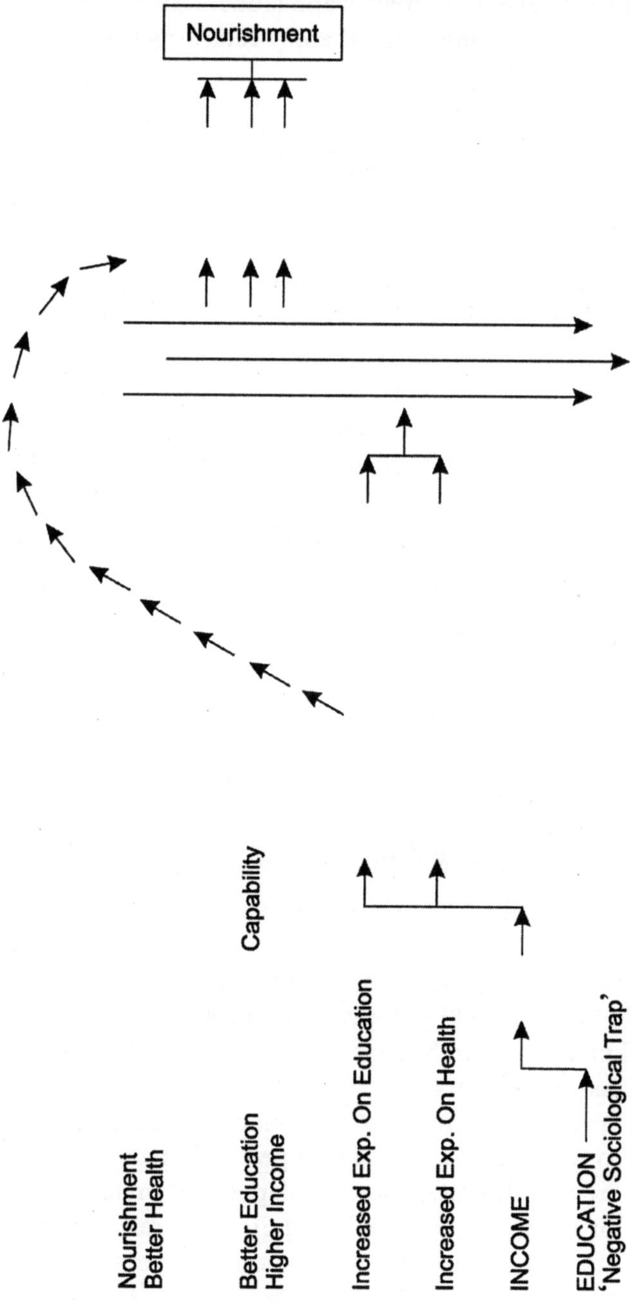

Fig. 12.1: Stairways to an Educated and Healthy Society
Sociological Big Push

revolution is necessary to transform increased expenditure on health and education into capability nourishment. The negative sociological factors act like a 'snake' in a 'snakes and ladders' game and try to pull down the development indicators, thereby retarding the development process as shown in Figure 12.1

Efforts must be made to create the sociological big push so as to jump to the capability nourishment phase directly without falling into the negative sociological trap. Once the process is out of the trap there is no looking back. The combined effect of better health and education will lead to capability nourishment and the ability to choose and make better use of an opportunity. As A.K. Sen[11] opines, health and education are two sources of freedom over tyranny and poverty (capability deprivation). A person's ability to make use of an economic opportunity that comes his/her way increases with the increase in the level of education and health care he/she receives. Sen defined freedom as expansion of choice and increased set of alternate value judgments. Therefore, as the freedom of all people expands, so does the development (as shown in Fig. 12.2).

Capability Development Nourishment → Ablity to make use of Opportunities better → Increased freedom & choice →

Fig. 12.2

CONCLUSION

Findings from the Secondary Data

1. Irongmara is a village inhabited by Bengali and Hindi speaking people.
2. It is divided into 10 groups and stretches across 10 sq km. It has a population over 10,000 plus presently (2006).
3. It is 21 km away from Silchar and is considered to be a satellite town of Assam University.
4. The birth of the University of Assam, Silchar, has given an identity to this unknown, undeveloped and uncared for village.
5. People here are illiterate, poor and dependent on agriculture.
6. The majority of the people living in the area are temporary inhabitants and comprise students and workers of the Assam University.

Findings from Primary Data

1. Assam University has a huge economic influence on Irongmara's socio-economic transition.
2. Most of the permanently settled people are now totally dependent on income generated by way of tenancy rent from students.
3. Positive educational externalities are generated by some students living there.
4. Some students also generate negative sociological externalities through drinking, quarreling amongst themselves and with the local people, etc.
5. The negative sociological externalities are more pronounced than the positive educational externality. This results in social degradation.
6. With a view to earn easy money, a section of the local businessmen also encourage the sale of liquor by opening new outlets.
7. Most of the people of Irongmara do not object to the social degradation as long as the money comes in. They tend to compromise social degradation with earning money.

Suggestions

1. Students of this university seem to be confined within their course curriculum. Academics is important but it is not everything. A greater widening of the thought process is required. Students of the university should start expanding their knowledge and outlook base beyond academics and start thinking beyond better grades and higher marks. This is possibly the main reason why the problems exist. The most frustrating fact is that it all boils down to the system framed by the university authorities that kills all creativity and any inquisitiveness and forces everyone to become stereotyped, programmed 'marks-addicts'.
2. Students should engage themselves in social activities through associations like the DEA—Down to Earth Association and USAI—the University Students' Association of Irongmara and organize cultural and sports-related activities to keep themselves active (and in the process stay away from delinquent activities and enhance a feeling of oneness).
3. The university authorities must modify its curricular so that cultural ethos and values can be introduced. They should make provisions to impart value education to the students, apart from academic education. No doubt a university should produce

technocrats, social scientists and professionals, but its foremost goal should be to create 'true human beings'.

4. In recent times, the role of community participation in the process of inculcating values in the minds of students has become a recognized fact. As such, community-oriented projects must be taken up in the Irongmara locality so that students can participate in them and this will help them in inculcating moral values.
5. 'Self-realization' on the part of the students and locals is required. A sense of self-esteem must develop among the students. Good education tends to inculcate good behaviour in human beings, and also a sense of responsibility. It is expected that university students act in a manner which creates a good environment in the locality.

The basic sociological and cultural set-up of Irongmara, historically, was never strong. People were always illiterate and hardly refined. Students, who came here, took this opportunity to exercise freedom and do whatever they liked. This was possibly because the environment of Irongmara was conducive for them to carry out their delinquent activities. Students mean money. So there was no one to protest initially. But gradually the atrocities reached a maximum and the locals started speaking out. Strange as it may seem, many locals exhibit the same behaviour as the students. Many, not all. Of course, the locals have the excuse of 'illiteracy'!

NOTES

1. S. Dass, *Spotlight on Assam*, Maharastra: Premier Book Service, 1980.
2. P.R. Bhattacharjee, 'Economic Backwardness of North Eastern Region in the light of the Theories of Underdevelopment', in P. Baisya (ed.), *Development Issues of N.E. India*, Gauhati: Lawyer's Book Stall, 1977.
3. Ibid.
4. See *http://assamuniversity.nic.in/au_objective.htm*.
5. Theodore W. Schultz, *Investment in Human Capital: The Role of Education and of Research*, New York: Free Press, 1971; Selma J. Mushkin, *Economics of Higher Education*, Washington D.C.: U.S. Govt. Print. Off., 1962.
6. Amartya K. Sen, *Development as Freedom*, Knopf Publishing Group, 2000.
7. Amartya K. Sen and Jean Drèze, *India—Economic Development & Social Opportunity*, Delhi: Oxford University Press, 1995.
8. Ibid.
9. Gunnar Myrdal, *Asian Drama—An Inquiry into the Poverty of Nations*, Delhi: Kalyani Publishers, 1968.
10. Gunnar Myrdal, *Economic Theory & Underdeveloped Region*, London: Duckworth, 1957.
11. Sen and Drèze, op. cit.

13

National Identity in a Frontier Area: The Case of Eastern Kazakhstan

YULIA GUZHVENKO

Post-Soviet Central Asia is a multiethnic region, and has experienced ethnic tensions. This is relevant to Eastern Kazakhstan, large border area between Turkic and Slavonic civilization enclaves, which is populated by two main ethnic groups—Kazakhs and Russians. In terms of international and national laws, this is indisputably the territory of Kazakhstan, but certain groups among ethnic Russians as well Russian-speaking minorities still have expectations that it may be separated and joined to Russia.[1] The purpose of this essay is to analyse from the historical and demographic points of view the ethnic structure and mutual attitudes of the main national groups in Eastern Kazakhstan: basically this is a representative sample of the growing ethnic tensions in the post-Soviet era.

According to archival sources, Kazakhs and Russians had interacted on this territory since eighteenth century. It is also well known that local Kazakh clans officially joined Russia, that is, adopted Russian authority in the nineteenth century. In early Soviet times (1920–5), this area was divided politically and administratively—Eastern Kazakhstan constituted the northern belt of the Kazakh ASSR, the newly established national unit later upgraded to a full-formatted 'union republic'. The demarcation of Middle Asia by Bolshevik authorities in the 1920s caused serious problems, which became explicit after independence in the early 1990s. This phenomenon may be illustrated by East Kazakhstan developments. The initial schemes of administrative border demarcation by Sibrevkom proposed that Semipalatinsk oblast (province), Atbasar and Akmola districts be attached to Kazakhstan because Kazakhs were in ethnic majority. But these territories also contained considerable Russian enclaves. Sources testify that the Soviet authorities had considered the option of redistributing the above-mentioned territories to RSFSR.[2] However, the key decree 'About formation of Kirghiz Soviet Socialist Republic'[3] didn't take into account the factor of a sizeable Russian population in the north-east part of Kazakhstan.

As for the current situation in the area under study, the demographic analysis shows a disproportion of allocation of Kazakhs and Russians. Russians are still numerically dominant but they have progressively met with social and political challenges as a non-titular nation. The Stalinist politics of deportation of entire ethnic groups during the Great Patriotic War, the industrialization of Central Asian borderlands as well the virgin soil campaign were the reasons for migration to Eastern Kazakhstan from European Russia and Siberia between the 1930s and 1950s. As a result of ethnic migration to Eastern Kazakhstan since 1926 till 1970, the Russian population increased two and a half times, while the Kazakhs decreased by more than seven and a half times because of negative natural and migration growth.[4] But the situation changed in late Soviet times, when the number of the population had primarily depended from natural growth. Thus, in 1970–9, the Kazakh population increased from 32.6 to 38.7 per cent in Eastern Kazakhstan. At the same time the number of non-titular nations (particular the Russians) progressively decreased.[5] Nevertheless, according to the 1989 census, the number of Kazakhs in Eastern Kazakhstan was 38.7 per cent, compared to the Russians at 51.6 per cent. One may say that Eastern Kazakhstan was actually the 'Russian' region inside Kazakhstan.

During Soviet times an attempt was made to create a unique Soviet nation, wiping away borders between different ethnics such as the Russians and the Kazakhs. Late-Soviet and post-Soviet projects strengthened the tendency to exalt titular ethnic groups. This was the cause of ethnic tension, especially in regions with a considerable Russian population. Eastern Kazakhstan is considered such a region. The break-up of the Soviet Union brought ethnic conflicts between Kazakhs and Russians in Eastern Kazakhstan to the forefront. The politics of the new Kazakhstan leadership led to the exaltation of the titular ethnic group, the Kazakhs. It was the Kazakh language that was recognized as the official state language, and this when the Russian-speakers were the major ethnic group in the eastern areas of new sovereign state. The reaction of the Russian-speakers to this language discrimination was mass migration from this area to Russia's border regions, such as the Altai province. Fortunately, this tendency is declining due to the balanced politics of the Kazakh as well the Russian authorities in the last several years. The formation of a new network of inter-state/inter-regional cooperation ('Altai—our common home') was one of the contributing factors in this mutual rapprochement, which has had an impact on ethnic attitudes as well.

As for some general migration/demographic trends, the number of the population in Eastern Kazakhstan has considerably decreased (see Table 13.1).

In 1997 Eastern Kazakhstan was reconfigured administratively to include Semipalatinsk oblast. This fact had influence on the ethnic and demographic situation: in Semipalatinsk oblast in 1993, the ethnic majority were the Kazakhs at 55.6 per cent, while the Russians were the ethnic minority at 34.5 per cent. By this time the Russians were the majority in Eastern Kazakhstan at 64.2 per cent, while the Kazakhs constituted only 29.1 per cent of the population.[6] After the uniting of 'Russian' Eastern Kazakhstan and Semipalatinsk oblast the correlation of the Kazakhs and the Russians became more or less comparable.

Currently the migration of the Russian-speakers from Eastern Kazakhstan has stabilized. The data of the census of 1999 shows that in Eastern Kazakhstan the Kazakhs accounted for 48.5 per cent of the population and the Russians 45.4 per cent.[7] This means that there is powerful potential for the outward migration of Russian-speakers from Eastern Kazakhstan, a point which should be carefully explored and taken into account by officials of both (Russian and Kazakh) sides from the academic, managerial, social, etc., points of view. At the

TABLE 13.1: DYNAMICS OF POPULATION IN EASTERN KAZAKHSTAN

Year	Number of population (at the beginning of year in thousand)	General growth in %	Natural growth in %	Migration growth in %
1994	1753.2	-19.5	7.9	-27.4
1995	1685.0	-68.2	6.0	-74.2
1996	1683.3	-46.7	1.6	-48.3
1997	1600.2	-38.1	-0.3	-37.8
1998	1562.3	-37.9	-2.0	-35.9
1999	1532.9	-29.4	-1.8	-27.6
2000	1510.8	-16.1	-1.8	-14.3
2001	1499.0	-17.8	-1.9	-15.9
2002	1482.4	-16.6	-1.6	-14.7
2003	1466.0	-16.4	-1.2	-15.0

Source: *Statistical Bulletin* 2, no. 3 (Ust-Kamenogorsk, 2003), pp. 99, 105.

beginning of 2005 the Kazakh population increased to 51.8 per cent while the Russians decreased to 43 per cent.[8] This however hardly changes the ethnic profile of this region where ethnic Russians were predominant (see Table 13.2).

In sovereign Kazakhstan, like in other former Soviet republics, the status of Russians, who earlier were considered as 'senior brother', changed. The post-Soviet Kazakhstani community has new demands, namely, proficiency in the Kazakh language.

The politics of exaltation of Kazakhs is manifested in different spheres of public life. Kazakhstan's community: education increased the number of Kazakh students who could study at universities. In the sphere of labour, the representatives of authority are Kazakhs; the Russians work in industry. Russian-speakers cannot hope for a career growth without being proficient in the Kazakh language. These facts were and are the cause of ethnic tensions inside Kazakhstan, especially Eastern Kazakhstan. One may say that existing Kazakh identity includes the following aspects: Islam, Turkic-ness, nomad legacy and attachment to land.

First of all, the idea about national identity is connected with the linguistic situation in Kazakhstan. The development of sovereign Kazakhstan is evidence that the inculcation of the state language into the entire of sphere of public life (the most important is state proceedings) is a more difficult process then was anticipated in the beginning. In Soviet times, a whole generation of people who are Kazakhs grew up, and they worked in state government institutions, but these Kazakhs were unable to prepare documentation in the native language. The status of the Kazakh language was strengthened by 'Laws about languages in Republic of Kazakhstan' 1989, 1997, when it was recognized as an official language. On the other hand, the Russian language was designated as the 'language of interethnic communication'. Russian is used in state agencies, etc., but the Republic of Kazakhstan's leadership developed the goal to introduce Kazakh as the only language in official documentation. Consciousness of this fact in the mid-1990s, and discussions by the mass media[9] prompted the leadership of the republic to take concrete steps in this direction. In 1994 the State committee accomplished the process of translating Russian terms into Kazakh (terminological commission). Thereafter new dictionaries, textbooks and study aids for interpreters were issued. The terminological commission systematically corrected earlier confirmed terms, which were published in 'Kazakhstan truth'. The abundance of new terms, editing dictionaries and changes in the structure of the language within a short time have ensured that

TABLE 13.2: NATIONAL COMPOSITION OF SEMIPALATINSK AND EASTERN KAZAKHSTAN PROVINCES WITHIN CENSUSES 1939, 1959, 1970, 1979, 1989, 1999 (%)

Census	Semipalatinsk province					Eastern Kazakhstan				
	Russians	Kazakhs	Tatars	Ukrainians	Germans	Russians	Kazakhs	Tatars	Ukrainians	Germans
1939	49.0	36.0	3.1	7.6	4.4	68.3	21.9	1.0	5.1	4.4
1959	45.0	35.0	2.9	3.3	8.2	70.9	18.9	1.1	2.3	3.1
1970	40.9	43.6	2.6	2.6	6.6	69.5	23.2	1.0	2.0	2.6
1979	39.1	47.9	2.4	2.5	5.7	67.7	25.4	1.0	1.9	2.4
1989	36.0	51.9	2.3	2.3	5.3	65.9	27.2	1.0	1.7	2.4
	United Eastern Kazakhstan Province									
1999	45.4	48.5		1.1	2.1					
2005	43.0	51.8								

Sources: The Archives of Contemporary History of Eastern Kazakhstan Province. F.P-615, Op. 2, D. 1404; Alekseenko A.N., *The Nations of Eastern Kazakhstan*, Ust-Kamenogorsk, 1994, p. 9; *Germans in Kazakhstan in the End of XIX-XX* (based on the datas censuses 1897-1999), Ust-Kamenogorsk, 2002; The Archives of Contemporary History of Eastern Kazakhstan Province, F.P-615, Op. 2, D. 1430; Russian State Archives of Economy, F. 1562, Op. 336, D. 6279, pp. 220–4; Russian State Archives Economy, F. 1562, Op. 336, D. 6228, p. 144; Monitoring of the Ethnic and Religious Situation in Eastern Kazakhstan Province//*www.analitik.kz/modules.php?name=News&file=print&sid=65* (last visited 28 June 2006).

the classical (official) Kazakh language is available for the elite. The evidence from everyday occurrences testify to the fact that this is not always comprehensible to the mass of the Kazakhs and causes difficulties when used in paperwork, written speech and public life. The role of intermediary, as before, is played by the Russian language.

In Eastern Kazakhstan the state language, according to the 1999 census, is spoken by 55.4 per cent of the population. In the central and northern areas of Kazakhstan there exists a strong Russian ethnic component (Akmolinskaya oblast: 43.6 per cent, Karagandinskaya oblast: 46.4 per cent, Kostanayskaya oblast: 39.3 per cent, Pavlodarskaya oblast: 46.4 per cent, North Kazakhstan: 36.4 per cent). In ethnolinguistic terms, the East Kazakhstan area 'was divided' into two regions: Semipalatinsk, with the Kazakh language in the predominant position and strictly Eastern Kazakhstan (Rudny Altai) or Ust-Kamenogorsk. Regionalism in Eastern Kazakhstan reveals itself in the political decisions of the state on the language question.

The linguistic processes in Semipalatinsk region and Semipalatinsk were analysed by the Centre of the Sociological Monitoring and Social Prediction of Semipalatinsk State University named after Shakarim. A majority of the Kazakh respondents in 2005–6 showed Russian as their second language, which they spoke perfectly (79.1 per cent of the respondents).[10] The Kazakhs were unhappy that 78 per cent of their compatriots had not yet learnt Kazakh. The Russians realize the necessity of a state language, but obstacles remain. B. Anderson has noted that while it is possible to adopt each language, it's learning requires time and energy to the extent that the availability of the language is limited.

Sociological explorations have revealed that language contradictions reveal themselves in conflict situations in everyday life. As many 58.5 per cent of the respondents have noted that they happened to face situations, when ignorance of Kazakh or Russian was the reason for the conflicts.[11] In the 1990s, the number of schools with Kazakh as the medium of instruction grew, but at the beginning of 2000, in Kazakhstan and in Eastern Kazakhstan an inverse trend was noted. For instance, in 2002 57 mixed language schools opened.[12] These facts are indicative of the change in the priority in education in Kazakhstan. In the first post-Soviet decade Kazakhstan understood that economic development and the participation of the state in global processes required universal education, which, to a great extent, corresponded to education in the Russian language. Spreading the national system of education without knowledge of other languages limits the future of young specialists. It is therefore unlikely that the Kazakh language will be able to replace Russian in the cultural, educational and technical spaces and as the language of the daily press and mass media in the next 20–30 years.

In pre-school institutions, education in the state language is not widespread. This is because in Eastern Kazakhstan as a whole, the network of pre-school institutions is limited. There are only 69 kindergartens, and only 5 of them offer education and upbringing in the Kazakh language.[13] In several reports about operating the state language in Eastern Kazakhstan, it was noted that teachers of the state language with suitable qualifications are not available. By 2003, the position had improved and only 10.3 per cent of teachers did not have suitable qualification.[14] As the practice indicates, education in universities and professional colleges is built on the principle of division in two languages: Kazakh and Russian. An interview with an employee in the education system[15] revealed that teaching in the Kazakh language in social professions is more successful. The study of technical disciplines in the Kazakh language causes more difficulties, since it requires a special terminology. This is proved by the fact that only 22 per cent of students in technical universities get education in the state language.[16] In spite of these difficulties, in one of the leading universities in Eastern Kazakhstan, the State Technical University named after Serikbaev, 29 professions were submitted for instruction in the state language. Therefore, it is necessary to encourage students to complete for the title of 'the connoisseur of Kazakh language', with an award from the governor of Eastern Kazakhstan. Such competitions should also be instituted in separate universities of the region and republics.[17]

Everyday life also becomes the object of ethnolinguistic reform. At the beginning of 2000, a step-by-step inculcation of the state language ensured that all official and accountable documentation was in the Kazakh and Russian to get the people used to the paperwork and psychologically prepare them for the change. In spite of the fact that there is a strengthening of the ethnolinguistic construction on a national basis in the region, the sociological research done by the analytical centre Dana shows that the majority of the population in Eastern Kazakhstan has a negative attitude towards the national policies designed and pursued by the local and central governments, as they openly discriminate against Russian-speakers and violate their cultural and even human rights.

In the region, respondents not studying the Kazakh language

prevail over respondents who are. The highest percentage of respondents leaving the republic was in Eastern Kazakhstan (30 per cent), followed by Northern Kazakhstan (21.6 per cent) and Astana (23.9 per cent). Among the ethnic groups the potential to migrate was highest among the Germans (35.5 per cent), followed by Russians (29.9 per cent), the Ukrainians (19.2 per cent) and the Koreans (11.8 per cent).[18] Mass meetings, demonstrations and strikes were highest in Astana (4.3 per cent), Eastern Kazakhstan (1.7 per cent), Northern Kazakhstan (1.4 per cent).[19] The only point is when to start implementing the procedures in the different regions, cities, settlements. For example, in Semipalatinsk, the deadline was July 2007, in Ust-Kamenogorsk it was postponed to the middle of 2008. The reason is that Semipalatinsk is primarily a Kazakh city by population (Kazakhs accounts for 51.1 per cent and Russians 39.9 per cent) in comparison to Ust-Kamenogorsk, where Russians prevail ethnically (74.3 per cent, Kazakhs 19.4 per cent).[20] This case study revealed that the Russians in Semipalatinsk, are more proficient in the Kazakh language (and this is encouraged by the government) than those in Ust-Kamenogorsk or other Russian-dominated urban centres of Eastern Kazakhstan. The Kazakh leaders understand the specifics of the north-eastern regions and even of regional Eastern Kazakhstan, so the timeframe for the implementation of the state programme for the adoption of the Kazakh language in official paperwork differs within the region.

Awareness among the population of Ust-Kamenogorsk about the postponement of deadline to introduce Kazakh as the only language in official documentation from 2008 to 2010 is low. In a sociological study ordered by the government of Eastern Kazakhstan, to guage the level of awareness of the deadline, 55 per cent of the respondents said that they were hearing of it for the first time, 18 per cent knew about the deadline, 11 per cent had heard and approved of the new periods and 16 per cent had no information.[21] The report by Eastern Kazakhstan's government noted the need to develop a system of notification of the population about the deadline for the translation of the paperwork into the state language before 2008, since the lack of awareness among the people was leading to fresh outmigration. There was every need to inform people of the region about the decree on Kazakh as state language. Such information should be received by population proportionally.[22]

A survey of the ethnolinguistic characteristics of the main town of Eastern Kazakhstan, Ust-Kamenogorsk, allowed for the diversion of the population into several groups ranging from those with a desire to learn the state language to those who were unwilling to. Of those who participated in the survey, 13 per cent knew the language well, 8 per cent were seriously working towards learning it, 6 per cent intended to learn it and 9 per cent wished to learn the state language. Of the latter, 3 per cent wanted to learn the language but were prevented by the lack of qualified staff. Only 7 per cent of the respondents felt that there was no need to know the Kazakh language.

The high percentage of people who refused to answer is indicative of the doubts of the townspeople about the study of the state language.[23] Unwillingness among the middle-aged and elderly to study the state language is conditioned by the fact that representatives of these groups already occupy a certain social niche and mastered their profession in a period when knowledge of the language was not a priority. This also confirms the thesis of B. Anderson that each language is closed and requires time for its detailed mastering.[24] The younger generation, realizing the market situation and growing up in post-Soviet Kazakhstan, is more mobile and were interested in studying the state language.

At the same time, the conditions under which the youth in the age group of 18–29 years would be willing to remain in Kazakhstan included reinstatement of Russian as the state language, elimination of the disadvantageous ecological situation and a solution to the housing problem. Residents in the age group of 30–9 years outlined similar conditions for remaining in Kazakhstan. For people in the age group of 50–9 years, the main condition for further residence in Kazakhstan was increasing well-being and a solution to the ecological problems. For those of retirement age (60 and older), the important issues were well-being, improvement in the ecological situation in the city and equal rights for all ethnic groups.[25]

The present data shows that in Ust-Kamenogorsk, as long as ethnic attitudes are in conflict a latent disposition towards migration will exist. The analytical reports of the sociological research, which was conducted by the government of Eastern Kazakhstan, are indicative of the fact that the main source of the supposed conflict is the language policy, discontent of the population with regard to ethnic issues and the absence of Russian as the state language. The special situation in urban Ust-Kamenogorsk, where the majority of the population is Russian, can obstruct the institution of Kazakh as the state language. Having educated staff with knowledge of the Kazakh language in all state structures of the region and in Ust-Kamenogorsk is not sufficient. There is the realization that such a trend can obstruct the operation of the state structures.[26]

In 1990, the Kazakh language acquired an exalted status with the introduction of new terms and translations. The Kazakh language began to take the form that could correspond to the state language. Actions were organized in 1990 to prepare qualified staff to teach the Kazakh language. As a result, at the beginning of 2000 there was a phased introduction of the language in the paperwork and in public life. On the whole, the language policy and its implementation by the government within the framework of the given programme differ in Semipalatinsk and in Ust-Kamenogorsk. The difference is due to their ethnic specificities. In particular, there is a more positive attitude towards the programme in the Semipalatinsk subregion, where Kazakhs dominate, while among the Russian-speakers in Ust-Kamenogorsk there remain a host of problems such as unwillingness to study the state language and greater awareness among the population about the postponement of the deadline the translation of the paperwork into Kazakh.

The exalted status and position of the state language in Eastern Kazakhstan is an undoubted fact but it has an unstable base. This revealed itself in the drop in the demand for education in national schools at the beginning of 2000. There is also a preference among the population to send their children to mixed Kazakh–Russian schools. Certain problems exist in using the state language in the medical and technical professions. Difficulties have also arisen because Kazakh as state language had to incorporate Kazakh dialects or unify new forms. The uneasiness of the authorities in the development of the ethnolinguistic processes in the region is revealed in the constant sociological research of the disposition of the population in Eastern Kazakhstan. Although the, language policy stabilized at the beginning of 2000, at the same time there is the realization that it can intensify the uneasy relations between Russian-speakers and the titular ethnic group, particularly in Eastern Kazakhstan where there is a significant quota of Russian-speakers.

The problems pertaining to ethnic attitudes in the former Soviet area were highlighted after the break up of the USSR and the proclamation of the independence by the former union republic. The main reason for the change was a change in the status of the titular group and the Russian population, and, as a whole, Russian culture and language and the shaping of new state identities. Kazakhstan is a multinational state and thus it is not easy to prevent ethnic conflicts here. However, the local communities and government are striving to prevent ethnic conflict. One of major peacekeeping bodies is the Kazakhstan Assembly of Nations, which has asked for the preservation of all minor languages and traditions of all ethnic groups settled in Kazakhstan.

Ethnic attitude is a type of interaction of ethnic groups in different spheres—politics, culture, economy, everyday life and so on.[27] Ethnic interactions are an indicator of the image of the relations in society in different spheres of public life. In the first half of 1990s, ethnic attitudes in Eastern Kazakhstan were not a subject of special research in view of the intensification of ethnic tensions. Additionally, in view of the crisis in the economic sector all material expenses were directed on the re-animation of production. Kazakhstan society did not spend its resources on social necessities.

The press and interviews remain the main source of data on ethnic interactions in the first half of the 1990s, when flashes of nationalism in Semipalatinsk and Eastern Kazakhstan region were not an infrequent phenomenon. Reports about this in the press[28] and the analytical findings of experts,[29] indicate that the initiative of the young, independent state in the sphere of language was perceived negatively and resulted in migration from the region. In other words, the changed status of the non-titular ethnic groups and their social-economic position resulted in a significant deterioration in the position all Russian-speakers. The tension between the ethnic groups was expressed in everyday life, although overall the situation remained comparatively calm.

At the beginning of 2000, with increased economic stabilization in the region there was increased interest in social and national process. In that year questions about ethnic attitudes in Semipalatinsk sub-region as a whole, but in Semipalatinsk in particular, were regularly traced and studied by the Centre of Social Monitoring and Social Prediction of Semipalatinsk State University, named after Shakarim, under the direction of Professor A.P. Konovalov.[30] Similar studies were conducted in Ust-Kamenogorsk on the ethnic and religious situation in the city but these were intended for internal use by the government and are not available.

This study analyses the ethnic attitudes of the urban territories of Eastern Kazakhstan from the position of the region as a separate zone according to ethnic majority. For instance, the regions with a majority of Kazakhs are Abayskiy 98.6 per cent; Ayagozskiy 92 per cent; Beskaragayskiy 62.7 per cent; Zharminskiy 86.8 per cent; Zaysanskiy 92.4 per cent; Katon-Karagayskiy 77.5 per cent; Kokpektinskiy 77.2 per cent; Kurchumskiy 89.3 per cent; Tarbagatayskiy 98.3 per cent; Ulanskiy 62 per cent; Urdzharskiy 87.4 per cent.[31] Regions with a predominance of Russians are Borodulihinskiy 56.01 per cent; Glubokovskiy 74.1 per cent; Zyryanovskiy 79.1 per cent; Shemonaihinskiy 82.3 per cent.[32] The small towns of Eastern Kazakhstan are not an exception: 34.7 per cent Kazakhs and 57.6 per cent Russians live in Kurchatov; in Ridder 8.3 per cent are Kazakhs and 86.3 per cent Russian.[33] Increased migration flows of the rural population from southern depressed zone of the region to the urban north have transformed the ethnic structure of urban territory and resulted in a breakdown of socialcultural, economic and emotional links.

The data in Table 13.3 is witness to the fact that in the ethnic composition, the prevalence of the Kazakh population is fixed only in Semipalatinsk—59.6 per cent—while in Ust-Kamenogorsk and other towns of the region, Russians are in the majority (70.5 per cent). Such ethnic distribution has a significant influence on the socio-economic and ethno-political stability of urban territories and the region as a whole.

Sociological studies by the Centre of Social Monitoring and Social Prediction Semipalatinsk State University show that ethnic attitudes are more favourably portrayed among Semipalatinsk's Kazakhs. In 2004–5, only 65 per cent of Russians acknowledged ethnic attitudes as being favourable.[34] No less interesting is the data about the influence of ethnic tradition. As of 2006, only 87.2 per cent of Kazakh respondents in Semipalatinsk subregion referred to themselves as Muslim, while 12.8 per cent of Kazakhs professed Christianity. In the same period, however, 82.8 per cent of Russians said they were Christians, while 17.2 per cent of them chose Islam.[35] In the opinion of the author, the present data is indicative of the close ethnic interaction in Semipalatinsk: ethnic marriages and mixed family and the influence of representatives of ethnic groups on each other. On the other hand, individual field studies by the present author prove that quite often Russians are identified as Tatars who confess to Islam, and the Koreans consider themselves to be Russians, but profess to Islam.[36] Only a small part of the representatives expressed suspicions of ethnic encirclement. Russian respondents were well

TABLE 13.3: ETHNIC COMPOSITION OF URBAN TERRITORIES OF EASTERN KAZAKHSTAN (BEGINNING 2006)[37] (%)

Ethnic groups	Ust-Kamenogorsk	Semipalatinsk	Ridder	Kurchatov
Kazakhs	23.8	59.6	8.3	34.7
Russians	70.5	3.3	86.6	57.6

Source: Eastern Kazakhstan in Numerals 2006. Ust-Kamenogorsk, 2006, p. 29.

disposed towards Kazakhs and their cultural traditions.[38] But at the same time, the introduction of the state language was perceived by the Russian population as harmful to their national interest and led to their migration.

The main reason for the migration remains the reinforcement of the position of the state language.[39] Therefore, language problems vastly influence the sociocultural, and ethnic processes in the region. The main problem in the sphere of ethnic interactions remains, as before, the language problem—the introduction of Kazakh as state language and an insufficient legal base of support for the Russians. The Russian-speaking population is the main target of these developments: ill-considered measures by the government; prejudices by titular groups in the labour market; education and law. The protest of the Russian-speaking population is expressed in passive ways such as migration. Uncontrolled movements may heavily damage the socio-economic structure of both Russian and Kazakh regions and undermine the mutual confidence between the national groups, which constitute the friendliest folks within the Eurasian landmass.

In conclusion, one may suggest that the prospects of conflict resolution in Eastern Kazakhstan are still uncertain: they will depend on the political will of both sides involved (their leadership and communities, etc.); further development of a transitional economy, inter-regional cooperation, etc. The basis of the progress in this direction would be the idea of a Eurasian common ground—the historical and cultural similarities between Russians and Kazakhs, both eminent nations of the Central Asian space.

NOTES

1. These rumors were proved by the present author while doing fieldwork in Ust-Kamenogorsk in October 2003. For similar attitudes, see also A.N. Alekseenko, *Frontier Migration*, Moscow: Uralsk, 2002, p. 187.
2. *Altai Province—Kazakhstan 1917–1925: History of Administrative and State Demarcation*, Barnaul, 2001, pp. 86–7.
3. Ibid., p. 143.
4. Alekseenko, *Frontier Migration*, p. 189; 'Demographic Indigenization in Kazakhstan—A Station-Temporal Analysis', *The Journal of Central Asian Studies* 11, no. 1, 2000, p. 50.
5. Ibid.
6. 'Demographic indigenization in Kazakhstan', p. 52.
7. *Development of Eastern Kazakhstan 1998-2002*, Ust-Kamenogorsk, 2003, p. 24.
8. 'Review of Ethnic and Religious situation in Eastern Kazakhstan', available at *www.analitik.kz/modules.php?name=News&file=print&sid=65* (accessed on 28 June 2006).

9. A.I. Nurpesbekova, 'Why We do not Know Our Self-Language?', *Kazakhstan Truth*, 26 February 2000.
10. Ibid., p. 24.
11. Ibid., p. 26.
12. Sh. Azmuhambetov, 'State Language in the Age of Globalization', *Rudny Altai*, 15 February 2003.
13. *Information About Eastern Kazakhstan*, materials of akimat (government), Eastern Kazakhstan.
14. Azmuhambetov, 'State Language in the Age of Globalization'.
15. Fieldwork of author, Semipalatinsk, October–November 2006.
16. B. Zhumagulov, 'State Language and Official Paperwork', *Rudny Altai*, 20 May 2003.
17. Azmuhambetov, 'State Language in the Age of Globalization'.
18. B.B. Abdygaliev, *Politizatsiya Etnichnosti: Protsessy, Mekhanizmy, Posledstviya* (Political Ethnicity: Processes, Mechanisms, Consequences), Almaty, 2003, pp. 70–81.
19. Ibid.
20. *Development of Eastern Kazakhstan: Information-Analytic Collection*, Ust-Kamenogorsk, 2003, p. 57.
21. *Migration Attitudes of the Inhabitants of Ust-Kamenogorsk*, materials provided by akimat (government) of Eastern Kazakhstan.
22. Ibid.
23. 'Review of Ethnic and Religious Situation in Eastern Kazakhstan'.
24. B. Anderson, *Imagined Communities: Reflections on the Origin and Spread of Nationalism*, Moscow: Kuchkovo Pole, 2001, p. 166.
25. *Migration Attitudes of the Inhabitants Ust-Kamenogorsk*.
26. Fieldwork of author, Semipalatinsk, October 2006.
27. Yu. V. Arutunyan, L.M. Drobizheva and A.A. Susokolov, *Ethno Sociology: Textbook for Universities*, Moscow: Aspekt Press, 1999, p. 185.
28. 'To that has Brought Independence', *Rudny Altai*, 26 February 1996.
29. Alekseenko, *Frontier Migration*, p. 179.
30. A.P. Konovalov, *The National Processes in Republic Kazakhstan*, Semipalatinsk: Semei, 1999; A.P. Konovalov, *Development of the National Processes by Eyes Population of Semipalatinsk: Collection Material Sociological Research Carried Out in 2003*, Semipalatinsk, 2004; Konovalov and Nanbekova, *The Particularities of the Manifestation to Histories of the Solution National Contradiction in Consciousness Kazakhstani on Example of the Sociological Research in Semipalatinsk Subregion Eastern Kazakhstan Region (2004-2006)*.
31. *Development of Eastern Kazakhstan*, p. 57.
32. Ibid.
33. *Eastern Kazakhstan in 2006: Statistical Collection*, Ust-Kamenogorsk, 2006, p. 29.
34. Konovalov and Nanbekova, *The Particularities of the Manifestation to Histories of the Solution of National Contradiction in Consciousness Kazakhstan Example of the Sociological Research in Semipalatinsk subregion Eastern Kazakhstan Region (2004–2006)*, Semipalatinsk, p. 5.
35. Ibid., p. 11.
36. Fieldwork of present author, Semipalatinsk, February 2005.
37. *Eastern Kazakhstan in Numeral 2006*, Ust-Kamenogorsk, 2006, p. 29.
38. Fieldwork of author, Semipalatinsk, October–November 2006.
39. Konovalov and Nanbekova, *The Particularities of the Manifestation to Histories*, p. 14.

Review Articles

14

In Search of Good Governance: A Comparative Perspective

AMIYA K. CHAUDHURI

Jayanta Kumar Ray and Muntassir Mamoon, *Essays on Politics and Governance: in Bangladesh, India, Pakistan and Thailand*, Kolkata: Towards Freedom, 2007.

The book under review is the work of two scholars from India and Bangladesh, Jayanta Kumar Ray, former Centenary Professor of International Relations in the Department of History, Calcutta University, and Muntassir Mamoon, Professor of History in the University of Dhaka. It is a collaborative venture of two renowned historians of two very important neighbouring countries of South Asia. The authors have undertaken to study, in depth, the politics and governance of Pakistan, Bangladesh, Thailand and India. It is remarkable to note that each of these four countries has its own specificities with regard to processes of politics or 'non-party' political process of politics. These terms have of course not been used in the sense Rajni Kothari[1] used them, and later others used the terms democratic roots, constitutional framework and the often-stunted system of administration and governance. India is a stable democratic country but its social fragmentation in terms of castes and communities reflects the fragility of its politics at both central and state levels. Bangladesh, a newborn nation which was once a part of Pakistan, is a nation state which came to be shaped as an Islamic state where politics and religion were intertwined. It is difficult to find traces of democratic elements and institutions in Pakistan. Since the 1950s, when the demand for Bengali as the second language was rejected, to the Bengali people of Eastern Pakistan their state had appeared to be a colony of Urdu-speaking West Pakistan. The demand for Bengali statehood had been gaining strength based on the language movements that culminated in the birth of Bangladesh. A secular state with a democratic constitution came into being. But democracy was short lived. In fact, it is still going through a process of torturous transition. Thailand with its colonial hangover became independent with a constitutional monarchy. But the overarching military establishment made the present Thai state what it is today.

The ideas and interests of the two eminent authors that are apparent from the preface of the book converge on important topics like nationalism, colonialism, neocolonialism, internal colonialism, civil-military relations and challenges of good governance.[2] This last, but crucial item, is very important and constitutes the focus of the nature, structure and process of any government, be it democratic, benevolent authoritarian, civil or military. In this context the following comment made by an expert about the Indian state and government is apt and interesting: 'The monster is the modern centralized State in India and elsewhere, backed by [the] even more centralizing tendencies of corporate capitalism and the militarist doctrine of security that is taking possession of ruling classes everywhere. Such a structure of governance is kept alive by individuals with an insatiable appetite for power that is exercised without reference to any norms of accountability or civilized behaviour. India is not unique in being afflicted with this pervasive malady; it is unique in the sheer scale and variety of human oppression.'[3] Besides India, the observation correctly gives some understanding of the politics and governance of the other two South Asian countries, namely Bangladesh and Pakistan and one South-East Asian country namely, Thailand. The narratives attempt to capture the perspective of each country, in both its present and its recent past. But in comparison, the politico-electoral process in India is much more enduring and resilient because of its plural culture, democratic moorings and secular ethos.

In all the four countries, the authors, both sensitive historians and meticulous political observers, have diagnosed those dysfunctions of public administration that have repeatedly come to the forefront. In this perspective the solitary essay on Thailand gains great importance because it reveals similarities between South and South-East Asian countries on the one hand and the two regions and the United States of America on the other.[4] The essays included in this book were mostly written between 1973 and 2003 and present the readers with an assorted canvas of evolving historical moments of the respective countries. The subcontinental countries barring Thailand—an ASEAN country which is ruled by hereditary monarchy—share a common historical legacy of colonial domination but the post-colonial politics and systems of governance follow somewhat different trajectories. Bangladesh and Pakistan, in spite of their historical separation in 1971, share some common characteristics and can be classified in one group in contrast to the politico-administrative culture of Thailand. The US influence is also quite visible in the domain of civil-military relations, overtly in Pakistan and sometimes indirectly in Thailand. In the context of globalization, with the liberal ways of life, the political economy of the state, among others, is greatly determined by tourism as an industry. In this scenario India stands as a distinct entity in respect of its secular tradition, democratic values, administrative structures, representative institutions and decentralized governance—good or less than good.[5] Among the four states chosen by the eminent scholars, the Indian state may be taken as a referent. This volume includes ten papers in ten chapters dealing with different aspects of politics and governance in Pakistan, Bangladesh, Thailand and India. The ten essays can be put into four categories in terms of the degree of political change and governance as per their approximation to the definition of good governance.

Samar Sen's 'Frontier and the Liberation War', 'South Asia: History, Power and Legitimacy—Bangladesh Perspective', 'The Challenge of Governance in Bangladesh', 'Social Mobilization in Bangladesh in 1990s' and 'Technology Transfer: Aspects of Bangladesh Experience' would be included in the first category. 'Nationalism, Military and Politics' and 'Political Development in Pakistan 1947–1971' form the second. Historically Pakistan and Bangladesh were closer in respect of their system of values in the area of politics and governance. But Bangladesh, by enacting its new constitution in the early 1970s, chose to be a secular state, later to be taken over by the military dictatorship in 1975. In the next category, Thailand a South-East Asian monarchical soft State backed by the military, stands somewhat apart in respect of its ethno-political and cultural distinctiveness. It has been properly examined from a different perspective in the essay, 'Foreign Aid, Domestic Administration and the Rural Poor: A Case Study of Thailand'. On the other hand, for its politico-administrative stability as well as its democratic electoral processes glimpsed through a well laid out perspective, India, in the essays 'Anti-Public Administration in India', 'A plea for and Alternative Bureaucracy' may be regarded as a category by itself. But the borderlines of the discourse encompassing all the four States in their political processes, administration and governance, and other establishments and movements are not always well defined and often overlap.

To overthrow civilian administration the military establishment, where it is socially and temperamentally entrenched as in Pakistan as also to a great extent in Bangladesh since August 1975, may find numerous reasons. The two eminent authors have rightly observed, 'The following are the familiar factors which erode the legitimacy of a civilian Government: failure to resolve or suppress violent outbreaks or widespread disorder; large scale and visible corruption among civilian political leaders and officers; economic decline or stalemate caused by failures to prepare and/or carry out appropriate state policies; the adoption of illegal or unconstitutional measures to extend and/or to perpetuate the powers of a civilian regimes.'[6] The reasons are found to be unassailable in most countries of the third world, which frequently came under a sort of a military bureaucratic dispensation.

The primary responsibility of any government is to maintain internal security, law and order to ensure personal life and liberty of the people and properly look after the political economy of development. The sense of nationalism and a right perception about the civil-military equation in the institutionalized term among the people make a state what it should be in a democratic dialogue. This is where a distinction may be made between India and its nearest neighbours, Pakistan in the north-west and Bangladesh in the east. To trace the political development in Pakistan (1947–71), Professor Ray delves deep into the bureaucratic and political structures of that country with extreme caution when dealing with the two geographically-culturally separate regions.[7] Big business houses and top-ranking officials with the eager connivance of the ruling elites used to dominate the political structure and institutions till the military capture of power in Pakistan. Since the military regime of Ayub Khan in 1958, another factor, Inter State Intelligence (ISI), was added to the Pakistani state structure which was almost intermittently backed by the USA in its policy towards South Asia *vis-à-vis* its Cold War rival Soviet Russia. This was, to put it frankly, the undoing of Pakistan which was dismembered giving birth to Bangladesh. A political culture of democratic governance remained ever elusive in the contemporary history of Pakistan.

Professor Mamoon is a prolific writer and an eminently serious scholar of the history and politics of Bangladesh. Not only does he have a number of books to his credit but he also wrote several serious pieces as a freelance journalist in many Bangladeshi and Indian journals and newspapers. He critiques Samar Sen's Communist perspective of the 'Frontier' and the Bangladesh War of Independence in the same vein as he does the political-history of South Asian history, power and legitimacy, and almost a recent piece on social mobilization in Bangladesh in the 1990s in the perspective of Bangladesh.[8] Professor Mamoon in his conceptual frame of analysis of good governance in the essay on 'Challenges of Governance in South Asia' is Bangladesh-centric. Good governance[9] is, among other things, participatory, transparent and accountable, effective and equitable, and promotes the rule of law. It is to be noted that the governance of Bangladesh, not to speak of the existing caretaker government ever continuing its existence backed by the establishment of the barracks, has been analysed very cogently, section by section, such as colonial legacy, state dependency, role of the civil society, status of governance and a decentralized system or reforming governance from the grass-roots upwards. This is the story of the contemporary past before the present caretaker government took over to the conduct parliamentary elections in January 2007. From this essay it appears that if the prescriptions were followed, good governance in a country like Bangladesh would symbolize a paradigm shift. This is a valuable contribution of the author to the existing literatures on the subject.

Jayanta Kumar Ray's essays in the volume are seminal and deal with very interesting though sometimes controversial topics. Governance and administration are the two major areas of focus, which he has been concerned with for the last several years. One of his seminal works is *Administration in a Mixed Polity*,[10] which was published in 1981. To quote him, 'In a mixed polity, the line of distinction between the duty of a politician (viz., policy determination) and the duty of an administrator (viz., policy implementation) remains blurred.'[11] This remains one of the grey areas of public administration that many of the fraternity take advantage of. Accordingly, Professor Ray innovatively characterized the clan of the administrators as (a) promoters, (b) resistors, (c) accommodators, and (d) detractors. This interesting taxonomy of the people, who believe themselves to be the real rulers, helps in appreciating the contents of the essay, 'Anti-Public Administration in India'—a referent in the discussion of the countries being focused in the volume. Added to this are the nature and activities of elected lawmakers, 'actively engaged in crimes or visibly dependent on criminals, [who] not only persecute ordinary individuals but also honest high ranking officers (whose number naturally registers a rapid decline)'.[12] Self-aggrandizement, in whatever form, rather than the welfare of the people appears to be the objective of the politicians and many of the administrators servile to the men in power who care little for the observance of constitutional propriety and rules that matter for good governance.

In the next article Professor Ray dwells at length on India's foreign policy relations with Pakistan during 1947–71. This is a very perceptive essay particularly in view of the fact that in 1971 India, for its economic and demographic compulsions, had to help create an independent Bangladesh. This is one of the most significant issues that embittered Indo–Pak relations in respect of the long-standing and ever-unresolved problems in Kashmir. At the end of the essay, Professor Ray pleads for an alternative bureaucracy to the conventional one that we deal with. Professor Ray is deeply concerned with the process and redefinition of good governance. He has been working on the core of the subject for a long time. In his earlier work *India in Search for Good Governance*[13] he attempted to redefine the concept, 'Good governance is not a final product. It represents a continuous and an endless effort. The quest is for mass prosperity and liberal democracy, and the effort towards sustaining and upgrading whatever level of good governance has been accomplished.' In this connection he rightly picks up the thread to go into a detailed discussion on the constitutional obligation and position of decentralization and its implementation in the form of the *panchayati raj* system in several of the Indian states. His discussion on the West Bengal system as being totally centralized and often corrupt and partisan is bold and dispassionate which other local scholars for reasons of their own were unwilling or afraid to bring bolder focus. With regard to technology transfer, Professor Ray concentrates on Bangladesh as a country which he visited frequently for his field surveys.

Professor Yunus won the Nobel Prize for his outstanding work in Bangladesh, the innovative application of the concept of micro-finance and upkeep of the *Grameen Bank*. Long before, in the early 1980s, Professor Ray after one of his field surveys wrote about the possibilities of the miracle[14] that might have been achieved through the *Grameen Bank* in Bangladesh in the areas mostly populated by the cash-starved poorest sections of the people. But from a larger perspective, on the question of modern technology, based on his study of the macro-level developmental process of the late 1990s, he comments 'Bangladesh requires a massive and quick upgradation of its technological base if the majority of its population is to experience an appreciable rise in its standard of life in the near future'.[15] This observation is true of almost all developing countries, such as the South Asian and South-East Asian countries. It is a very detailed study touching on a number of areas where technological innovations and upgradation, both in the private and public domains, are urgently needed. Good governance, whatever may be the form, is the answer.

The last essay of the collaborative venture is on Thailand. Professor Ray is an expert on South and South-East Asian countries including Thailand. He worked extensively in Thailand during the 1970s and continues to do so. In this study he proposes to focus on some important aspects of America–Thailand interactions in the contemporary historical perspectives of foreign aid, domestic administration and the rural poor. The essay[16] attempts to highlight the American influence on the Thai policy makers, not only in foreign relation matters but also in domestic governance in respect of its economic development reorientation. The essay attempts to bring our many unknown facets of the Thai administration, be they related to agriculture, industry, rural poor, the bureaucratic culture or even insurgency. It may be regarded as an original contribution by the author since many of the themes discussed and documents mentioned are not usually accessible to ordinary researchers.

The book is a remarkable contribution to Area Studies. This serious and painstaking study undertaken by the two renowned professors and scholars of history deserves the unreserved gratitude of not just the researchers of Area Studies but scholars, academics, journalists and ordinary readers as well.

NOTES

1. Rajni Kothari, *State Against Democracy: In Search of Humane Governance*, Delhi: Ajanta Publications, 1988.
2. Jayanta Kumar Ray, *India in Search of Good Governance*, Kolkata: K.P. Bagchi & Company, 2001.
3. Kothari, *State Against Democracy*.
4. Jayanta Kumar Ray and Muntassir Mamoon, *Essays on Politics and Governance*, Kolkata: Towards Freedom, 2007 (hereafter *Essays on Politics and Governance*).
5. Ray, *In Search of Good Governance*, and *Administration in a Mixed Polity*, Delhi: Macmillan India Limited, 1981; Muntassir Mamoon and Jayanta Kumar Ray, *Civil Society in Bangladesh: Resilience and Retreat*, Kolkata: Firma KLM Ltd., 1996; and Muntassir Mamoon, *The Vanquished Generals and the Liberation War of Bangladesh*, Dhaka: Somoy Prokashan, 2000, and *South Asia: History, Power, Legitimacy, Bangladesh Perspective*, Dhaka: International Centre for Bengal Studies, 2005.
6. *Essays on Politics and Governance*, p. 2.
7. Ray, 'Political Development in Pakistan 1047–71: Role of Bureaucracy', *Essays on Politics and Governance*, pp. 22–56.
8. Mamoon, Chapters 3 and 4, *Essays on Politics and Governance*.
9. 'Governance for Sustainable Human Development', a policy paper, UNDP, 1997.

10. Ray, *Administration in a Mixed Polity.*
11. Ibid., p. 7.
12. *Essays on Politics and Governance*, p. 173.
13. Ray, *India in Search of Good Governance.*
14. Jayanta Kumar Ray, *To Chase a Miracle: A Study of the Grameen Bank of Bangladesh*, Dhaka: University Press Limited, 1987.
15. Ray, *Essays on Politics*, p. 193.
16. Ibid., pp. 249–313.

15

Rural Societies and Economies of Post-Communist States

NAJAM ABBAS

Osamu Ieda (ed.), *Transformation and Diversification of Rural Societies in Eastern Europe and Russia,* Sapporo: Slavic Research Centre, Hokkaido University, 2002.

Osamu Ieda (ed.), *The New Structure of the Rural Economy of Post-Communist Countries*, Sapporo: Slavic Research Centre, Hokkaido University, 2001.

Post-Communist rural societies are still undergoing the transformation process, varying widely even within a single country, partly as a result of the varied routes taken to pursue agricultural transformation. These books introduce the readers to the deeper dimensions of changes occurring in the post-Socialist rural societies. The contributions describe the difficulties experienced following the privatization of land and farming enterprises, changing employment and dwindling living standards as well as how a near absence of services affects rural life.

These books offer a collection of the essays of a workshop held to examine new aspects of rural economic transformation after the post-Communist privatization of agriculture in the mid-1990s, discussing these aspects from a Eurasia-wide, interdisciplinary perspective.

Though the books chronicle the dimensions of change experienced in relation to rural transformation in post-Socialist East European states, the framework of analysis can prove a tool for drawing comparisons between and contrasts with Central Asian states and other former Soviet nations too, as the following paragraphs will illustrate.

Zemphira Kalugina, in 'Rural Transformation in Russia: Inconsistencies and Results', touches upon the issue of food provision in recent decades. During the course of the ongoing agrarian transformation and partial disintegration of collective farming, the protracted and complicated character of the establishment of new economic forms in the agro-industrial complex, the role of part-time farming as the most flexible, steady and self-regulatory entity has increased. However, citing factors like the public psyche, the level of industrial potential, the status of legislation, the socio-political conditions in the country and the time required for coping with a transition, Kalugina concludes that, in the foreseeable future, autonomous farms cannot become a dominant form of agricultural production in the Russian countryside.

Referring to the downside of the changes the rural sector is undergoing, Kalugina's comprehensive analysis attributes the reduction in agricultural production, and the emergent trend of a decline in the household's output to several factors, the first being the dismantling of agriculture subsidies under which collective farms had access to fodder, seeds, agriculture equipment, fuel and parts for mechanized farming and transport vehicles under privileged conditions. Secondly, the financial possibilities of an average rural family have substantially diminished, resulting in lowered living standards and depreciation of savings. Thirdly, the labour potential of a typical rural family has been practically exhausted and they are unable to put in physical labour beyond a limited extent. There are apprehensions that if part-time farms are classified from the informal into the formal sector of economy, it will bring further hardships to the rural population. Though the numbers of collective and state farms have been reduced, and forms of mixed ownership have emerged, there is a need to keep in mind the merits and the social price of such transformations.

Following the reforms, the living standards of both the urban and the rural population have declined along with their consumption of staple food. A general increase is noticed in the consumption of potatoes and baked products. Malnutrition, among other factors, is negatively reflected in the state of health of the population, mortality rate and life expectancy figures. It is observed that the wages of agriculture workers remain less than the national average, below the subsistence level, and even then they are paid after a delay of several months. Additionally, the remunerations do not correspond to a worker's contribution or qualifications. Privatized farms do not possess the capacity to address the problems of their employees. Such circumstances cause a loss of motivation towards professional quality, productivity or work efficiency, especially among the rural youth who do not see any prestige in working in the public sector. Though local governments are obliged to manage the social and cultural services of their localities, they continue to lack sufficient financial means and technological capabilities to deliver. This in turn contributes to a substantial worsening of social services provision in the rural areas.

An essay titled 'Household Capital and Structural Change in Employment & Income in Rural Russia from 1991–1999', by David O'Brien and Valeri Patsiorkovski notes that in the 1990s the rural sector in Russia (as elsewhere) underwent substantial changes in institutions and social organization. They attempt to identify long-term aggregate trends in economic behaviour and emerging incremental institutional changes at the local level. Their joint contribution also examines the differences between households and villages with respect to their abilities to take advantage of new opportunities in entrepreneurial activities. Both point out that the lack of material infrastructure, poor physical capital and reduced plot size have increased the importance of household manual labour as a form of human capital. Drawing attention to the structural changes in the rural areas, the authors list factors such as a substantial shift in the nature of employment and earning level in the villages, which in turn has brought profound effect on a rural households' income.

When discussing the post-Socialist in transition economies, agriculture can be treated as a distinctive sphere, to which the usual approaches and criteria for the transition to a market economy cannot be applied. As a consequence of the dissolution of the Socialist regimes, new farming structures have emerged which are quite different from those working under market economies elsewhere, notes Rihito Yamamura. His essay, 'A New Phase of Post-Socialist Structural Changes in Russian Agriculture', focuses on the changes in individual private farms and notes that a majority of existing cooperative farms are member-oriented than market-oriented and are yet to reach efficiency under the new market economy conditions. Citing recent Russian agricultural statistics, Yamamura notes that the 'bulk of vegetables and potatoes are now produced in various types of small plots owned by village and city dwellers. More than a half of animal production comes from subsistence level farming by villagers' (p. 120). Yamamura fears that while the individual private sector overall seems to have entered a stagnant stage, the structure within the sector has been changing more dynamically.

Turning to the changes in the peasant farm sector, it is noted that the declining trend in this stratum is actually stronger than the statistical figures indicate. Most of the peasant farms have suffered from disequilibrium between three main resources, namely, labour, land and capital. Peasant farms, usually created as typical family farms and relying mainly on labour resources from their immediate relatives, still have to arrange necessary land and capital resources. Even when farmers succeed in acquiring the necessary machines, they cannot use them to maximum advantage because the land initially given to them was limited and farmers could not freely expand their farm size by land purchase or leasing. On the other hand, peasant farms or individual groups of families equipped with machines have been faced with a 'deficit of land'.

Gejza Blaas' quest, titled 'Is the Completion of Agricultural Reforms in Central and Eastern European Countries Conditional on a Move to Family Farming?' draws attention to eight factors affecting farm transformation which are worth noting:

1. The termination or significant reduction of state intervention in the agricultural sector;
2. Price and trade liberalization;
3. The decline in demand for domestic food and the loss of foreign markets;
4. Income deficiency in the farm sector caused by a price-cost squeeze;
5. The lack of adequate infrastructure on the input side and insufficient marketing channels, the lack of a financial infrastructure adapted to the needs of small and middle-sized entrepreneurs, and a lack of loan schemes designed to meet the needs of the farmers;
6. The lack of appropriate finance, partly connected with a more general problem—the insufficient progress in the identification of land titles and land consolidation;
7. The fragmentation of land ownership;
8. The deficit in the skills necessary in individual farming among those who might start a farm business as well as a lack of starting capital.

Is there some hope that the restructuring process will provide opportunities for new integration and the reconstruction of rural economies and societies? In Hungary's case, Osamu Ieda notes that the general business conditions became progressively worse after agricultural privatization. The market for Hungarian agricultural produce disappeared along with its buyers in the former Soviet economy. The price of agricultural products went into decline and increasing competition with Western European producers had a serious impact.

Writing on 'Agricultural Restructuring in Hungary and Its Social Impacts', Katalin Kovács thinks that as in other post-Socialist countries, Hungarian policies on land restitution and property de-collectivization have resulted in a fragmented property structure, where property and land are often used inefficiently and inappropriately. He notes that among the various rural sectors, livestock production struggled most to make a recovery. The end of subsidized feed supplies and the provision of transport and marketing services (which were formerly arranged under the collective farms) had a significant impact on poultry production.

Kovacs' description of how those who wished to pursue a change of course from the collective practice venture in Hungary portrays well the plight of farmers elsewhere in the post-Socialist countries: 'Those who left the cooperatives in a hope to operate a privatised enterprise subsequently observed some hard facts: their holding was too small and the assets that they had taken from [the] cooperative were insufficient for the task, the old machinery was depreciating and options to acquire machinery from the cooperative were fewer, nor could they afford any machinery on their own. The banks won't extend loans to such farmers as they had nothing to offer as security. State resources could not compensate for the absence of personal resources, since the change in structure was not supported by any injection of capital' (p. 263). Furthermore, those starting anew or from scratch were further hindered by a lack of cooperation between private farmers. The collapse of large-scale farms contributed to a sharp rise in rural unemployment. The large number of jobs that disappeared after the transformation could not be replaced with new opportunities in rural areas, in either the farming sector or elsewhere. Under such conditions, plot farming has become essential for masses of rural households for sheer survival. What gives serious cause for concern, however, is the problem of rural poverty which, although connected with agricultural restructuring, cannot be solved within the agricultural sector. Privatization of land among other things allowed many families to survive relying on a style of agricultural activity which is subsistence-oriented and does not allow selling more than what is surplus. All this means that agriculture is no longer the backbone of the rural economy as it once was.

Tomas Doucha's contribution, 'Agriculture and Rural Development in the Czech Republic', observes that the 'passivity of the rural problem is another serious barrier to rural development and to the development of smaller individual (family) farming or other small businesses'. He draws attention to those aspects of rural development that need consideration. A decent rural living depends the on the services available to the rural people. A substantial decline is noted in the transport services while at the same time prices for the services have been rising drastically. This has proved a very negative measure for the rural areas where people need to commute big distances to farms and markets. Local heating, which was once provided by collective or state farms, is non-functional, unavailable or unaffordable. A rise in energy costs makes electrical heating very expensive and unsuitable for heating rural households.

'Agricultural Reform in Slovakia: Changing Institutions and Structure' is the title of Gejza Blaas' essay which reminds us of the common challenges experienced elsewhere as he lists the six adverse conditions that accompanied the restructuring process: (1) little reward for doing business in agriculture due to unfavourable terms of trade; (2) restricted availability of loan capital and liquidity problems; (3) fragmented ownership of land and underdeveloped markets for land; (4) highly ineffective laws relating to bankruptcy procedures; (5) growing unemployment in rural areas; and (6) comparatively high levels of social dependency of the rural population on collective farming as their main source of subsistence.

Through their individual essays tracing past attempts from the history of Russian agricultural reformation Ilya Gerasimov and Yoshida Hiroshi underline that a fresh round of modernization requires a reorientation of the people while warning that the outcome may not be the same at different places.

In their joint essay 'Farm Transformation and Restructuring in Czech Agriculture' Tomas Doucha and Emil Divila take stock of how things have evolved between 1991 and 2001. The two authors assert that the key differences in the farm structure development in the transitional countries are derived from four crucial factors:

(a) The historical background and heritage that couldn't be overcome in ten years;
(b) The applied agricultural policies;
(c) The development of the institutional framework of the society;
(d) The development of the national economy.

These books may serve as a vantage point for the English audience to familiarize itself with issues, experts and recent scholarship. The two works give the reader have a cross-country, comparative picture of how changes have evolved in the rural parts of post-Socialist societies. Rural transformation is a dynamic, ongoing process of which many pertinent and significant elements can still be observed in Central Asia, for example. There is a need to multiply such intellectual collaboration to further enrich our understanding of how and why the lives of the millions engaged in the rural sector in post-Socialist societies are undergoing changes and how they cope with them.

16

'Between Heaven and Hell': Romancing Siberia or Portraying Gloom?

SUCHANDANA CHATTERJEE

Nicolas Werth, *Cannibal Island: Death in a Siberian Gulag*, Princeton, N.J.: Princeton University Press, 2007.

Fiona Hill and Clifford Gaddy, *How Communist Planners Left Russia Out in the Cold*, Washington D.C.: Brookings Institution Press, 2003.

Kuroshima Denji, 'Siberia Under Snow' (translation and introduction by Lawrence Rogers), *Critical Asian Studies*, 38 (2): 2006.

Victor L. Mote, 'Stalin's Railway to Nowhere: "The Dead Road" (1947-1953)', *Sibirica*, vol. 3, no. 1, 2003.

Valentin Rasputin, *Siberia, Siberia*, Illinois: Northwestern University Press, 1997.

John Givens, 'Siberia as "Volia": Vasilii Shukshin's "Search for Freedom"', in Galya Diment and Yuri Slezkine (eds.), *Between Heaven and Hell: The Myth of Siberia in Russian Culture*, New York: St. Martin's Press, 1993.

The public image of Siberia is that of a limitless space, a wilderness, a remote terrain with lack of connectivity and a dumping ground for convicts and exiles. The optimism about federal governance since the Siberian Accord of 1991 has faded and there is an implicit urge to write about past failures, highlighting megalomaniac ventures and abandoned projects in Siberia during the 1930s and 1940s. Siberia primarily continues to be the region that has disconnected men from their cozy locales. To the majority of exiles and deportees, Siberia as a colony was unattractive because it meant isolation from the motherland. The severe physical conditions were unbearable and made life unpleasant. What was also difficult to fathom was the cultural environment, represented by people of the Steppe—both Russian as well as native. The Siberian wilderness was like a psychological bind for them: an inhospitable terrain, remote location and a metaphor for gloom. Those who were engaged in perilous projects along the wartorn Manchurian or Chinese frontiers of Siberia in the 1930s seemed to lack normal human values and feelings. Japan's proletarian writer Kuroshima Denji (1898–1943) felt Japanese militarymen lacked compassion—a quality one could not possibly learn to appreciate in the snows of Siberia. It was as if the brutal men were there to have fun, as if there was no law in Siberia.

The brutality comes into full view in the numbing descriptions of Stalinist repressions in 1933—the deportation camps of Nazino Island in western Siberia. Nicolas Werth's *Cannibal Island: Death in a Siberian Gulag* (2007) describes the plight of the deportees who were city dwellers and were labelled as *kulaks* and 'special settlers' representing several ethnic groups. The 'déclassé and socially harmful elements' were left to their fate on the little island that stood at the confluence of the Ob and the Nazina rivers, about 800 km north of the Siberian city of Tomsk. Werth's findings, mostly based on the enquiry commission's reports and other documents related to the deportation and collections from the regional archives of Novosibirsk and Tomsk, tend to draw attention to the 'decivilization' process, narrated in some gory detail, about the cannibalism that was practised by the deportees on that island in order to live and survive. The Cannibal Island, or the Dead Island as it was called, has become the symbol of Stalin's brutality in transforming urban spaces through a series of deportation plans. City-based dwellers were deported to western Siberia and Kazakhstan to 'exploit' opportunities of timber, mining and agricultural resources in the Soviet Far East—a scheme which Werth considers to be utopian. Identified as labour colonists, they were expected to free the state from the expenses of supporting them. Also, they were expected to support themselves by engaging in small-scale operations like mining, fishing and small crafts. The plan was grandiose and inevitably led to insurmountable costs because the camps were located in uninhabited regions with little local transportation facilities.

There have been other writings about abandoned projects in Siberia. The Trans-Siberian Railway was the epitome of long-distance connectivity in Russia, criss-crossing Siberia and touching the eastern and western fringes of Russian territory. According to Victor L. Mote, however, the construction of the Northern Trans-Siberian Mainline, paralleling the Arctic Circle between Chum Station and the Chukchi Peninsula and in the vicinity of the Ob River, was abandoned halfway in 1953. The purpose was to pose Soviet socialism as picture perfect in the Soviet north just after the Second World War and also to utilize the massive resource (oil and gas) base in Siberia, which might have appealed to the whims and fancies of no more than eight people in the Soviet leadership. The leadership designed great plans 'to transform Nature', almost inattentive to the fact that it entailed the dislocation of no less than 250,000 people in the Ob-Yenisei basin. This workforce worked as slaves, and according to memoirs of project engineers, lived 'a dog's life'. The 'Dead Road' was like a curse and those who wanted to escape the curse to the tundra on stolen bicycles could not fight the bitter cold. Stalin's plan of building a railway network in Siberia's wooded Tundra region paralleling the Arctic Circle was unaccomplished because of its unprecedented length. The gigantic enterprise of bringing in labourers into a region where railway infrastructure was totally absent was abandoned midway and the Trans-Polar Railway seems to have remained dead ever since.

So the impression is that because of her remote location Siberia has been unlucky. Also, size is a factor which often seems to be a disadvantage: Russia's huge size is certainly not its strength. Rather, it has restricted the pace of economic development. According to Fiona Hill and Clifford Gaddy, one should not even think of programmes for Siberian redevelopment because it has ceased to be a self-sufficient economic space. There is also labour movement from the Siberian regions (the only exception being Tajik and Kyrgyz immigrant workers) and hence one cannot expect that with a labour shortage in the Far Eastern sector, there will be substantial and realistic development. Moreover, what is predicted is the continuity of the Gulag legacy because immigrant workers would hardly have prospects of 'a new employment' and would face the difficulties of sustainability. In the long run, this would result in social upheavals—an argument that is being put forward by the anti-immigration lobbies in Russia. The problem, therefore, lies not merely in whether the exodus of Chinese labourers to the Far East is going to create problems or not. There are also indications of social rupture in Siberia on a scale which possibly cannot be imagined.

Such apprehensions also exist among the concerned lobbies in Russia, represented by the demographer Zhanna Zaionchovskaya who advises caution in undertaking plans to develop a Siberian Federal District. According to British geographer Michael Bradshaw, one has to take a leaner approach to Siberian development. With such critical views about localized development, with the decrease of subsidies and other Soviet-era benefits, with increasing pressures to adjust to the global economy, one needs to rethink strategies like relocating urban development towards the Pacific coast in terms of the economic advantages that it can offer.

According to the two Carnegie scholars, the idea of stimulation of Russian economic growth at the cost of a re-utilization of Siberian resources (e.g. by diverting the water of the Irtysh to irrigate the cotton fields of Central Asia) is redundant and is equivalent to what the Soviets did half a century ago. The same caution needs to be applied to other assets of Siberia like the forestry complex and the machine-building complexes. Both think that human errors of the past should not be repeated. The factor of distance was the main weakness of Siberia. Soviet economic planners committed the gravest mistake of choosing distant locales of Siberia for expanding Russia's economy and using them as reserves for Russia's demographic expansion. Siberia was mismanaged right from the start and this poses serious problems for the future.

A shade different from these gloomy projections is the narrative of Vladimir Zenzinov, the exiled explorer who was among the Chukchis and the Yakuts just after 1910 and got the flavour of freedom in Northern Siberia. He was among those who were looking for escape from dark dingy cells and penal colonies. For Zenzinov, the Siberian journey was far more exciting and it was an interlude with happy memories. Even as Zenzinov portrayed the road to 'oblivion', he spoke of the most pleasurable moments in his life in the Yakutsk territory. He was craving for freedom after 18 months of imprisonment and his Yakutsk experience gave him all that—'free spaces, limitless snow fields, movement, an endless change of scenic effects and overhead the open skies!'

The practical concerns and the approach of shifting the gaze from Russia's southern tier along the Trans-Siberian Railway to the Far East are very different from the Sibiriaks' emotional concerns. The Irkutsk-based writer, Valentin Rasputin, represents the village prose movement in Soviet literature and praises the landscape of Siberia and its setting—as a place of unrestricted space and individual freedom. For him, 'Siberia is in no hurry to reveal itself, and it placed its finest creations with love and good taste in its heartland' (Rasputin 1997: 61). Vasily Shukshin (1929–74), a displaced filmmaker who belonged to the Altai region, missed his childhood days in Siberia. To him, Siberia was a land of freedom (*volia*) and the Siberian expanses did not represent the monolithic face of penal exile but a space for artistic freedom. Shukshin, like Rasputin, was nostalgic and yearned 'to go to home' to Siberia which was a distant paradise (Givens, 1993: 179).

The sensitivities of Rasputin or Shukshin are similar to the esoteric ideas of the early twentieth-century Russian artist Nicholas Roerich. Roerich was obsessed with the pristine and divine beauty that he discovered in the mountains of High Asia. In the nineteenth century too Siberian 'insiders' portrayed Siberia as a kingdom of Nature.

Such varying impressions of Siberia are in plenty. Fiona Hill and Clifford Gaddy represent visions of an approaching apocalypse. These writings are essentially policy-based and do not take into consideration the aesthetic values or the esoteric ideas of the Sibiriaks and the wayfarers. The literary genres of Siberia are also sometimes left in the shade. What are also not taken into account are the sanctity of a Turko-Mongol heritage and the Buddhist-shamanist linkages or the borderland cultures of a widely diverse terrain called Siberia.

Research Notes

17

Diaspora Studies in India

BINODA K. MISHRA

Diaspora Studies has emerged as an important new field of study within the post-modern discourse. It is being pitted against the concepts of nation and nationalism in an attempt to refigure the relations of citizens and nation states. However, the term 'diaspora' is often used with reference to transnationalism and globalism thus hiding the nuances of the concept of diaspora. In India, Diaspora Studies remains a UGC Special Area Studies Programme and is yet to receive full recognition as a separate discipline. This is because it is a very new phenomenon in terms of its contributions to the Indian economy and image. However, it has received acceptance in litearture, culture, and sociological studies. Basically Non-Resident Indians have helped the study go beyond the taken-for-granted notion of hyphenated identity.

Though one of the oldest diasporas in the world, the Indian diaspora was never of any interest to independent India. It is an irony that India chose to forget her diaspora which played the most significant role in her freedom struggle. The condition of the Indian diaspora under the colonial masters formed a core issue for the freedom struggle. The Indian National Congress attached so much importance to overseas Indians that it opened a branch called 'Overseas Indian Affairs' under Jawaharlal Nehru. The plight of Indians in South Africa, Fiji and Mauritius was used for mobilizing Indian sentiments against the colonial masters. It was the diaspora that provided money, manpower and network to the militant nationalist movement. Examples of the Gadr Party, the Indian National Army and many more fill the history of the Indian independence movement showing the active involvement of the Indian diaspora. The Indian National Congress acknowledged the importance of the Indian diaspora in unambiguous terms. In the words of B. Pattabhi Sitaramayya the official party historian of the INC:

Indians abroad, it may look like a paradox to say so, paved the way really for Indian emancipation. It was the gospel of passive resistance that was conceived, developed and implemented in Transvaal in 1908 . . . [that] paved the way for the development of non-cooperation, passive resistance, civil disobedience and satyagraha. . . . We therefore owe all that we are to the initiative, the originality, that daring and the sacrifice of the Indians abroad.[1]

After Independence, India took little interest in overseas Indians. The plight of indentured labours and the discrimination against Indian traders were soon forgotten. The post-Independence leadership in India 'adopted an attitude of studied indifference to the overseas Indians'.[2] This was in contrast to the INC's promise to overseas Indians during colonial times. In 1939, in a message to the Indian National Congress of South Africa, Nehru wrote, 'India is weak today and cannot do much for her children abroad . . . a day will come when her long arm will shelter and protect them and her strength will compel justice for them.'[3] Nehru repeated the same promise on 18 March 1946 while addressing a public gathering. He promised, 'when India attains independence, she would immediately decide who her nationals were and Indians overseas would be Indian nationals unless they choose to be otherwise.'[4]

When he became the first prime minister of the country, Nehru asked the expatriates to assimilate into the host societies and enhance India's image by contributing to the local economy and maintaining social harmony with the indigenous ethnic groups in the host societies. In the Constituent Assembly, on 8 March 1948, Nehru dissociated the expatriates politically by declaring that those overseas Indians who are not Indian nationals do not interest India politically and India would have only cultural, emotional and humanitarian interest in them. The Citizenship Act of 1955 formalized the dissociation of the expatriates.

This sudden apathy towards the overseas Indian population can have two explanations. (1) the Cold War-characterized international system called for careful planning of foreign policy by the group of nations that obtained independence in the aftermath of World War II. Nehru visualized an idealist posture for India which would take the country to the rank of a world leader. Thus, he launched the Non-Alignment movement and advocated *Panchasheel* (five principles of peaceful coexistence). Both these guiding principles of Indian foreign policy prevented India from taking any effective measures regarding the sufferings of overseas Indians, as it would amount to interference in another country's internal affairs; (2) after Independence, India had the daunting task of building a nation on the European model encompassing cultural, religious and ethnic diversities. It had limited resources to carry out this process and thus expediently chose to ignore the millions suffering abroad sincc it would have put tremendous pressure on the resources of the country and on the immature political system. Indians suffered in Myanmar (then Burma), in Kenya, in Uganda and in Guyana. This deliberate distancing was continued by successive governments despite pleas from the suffering Indians in Kenya and Uganda in the early 1970s.

It is inexplicable as to why a nation which seemed to have 'condemned her diaspora to extinction' is currently so possessive about it. Given the obsession of the recent governments with the Indian Diaspora, one would be tempted to think it to be an assertion of 'Rising Indian Nationalism' and a timely act to keep the promise that Nehru made to India's overseas children before Independence. But a little probing reveals that such sudden love for the expatriates is merely a desperate economic measure, without much thought being given to the complexities involved in engaging the diaspora. For the first time, the Indian leadership thought of the Indian diaspora when a non-Congress government came to power at the centre. The Indian government showed legitimate concern for the overseas Indians. This concern was based on the realization of their economic potential particularly of those who had emigrated to the Gulf region and were sending substantial remittances to the country. Banking was partially reformed to facilitate the flow of foreign currency. Terms such as Non-Resident Indian (NRI) and People of Indian Origin (PIO) appeared in the official lexicon of India. This was followed by some cautious engagement with the Indian diaspora by Rajiv Gandhi. The response of the Indian government to the crisis in Fiji was proactive in contrast to the official response to the Kenyan and Ugandan crises of the 1970s, when India had chosen to ignore the plight of the Indians there on the pretext of non-interference in the internal matters of other countries.

The actual re-engagement with the diaspora began with the economic crisis of 1990–1. India's foreign exchange situation was worsening and India was on the verge of defaulting on its international financial commitments. The Indian government realized that in the fast-emerging global economy, in order to survive, the country required heavy investment in infrastructure and the government was in no position to take up the job alone. This triggered the process of liberalization which provided incentives for foreign investment. Realizing the economic might of those Indians who had left just after the Independence, India wanted to use them as cash cows for its economic development.

Social science has always remained utilitarian in India. A subject attracts the interest of scholars only when it promises some policy relevance and the government takes active interest in promoting the subject. Diaspora Studies never formed a part of the curriculum of any university or other academic institution in the country till recently. The problems partly due to the nature of the Indian diaspora. Since independent India chose to forget its diaspora which had played such an important role in the Freedom movement, the identity of diasporic Indians could not be articulated properly. The concept of Indian diaspora was lost among parochial identities based on language, region, ethnicity and religion.

A substantial section of the literature, which is now clubbed under Diaspora Studies, is actually literature on migration, identity formation of particular sections of Indian population and the problems of assimilation in the host societies. Literature on the Sikh diaspora is particularly rich owing to the political role of the Sikhs in the Secessionist movement for the creation of a separate Khalistan state. Literature on the migration of early Indians, particularly from the southern part of the country to South-East Asian countries, makes up the bulk of the literature on the Indian diaspora. However, given the long history of Indian diaspora formation and its diverse nature, it is hardly possible for any particular discipline to deal with all its aspects. In the words of N. Jayaram, 'the agenda of *Indian Diaspora* as an area of academic study is necessarily multi-disciplinary in nature'.[5] The various aspects that need to be studied under the subject matter of Diaspora Studies can be listed as below.

Study on Indian diaspora involves study on migration dynamics. India has a long history of migration. It has both internal and external factors. While the ancient migration had entrepreneurship as the prime motive, migration under the yoke of colonialism had economic compulsions in the homeland and exploitative designs of the colonial masters to satisfy their industrial requirements as the determining factors. This was in contrast to the bulk of outward migration that began after Independence and is still continuing, which is based neither on entrepreneurship nor on economic compulsions but on economic rationality. Given the long history and varying factors involved, this has attracted the interest of not only historians but also anthropologists and geographers. The second important aspect of Diaspora Studies is the nature of the relationship of the immigrants with the host land. Where Indians constitute the bulk of the population they have certainly changed the social demography of that society and 1created new social, economic, political and cultural complexes generating interest among economists, sociologists, political scientists, historians and specialists on cultural studies.

A similar interest is also found on the homeland connection of the Indian diaspora. The homeland relationship of the Indian diaspora has more facets than the much-hyped economic relationship. While economists are calculating the potential of the Indian diaspora in terms of investment in the home country, political scientists are engaged in finding out the political ramifications of the relationship of the overseas Indians with the homeland, which have various colours, such as religious, ethnic and linguistic. Historians are also interested in determining the nature of the engagement India should have with its diaspora based on their nature and time of migration from the country. A section in the academia is also interested in exploring the possibility of using the diaspora as an agent for promoting Indian interests at various international forums. The cultural aspect of the homeland relationship of the Indian diaspora has emerged as a very important area of study. The uniqueness of Indian culture has allowed it to survive in the memory and habits of the Indians even after generations. Thus, it is being treated as the most important strand of relationship between India and her overseas population.

The Maulana Abul Kalam Azad Institute of Asian Studies, as a part of its academic commitment to engaging with contemporary issues, tried to give a fillip to the academic discussion on Indian diaspora by organizing a national and an international conference on the subject involving scholars from both within the country and abroad. The national conference titled 'Indian Diaspora: Past, Present and Future', organized in collaboration with the Indian Institute of Advanced Studies, Shimla, focused on the development of the Indian diaspora from ancient times till the present with its gender dimension. The relationship between internal migration and diasporic migration during the colonial period was clearly established. A major section of the discussion focused on the position of Indians in various parts of the world. Scholars delved into the history and the current socio-economic and political position of Indians in countries of Asia, Europe and America facilitating a comparative assessment of the position of Indians in various parts of the world and its co-relationship with the nature of the socio-political system of the host country. The other major aspect of the Indian diaspora that attracted interest was its utility for India and how the Government of India is dealing with it. While there was a positive prognosis about the role of the Indian diaspora as a development agent for India, the diaspora policy of the government came under scrutiny.

The discussions served as a curtain-raiser for further engagement with the concept. In January 2007 an international conference was organized which involved scholars from both within the country and the Indian diaspora, as well as other foreign scholars who have studied the Indian diaspora. The entire concept of Indian diaspora was discussed with all its nuances. Apart from the history of the diaspora formation, the nature of the relationship of different generations of the diaspora with India was an interesting finding. The older the diaspora, the more nostalgic they were about their Indian connection; the expectations of the diaspora also varied with the length of migration. The pre-colonial migrants and the migrants under the colonial yoke are more interested in a cultural relationship with India whereas the younger diaspora, particularly those who migrated in search of greener pastures outside the country, were found to be more interested in a political and economic relation with their original homeland. From the discussion it was evident that while a majority of the diaspora was in favour of India pursuing a diaspora policy which would help them keep their Indian identity culturally alive, the Indian government policy seems to be more favourably predisposed towards the contemporary diaspora that is termed as the *Dollar Diaspora*.

In retrospect, more than an analysis the conference proved to be a forum for determining the future of India's engagement with its more than 20 million diaspora. The views differed substantially. Though the utility of the diaspora for the development of the country was realized by all, there was strong caution about the fallouts of such engagement. The potential of the Indian diaspora playing a disintegrative and disruptive role in the country was identified as an area of concern in the evolving relationship of the diaspora with the home country. The conference identified a large number of potential research areas which can establish Diaspora Studies as a distinct field of study with a multidisciplinary approach, and contribute towards fruitful engagement of India with its diaspora.

NOTES

1. B. Pattabhi Sitaramayya, *The Encyclopedia of the Indian Diaspora*, vol. 1, Delhi: Oxford University Press, 2007, p. 84.
2. Aparajito Gangopadhyaya, 'India's Policy Towards its Diaspora: Continuity and Change', *India Quarterly*, vol. 61, no. 4, October-December 2006, p. 98.
3. *Selected Works of Jawaharlal Nehru*, Delhi: Orient Longman, 1976, p. 618.
4. *The Encyclopedia of the Indian Diaspora*, p. 84.
5. N. Jayaram (ed.), *The Indian Diaspora: Dynamics of Migaration*, Delhi: Sage, 2004, p. 23.

18

Refugees in Malda District: The Past and Present Scenario

MONIKA MANDAL

Migration and the associated problem of refugees that it creates are common to most states. For instance, the inflow of refugees started from East Bengal to West Bengal at the time of the outbreak of the Noakhali riots in 1946. Thereafter, in the aftermath of the Independence of India and the formation of Pakistan, the influx of refugees continued. Apart from Noakhali, the refugees also came from Khulna, Chattagram, Barisal, Maymensingh, Rajshahi and Faridpur districts of East Pakistan to Malda and elsewhere. This research note is based on an examination of a number of studies and surveys conducted at various existing refugee colonies in Malda district and on my own interviews in the refugee colonies in July 2007.

Refugee families reached the district of Malda at different times from 1946 onwards and various attempts were made for their rehabilitation. These colonies are situated in the border areas of Malda district: Malda, English Bazar, Gazole, Habibpur, Bamongola and Kaliachak Police Station (PS) of the district. I have visited the colonies and talked with the displaced people who came from East Pakistan to West Bengal after Partition. The refugee colonies are situated mostly by the banks of the river Kalendi in English Bazar, and the Mahananda in Kaliachak. For the post-1950s displaced persons 38 squatters' colonies were set up between 1 January 1951 and 25 March 1971. These 38 colonies are part of the 607 groups of refugee colonies (see Table 18.2). The colonies are located under the following police stations: 7 in PS Malda, 3 in PS English Bazar, 10 in PS Gazole, 14 in PS Habibpur, 2 in PS Bamongola and 1 in PS Kaliachak. There are also 6 undeveloped government-sponsored colonies outside the Calcutta Metropolitan Development (CMD) urban area, 9 undeveloped government-sponsored colonies outside the CMD rural area and 42 private colonies outside the CMD rural area. In PS Gazole there are 6 government-sponsored colonies.

Non-camp-dweller refugees who came to Malda district over a period of time after the 1950s for settlement were of two categories. The first consisted of those in the services of the army, the railways and the police in India, who decided to leave their home permanently and brought their families to their respective places of work. Some of those families found a place in the district by availing themselves of schemes meant for refugees. There was another class of refugees who came to West Bengal and lived with their relatives and/or in camps for a short period. They got employment in state government departments and were posted in Malda district where they decided to settle. Some of the agriculturist refugee families were also gradually settled in Malda district. Normally, a group of refugee families would join together and purchase lands from private owners and set up colonies in different locations depending on the availability of such land. In the course of time some of these families sold their homestead land to others and moved elsewhere for rehabilitation.

The quantum of assistance provided by the government from 1948 onwards under these schemes has varied slightly in accordance with the location of the established colonies. It was in the form of the cost of homestead land of three-fifths of a *cottah* and 15 *cottahs* per family at Rs. 25 per *cottah* for cultivated land. So, a house-building loan of Rs. 500 per family and a lump-sum amount of Rs 1,000 to 1,250 per family for the purchase of cultivated land and/or for small trade was provided. In the case of rural agricultural families a similar amount was given for the purchase of cultivated land—around 3 *bighas* per family—apart from house-building and lump-sum loans. Later, the government waived off the loan portions of the financial assistance.

These colonies are situated in Khas Land. The estimated average of the land price per *cottah* prevailing at present in urban areas is Rs. 8,000 and in rural area Rs. 250. A greater number of the refugees of depended on cultivation and 35 colonies are in rural areas. The largest population is in P.S. Habibpur Moza-Dalla, Dalla Colony, where there are 539 displaced persons' families. In the course of time, since the establishment of the colonies, the concerned local municipal authority, panchayat samities and other government agencies have undertaken infrastructure development such as roads, school buildings, sinking of tube wells, etc., in the colonies. The colonies are located such that educational facilities, health centres and hospitals are available in areas which are within easy reach by road connections.

Modern urban colonies—two in English Bazar Baraburitala Krishna Pally Colony and Paschim Sarbamangala Pally Colony and one in Gazole Adina Colony—were planned by the state government in 1948, and are located under the English Bazar and Gazole police station, district malda. A door-to-door survey was conducted from 11 June to 17 June 2007 to collect data and particulars to assess the development of refugee families residing in there colonies (Table 18.1).

A brief summary follows of some of the experiences of the displaced people as recounted by them during interviews. Paresh Chandra Das, when asked when he had arrived in the colony said that at the time of the outbreak of the riots and disturbances in East Pakistan during 1946 and 1950, he was employed by the Indian army and evacuated his family to West Bengal. He also pointed out that he settled in the English Bazar Baraburitala Krishna Pally Colony with the assistance

TABLE 18.1: DEVELOPMENT INDICATORS OF REFUGEE FAMILIES IN SELECTED AREAS OF MALDA

1.	Family income per month	Rs. 2000–4000 (27.3 %) Rs. 5000–10000 (36.4 %) Rs. 10001–20000 (9 %) Above Rs. 20000 (27.3 %)	
2.	Source of income	Service—50 %, Business—10.5 %, Professional—10.5 %, Unemployed—29 %.	
3.	Average family size	At the time of entry Adult: Male—1, Female—1 Child—1, Total—3	
	At present	Male—4, Female—3, Children: Male—1, Female—1, Total—9	
4.	Education:	Male	Female
	Graduate & above	37.5 %	25.0 %
	Professionals	06.3 %	-
	SF & above	0.6.3 %	06.3 %
	Under SF	09.3 %	09.3 %
	Illiterate	-	-
	Total	59.4 %	40.6 %
5.	Family members living outside	11.6 %	
6.	Marital status	63.6 % of men & women have marital relations with West Bengal families.	

Source: Table based on primary survey by the author from 11 June to 17 June 2007 in selected areas of Malda.

of the Refugee and Rehabilitation Department, which had planned those colonies at the English Bazar to rehabilitate the families of the displaced persons of East Pakistan, who had been employed in the Indian army. This was a planned colony with about 263 plots, each of about 8 *cottahs* for homestead purposes with wide roads on vested land belonging to the state government. The government allotted the plots to the displaced families of armed services personnel, but many of the persons in the army from East Pakistan did not wish to be rehabilitated in the district of Malda in the 1950s and preferred to stay around Calcutta Metropolitan City.

On being asked whether only those employed by the Indian army service had been allotted land in this colony, Mr Das said that subsequently, on the demand from other displaced families from East Bengal whose heads of households were in service in other civil departments of the state government, it was decided to allot the balance of the plots to other categories in state government service. This was done after 1960. Most of the displaced persons got employment in state government departments between 1950 and 1955. The state government decided that the plots would be given on a 99-year-leasehold basis. But later the government decided to sell the plots to the displaced persons in government service at Rs. 682 per *cottah* payable in instalments. Some persons did not pay any instalment at all, while some persons paid only a few instalments, and remaining persons paid the total value of the land.

The government transferred the title of the land in the form of a sale deed without any attachment, which means that the free title holder is in a position to resell the said plots. Those persons who made part payment for the occupied plots were given the title of the plots with attachment of a condition in the deed that they could not sell their plots for 12 years. Those who did not pay any premium for the plots were given the title on a 99-year-leasehold basis without any right to sell or transfer the title to anybody. About 50 per cent of these plots have already been sold by the displaced persons/allottees. All the existing families of displaced persons are well settled economically and educationally, in pukka buildings except for six such families with low incomes and less education who are living in country-type hutments. All the Municipal facilities like water, electricity, health care, transport, educational facilities are open to them. The average family size has increased to nine from three members per family. This is a special type of well-planned refugee colony, with all modern facilities that had been planned for those displaced persons who were holders of government service. It is the only colony of its kind in the district.

Chapal Bagchi said that he migrated to West Bengal in 1961 from his native district of Rajshahi in Bangladesh. He was recruited in 1963 by the Indian army. At the time of his recruitment he had no evidence of Indian citizenship as he had lost all his personal belongings during his migration from Bangladesh. Bagchi's parents were residents of village Balubhara, PS Badalgachi, Rajshahi, Bangladesh (East Pakistan), and migrated to India in 1956 and since then they have been living in Madhyam Kendua, PS Habibpur, Malda. In 1971, their other children joined them. Now they are all permanent residents here. Until recently, a ration card was considered proof of residence, but there was no difficulty in obtaining a fake one. Now, however, with the voter identity card considered a proof of identity, a ration card is no longer good enough to prove residency, which makes things a little more difficult for migrants.

Gita Sarkar a housewife who came alone from East Bengal to West Bengal, when I asked whether she had faced any problems while crossing the border, replied that her husband had been killed in the 1971 war. She had asked for help from the BSF to cross the border. But they molested her. In fact, this is true of a number of cases most of which remain unreported. Now she is a permanent resident in Digalbari Colony, Mouza Harinandanbati, PS Bamongola. This colony is in the rural area. She is employed a field worker.

Ranu Davi in Kutubsahar colony, PS Gazole, described the miserable history of her journey to this colony. She first arrived in Kutubsahar camp with her three children from East Pakistan. She was an evacuee, totally destitute, widowed and not enrolled in any camp. The SDO wrote out an order asking her to be admitted at Kutubsahar camp. As she had no way to go there (12 miles), the SDO took her and also provided food and accommodation. The camp has since closed. In Kutubsahar Mouza there are three colonies, namely, Kutubsahar-Golghar Colony, Kutubsahar Colony and Ghosani Bag Colony, PS Gazole. There are only 56 families in Kutubsahar Colony.

In the course of the interviews, it was revealed how the colonies had been established since 1948 by the refugee populations in the district of Malda. Refugee families took the initiative to get settled by establishing colonies after purchasing land from private owners under the *Bynanama-Amalanama* schemes of rehabilitation by the government. They built houses and started trade/business with the financial assistance provided by the government for the purpose.

TABLE 18.2: LIST OF 607 GROUPS OF DISPLACED PERSONS' SQUATTERS' COLONIES

Sr. No.	Name of colonies	Location	No. of displaced persons families	Rural/ urban	Public/ private land
1	Mangalbari Colony	Mouza Mangalbari Samandi P.O Malda	60	rural	Khas land
2	Khaihata Colony	-do-	33	-do-	-do-
3	Ganghi Colony	-do-	69	-do-	-do-
4	Charlaxmipur Colony	Mouza Mubarakpur PS Malda	101	-do-	NER land
5	Khanpur Colony	-do-	35	-do-	Khas land
6	Baglahagi Colony	Mouza Baglahagi, JL no. 55, PS Malda	85	-do-	-do-
7	Fuldanga Colony	Mouza Fuldanga, PS Malda	25	-do-	Private land
8	Bilbari-Nazir Khani Colony	Mouza Nazir Khani Bilbari Colony, PS English Bazar	37	-do-	-do-
9	Buraburitala Krisha Pally Colony	Mouza Pirojpur, PS English Bazar	263	Urban	-do-
10	Paschim Sarbamangala Pally Colony	Mouza Maheshmati, PS English Bazar	25	-do-	CAD Gov. of India
11	Adina Colony	Mouza Adina, JL no. 39, PS Gazole	279	-do-	Khas land
12	Uttar Mahimnagar & Kanchan Nagar	Kanchan GP, PS Gazole	46	Rural	-do-
13	Gobindapur Colony	-do-	28	-do-	-do-
14	Duba Khokson Colony	Chaknagar GP, PS Gazole	60	-do-	-do-
15	Kadubari Colony	-do-	70	-do-	-do-
16	Chandrali Colony	Bairgachi GP(1), PS Gazole	25	-do-	-do-
17	Boilari Colony	Ranigunj GP, PS Gazole	25	-do-	-do-
18	Kutubsahar Golghar Colony	Mouza Kutubsahar, PS Gazole	140	Rural	Khas land
19	Ghosani Bag Colony	Mouza Kutubsahar, PS Gazole	111	-do-	Khas land
20	Chinidana Colony	Mouza Pandua, PS Gazole	38	-do-	Private land
21	Kutubsahar Colony	Mouza Kutubsahar, PS Gazole	56	-do-	Khas land
22	Dalla Colony	Mouza Dalla, PS Habibpur	539	-do-	-do-
23	Parbatidanga Colony	Mouza Chakli, PS -do-	248	-do-	-do-

24	Agra Colony	Mouza Agra, PS -do-	79	-do-	-do-
25	Telnai Colony	Mouza Telnai, PS -do-	89	-do-	-do-
26	Harischandrapur & Aragachi Colony	Mouza Harischandra-pur & Aragachi, PS -do-	149	-do-	-do-
27	Nandagar & Poali Colony	Mouza Partharnan-dagar & Poali, PS -do-	45	-do-	-do-
28	Pathar Sasuli Colony	Mouza Pathar Sasuli PS -do-	62	-do-	-do-
29	Dharanda & Jugi Pathar Colony	Mouza Dharanda & Pathar Jugi, PS -do-	25	-do-	-do-
30	Kuchiamore Colony	Mouza Kuchiamore PS -do-	77	-do-	-do-
31	Kendua Colony	Mouza Kendua PS -do-	100	do	NF Rail-way land
32	Chaitangachi Madhyam Kendua	-do-	114	-do-	Khas land
33	Bulbulchandi Rice MU Colony	-do-	117	-do-	-do-
34	Bakshinagar Colony	Mouza Bakshinagar PS -do-	73	-do-	NF Rail-way land
35	Javdebpur Colony	PS Habibpur	25	-do-	Khas land
36	Digalbari Colony	Mouza Harinandabati, PS Bamangola	52	Rural	-do-
37	Barwadanga Colony	Mouza Nandinadaha, PS -do-	85	-do-	-do-
38	Bhangatola Colony	Mouza Lakshmipur, JL no. 36 PS Kaliachak	250	-do-	NF Railway land

Source: Government of West Bengal, *Manual of Refugee Relief and Rehabilitation*, vol. 1, Kolkata: Refugee Relief and Rehabilitation Department, 2001.

Some of the families were agriculturists and manual labourers. It was also observed that among the refugees surveyed, particularly in the rural area of Malda, non-agricultural families and persons actually outnumbered the people belonging to the agricultural class. Among the displaced populations found in the town area, those who had depended on trade and commerce in East Pakistan formed the majority. Agricultural family units had moved into the villages of Bankura.

It is important to keep in mind that the 'cultural characteristics' of the Bengali-speaking Hindu refugees from East Bengal and the Bengali-speaking people of West Bengal are definitely not so different as to reduce them into two alien groups within the same cultural environment. The Bengali language is the mother tongue of the people of Malda in West Bengal and East Bengal with only different dialects. With the passage of time, the East Bengalis adapted themselves to the dialect of Malda, thus reducing the division. Both share a similar cultural heritage and a common history. Inter-marriage brought them even closer and gradually they lost their 'refugee character'.

Though much illegal immigration takes place with the help of agents, who cleverly maintain good relations with the Border Security Force (BSF), the Bangladesh Rifles (BDR) and the police, many immigrants come across with the help of friendly neighbours on Indian side of the border, or of friends and relatives who have already migrated. People on both sides of the border share the same physiological features and the same language (though the accent may be different). Once across the border, the immigrants simply mingle with the locals, sometimes taking on new names.

Book Reviews

India after Gandhi: The History of the World's Largest Democracy

Ramachandra Guha
New Delhi: Picador, 2007

KRISHNAN SRINIVASAN

As a conspectus of the Indian story since Independence, this book is adequate. The prose is easy and undemanding. Why was it commissioned by Picador in India's 60th year? To cash in on the anniversary year interest, of course. The book would serve as a bird's eye-view of India for a would-be tourist or as a familiar narrative to the Indian reader, but this is not a work for the researcher or scholar.

The book, despite copious end-notes, shows no sign of the fruits of original research though there is a mention of exclusive access to P.N. Haksar's essays. The text could have been put together from a close reading of the daily newspapers over the years. It ranks as history only in the sense that the work of Lapierre and Collins or William Dalrymple is history. It may be classified as popular history; a chronology for the general readership. And it is not history in the additional sense that there is no analysis, no insights, no new illumination. Yet more than once, Ramachandra Guha refers to himself as a historian, which is mystifying until one comes across a reference to A.G. Noorani, who is also described as a historian —which Noorani is not by any manner of means, and is referred to in another paragraph as 'a constitutional expert'. Apparently for Guha, anyone who writes a commentary or even makes a statement on contemporary matters is a historian.

Nehru dies in the text on page 387, and Indira Gandhi on page 570, when there are only 200 pages left to the text and 23 years of the Indian story still to go. It is evident that the balance of the text is completely stilted. One discerns almost nothing of the views of the author himself, apart from his bestowal of a frequent and irritating epithet concerning an individual, such as 'great Cambridge historian', 'brilliant Cambridge-educated physicist', 'celebrated Cambridge-educated economist', 'brilliant low-caste lawyer', 'great German sociologist', 'great British biologist', 'fellow traveler P.N. Haksar', 'well-trained barrister', 'hard-working law minister' and so on *ad nauseam*.

The author makes obvious efforts to appeal to the Western readership. For much of the book he quotes, either to justify or contradict, several secondary sources from mainly British authors; and in the latter half, from American sources. Even English-language sources from nearer India; the neighbourhood, South-East Asia and the Gulf, are ignored, except for a few selections from Pakistan.

The book despite its length is surprisingly episodic. Since there is inevitably a need to retrace the narrative to follow a separate trend or development, there is considerable repetition, it is a pity Guha does not trust the reader's memory and chooses to give the same short introduction to persons who appear a second or third time, such as K.M. Pannikar, who is invariably described as 'a historian'.

There is the obligatory reference to Bollywood, and music, theatre and Indian cricket, without making it clear what their relevance is to the history of the world's biggest democracy. There are no similar references to literature, art or architecture. Guha descends to Indian-style colloquialisms, so we read about 'sticking to social work', 'liquidating her physically', 'tin-pot dictatorship', 'going down the tube', and 'outside of the cinema'. There are irrelevant flourishes like verses from Ghalib, and all too rare shafts of humour, along with highly contentious personal opinions, with no particular context, such as 'Intellectuals have always had a curious fascination for the men of power'. Is that so, or is it the other way round? In any event, it seems to characterize Guha's own inclinations.

India's and China's Recent Experience with Reform and Growth

Edited by Wanda Tseng and David Cowen
Houndsmills, Basingstoke: Palgrave Macmillan and International Monetary Fund, 2007.

KRISHNAN SRINIVASAN

This is a paperback version of a book first published in hard cover in 2005. It consists of a number of essays, this time twelve in number, written by as many as 22 authors, on reform and growth in India and China.

This does not imply that comparisons and contrasts are always made, since only 3 of the twelve pieces deal with both countries. Three deal only with China, five only with India, and one with neither. There is nothing on India's trade; and nothing on China's services.

The two persons described as editors have not contributed to any of the essays, and considering the number of persons they have named in the acknowledgements, one has to wonder what input the editors have themselves bestowed on the book.

The copyright of the book and the co-publisher is the International Monetary Fund, and it can thus be deduced that this volume is not for the layman or the general reader. It is specialized and technical in tone and is designed for policy makers. It is very strong on financial aspects in the two countries and much less so on trade matters, and exiguous on political imperatives and compulsions.

Having said this, the first article itself, by Meghnad Desai called 'India and China; an essay in Comparative Political Economy', is a superb piece of writing—analytical, perceptive, and far-sighted. It pointedly draws the appropriate contrasts and comes to the rational conclusions. It will be mandatory reading for anyone concerned with the future of the two countries, and it will be worth obtaining this book for Desai's essay alone.

The New Asian Power Dynamic

Edited by M. Rasgotra, Foreword by Brajesh Misra
New Delhi: Sage, 2007

KRISHNAN SRINIVASAN

This book follows the current trend of putting together a collection of essays by various writers on a general and rather loosely articulated theme, and adding a foreword and an introduction by an editor. Rasgotra and Misra are a rather blatantly obvious selling point; whereas their respective contributions are, especially in the latter case, extremely limited. In the former case, Rasgotra's introduction reads well and is elegantly set out in its argumentation, but it is not clear what editorial functions he has exercised, since he gives no indication of having seen, let alone been influenced by, any of the other contributions other than the conclusions of K. Raghunath. As is the case when various contributions are strung together in this manner, the quality varies from the good to the mediocre with the indifferent in between.

Of the 12 contributions, four are on China, three on India, one covers both, there is one on Japan and one on Russia. Of these ten pieces of varied quality, three are written by one author, D.S. Rajan. Then we have the introduction by Rasgotra and the conclusions by another former foreign secretary, K. Raghunath.

The book would have benefitted from better copy editing and proofreading; the printer's devils in the text are irritating.

One of the essays, by Pushpita Das, is a mere listing, without any commentary, of Indo-Chinese agreements concluded between 2000 and 2005, and is of such tedium that, if it had to be included, should have been consigned at best to an annex. The various contributors, apart from Raghunath, seem unaware of the essays written by others; the one-time US deputy secretary of state Zoellick is quoted—the same textual reference—by more than one author.

After a good introduction, which is in fact more of an overview, by Rasgotra (but why did he have to write; 'one prays for the rise of another Indira Gandhi to lead the Indian nation'?) the piece by Alka Acharya on Chinese foreign policy is replete with allusions and references to secondary texts, hardly allowing her space for any original thought. Besides, does she really think 'the notion of human rights and democracy' is exclusively Western? Gurmeet Kanwal's essay on China's military modernization draws much from Western sources, but is informative, though his conclusions about India's having to establish credible deterrence against China's nuclear and missile programme might be considered rather wishful thinking. Rajan writes three essays on China, its relations with the US, and with India. His piece on US perceptions on China is largely drawn from published American sources, and the best of his three contributions is the one on Indo-Chinese relations.

Jayshree Sengupta's essay on US economic ties with India and China makes coherent reading; and an excellent essay follows from Harinder Sekhon on Indo-American relations—analytical, clear and persuasive. Another excellent essay is by Arjun Asrani on Japan and Asian security: Asrani is well informed and authoritative on this subject. M.K. Bhadrakumar's essay on Russia-US relations follows, which shows admirable balance between US and Russian sources, though to make his points, he overstates the distrust and opposition to the US from both Russia and China—a point which is not substantiated by the other essays in the same book.

The final essay is described as 'Overview and Conclusions' but is in effect a self-standing piece by Raghunath. It is more Indo-centric than many of the others. He makes some telling general remarks, but is less impressive when it comes to specifics, and is least effective when he tabulates his comments in 1-2-3 or a-b-c format; and assertions such as Indian nuclear weapon tests have enhanced respect for India in China may be treated as contestable.

Mru: Hill People on the Border of Bangladesh

Claus Dieter Brauns and Lorenz G. Loeffler
Basel: Birkhaeuser Verlag, 1990

SWAPNA BHATTACHARYA (CHAKRABORTI)

The book, *Mru: Hill People on the Border of Bangladesh*, by Claus Dieter Brauns and Lorenz G. Loeffler, published by the famed publisher Birkhaeuser of Basel in 1990, first appeared in 1989 with the original German title *Bergbewohner im Grenzgebiet von Bangladesh*. The English translation has been done by Doris Wagner-Glenn. The book is about a tribal group, called Mru—an up-hill tribe from the Chittagong Hill Tracts (CHT) of Bangladesh. But, in reality, it narrates hitherto unexplored details of all the ethnic groups of this entire border region of Bangladesh. Lying as it is, in the south-eastern fringe of Bangladesh CHT, attracted the attention of the British policy makers, administrators and ethnographers not only due to its strategic location between the Burmese Empire (modern Myanmar) and the Indian subcontinent, but also owing to its vast natural resources, forest in particular. CHT makes 10 per cent of the total area of Bangladesh, but has a population of about 1.2 million. The area has hills and plains, with four rivers, Feni, Karnafuli, Sangu and Matamuri flowing across the area. Any scholar on CHT would, while recognizing the contributions of Captain T.H. Lewin, R.H. Hutchinson, J.P. Mills, Levi Strauss, Lucien Bernot, automatically place the author of the book Lorenz G. Loeffler along with those great names. Loeffler was a full Professor for Cultural and Social Anthropology at the University of Zurich, Switzerland. The CHT study has come a long way since 1960s and 1970s. But, Professor Loeffler's name enjoys a special respect across the scholarly world, including in Bangladesh and

India, not only for his profound knowledge of the culture, society and language of CHT of Bangladesh, Lushai Hills/modern Mizoram of India, and Arakan (modern Rakhine State) of Myanmar, but also for his real love and concern for the Chakmas and their kinsmen beyond the border.

Historically speaking, the people of CHT got integrated into a territorial system which comprised three Chiefs and their respective three circles: Chakma Chief in Central Karnafuli Valley, Mong Chief in North Karnafuli Valley and Bohmong Chief in South Karnafuli Valley. The people of CHT are well known for their skill in basketry, in weaving, in domestication of cattle, and above all, for their inborn talent in the meaningful management of the wealth of the nature. An aspect, highlighted in the present work, which would capture anyone's attention, is the hill–plains dichotomy within the Hill Tracts itself. This has been elaborated in the book in following way: 'Living in an era already strongly influenced by the economic system of the plains, the concerned Chakma and Marma were surely not people with whom other hill people would have felt any particular solidarity' (p. 40). Languages of this region remain an extremely valuable cultural asset as they belong to the Tibeto–Burman group of the great Sino–Tibetan language family. In contrast to Sanskritic (Indo–Aryan) languages, in Tibeto–Burman languages, various tones determine the meaning of the words. On the other hand, as the glossary of the book under review shows, constant interaction with Mughal rulers (Mughals annexed Chittagong in 1666) of India on the one side, and Buddhist rulers of Arakan on the other, CHT languages, the Chakma language in particular, have adopted a large number of Persian and Arakanese words. For the benefit of those, who are not so familiar with the languages of Myanmar, I must mention here that the Arakanese (Rakhine) is very similar to the Burmese language.

The book is unique in the sense that it gives a lot of attention to the various avenues of social and economic interaction between the tribal Hill people and the people from the Chittagong Plains, who were predominantly Muslims. The Chakmas, as their language indicates, experienced the closest relation with the Bengali-speaking people from the Plains. On the other hand, the Mru language is, as the author argues, a bit isolated type. Mru, though a Tibeto–Burman language, cannot however be brought under either the category of Burmese, or Naga-Chin group. This observation of Loeffler certainly indicates that the Mru people, found themselves constantly cornered, and took distance from the valley dwellers and preferred to (or forced to?)

maintain isolation. This 248 paged book with brilliant photographs, illustrations, maps, index, glossary and bibliography presents itself to be an invaluable contribution to the regional history of South and South-East Asia. No other work ever before has documented with such insightful information and photographs of the little known civilization and culture of such a remote corner of the world.

Seen from the viewpoint of kinship relation, the Mrus are co-brethren of the Murungs of the present Rakhine State (Arakan) of Myanmar. The Mrus should not be confused with the Mrungs or Hill Tipperas, though, all the ethnic groups of CHT came in various waves—from central and western Myanmar before they migrated to such directions as north-eastern India and CHT. Within CHT tribes, culturally, the Mrus, as the author argues, stand closest to the Khumis, who also came from Arakan.

The Chakmas, the Marmas and the Tipperas constitute the major body of the tribal population of CHT, while among the minor ones come: Tongchengya, Mru, Mrung/Riang, Bawm, Khumi, Sak, Pangkhua, Khyang and Lushai. Bawm and the Pangkhua people are closest to the Lushais. Thus, an immensely important message is conveyed in the book under discussion, as to how isolated became the Bawms and Pangkhuas of CHT when their kinsmen (Lushais of present Mizoram) got their own state, Mizoram, within India. According to an estimation, in 1981, the Mru people numbered 22,000 only. Though a few Mru settlements are located in the valley of Matamuri River, most of the Mru live in the interior part of the Hills. The uniqueness of the area called CHT lies in the fact that this particular area, like the north-eastern India, is a meeting point of South-East Asian and South Asian people. As the book has successfully demonstrated, for many of these border region people, phrases like 'Nation', 'State', 'Independence', 'Transfer of Power' carried no meaning at all. The British colonial rule 'excluded' their area from the administration of the mainland. Or, as in the case of CHT, all the minor tribes were thrown upon the mercy of the major tribes: the Chakmas, the Marmas and the Tipperas. Thus, two Rajas (Chiefs), the Marma Bohmong and Chakma Raja, became most powerful (see page 30) and acted as 'representatives' of their colonial masters, rather than their own people.

As a result of the colonial policy of centralization, as the book effectively shows—a clan-based society, dependent on the nature and her resources suddenly got transformed into an well-defined territory with a totally alien geographical (District, Circle, Mouza, etc.) hierarchy. State-employed middlemen appeared as the agents of the Colonial State to 'manage' the tribal affairs. These managers were known with the names *karabari*. The most important for the British rulers, as the book itself says, was the tax collection, which symbolically and also in practical sense meant acceptance of the colonial authority over land, nature and the people. The oft-quoted argument of 'protection' of the Tribal Hill people from the exploitation of the Plains' people was only too apologetically phrased. Or, one could even go to the extent of arguing that introduction of colonial economic order which discouraged mobility of the people from one mountain top to the other, practising 'slash-and-burn' system, in reality, aimed at rapid introduction of plough cultivation which would lead to the much-needed centralization of tax system. Exploitation of the forest resources could only be possible if and when the jhum cultivators settled as docile tax paying plough cultivators. As the author rightly argues, the valley-dwelling groups like the Chakmas, Marmas and the Tipperas responded quite positively to this colonial call. Thereby a barrier was created between them and their co-brethren, Mrus, Khumis, Saks, Bawms, etc.

I must admit that one gets enthralled having such an amazing academic product in hand which is not only the result of unprecedented labour on the part of the author and the photographer, but also carries the memory of their extremely challenging, at times even risky adventures in those early period when things were extremely uncertain, even more: unsafe. The text written by Lorenz G. Loeffler and the photographs done by C.D Brauns nicely complement each other. Let me first introduce the brilliant photographer Claus Dieter Brauns, who is a free-lance photographer and journalist with a genuine passion for the geography and ethnography of South and South-East Asia. This highly talented scholar-photographer went to this 'Backward Tribal Area' of Pakistan being fascinated with the pristine natural beauty and the unique human resources. After all, the area was (as is still now) so very different from the plains of Chittagong! The then Government of Pakistan normally did not encourage entry of outsiders into this sensitive area, let alone such people as foreign photographers and anthropologists! After all, the wound of the Partition was still fresh in the minds of the common people, who had suffered the most. Disappointment of the Buddhist people of CHT for the irrational inclusion of their area into Pakistan can be well understood. The cultural affiliates of the people of the CHT were actually the Hindus and Buddhists of India or the Buddhists of Myanmar.

Thus, CHT was seen as potentially a trouble-generating area. Such a region bordering the Arakan (Rakhine) state of Myanmar (Burma) and Lushai Hills of India (present Mizoram state) took away the sleep of the Pakistani rulers. The disastrous impact of the construction of the Kaptai Hydro-electric Project was visible in the form of displacement of thousands of people from their lands in early 1960s. Thousands of acres of cultivable land went under water, and a large number of displaced people migrated to the Indian territory of present Arunachal Pradesh. Brauns made it in those days of 1960s and 1970s to undertake such an operation as photographing the tribal people and their lives as went off in the lap of the high land of Chittagong. The editorial Board of the American *National Geographic* magazine was impressed by such endeavour and extended support. In pages 20–1 Brauns narrates his experience of being in the area during 1971, when the Bangladesh Liberation War against the military regime of Pakistan had broken out. The photographer could just manage to sneak out, and survived. The present volume contains several out of this extremely valuable collection of the 6000 photographs that he took for the *National Geographic.* In this book with 248 pages one finds photographs of various sizes published with proper illustrations on almost all the pages.

Loeffler's adventure in the Hill Tracts was provoked by his earlier works (Doctoral dissertation) on cattle ceremonies of South-East Asia. In 1955–7 Loeffler first visited the CHT and started his works with the Mrus. He got a Mru teacher who was also his guide. The teacher-guide was equally competent in Bangla/Bengali, Marma and Lushai languages. As we all know, Lushai is the language of the Lushai Hills, which later got the name 'Mizoram' .The book reflects upon how the Lushais got the name, 'Mizo' which means 'the Highlanders'. What makes the work so unique is the vast range of information that is available: it starts from the description of state of research on the CHT and ends up in the love song of the Mru people.

The subjects of the text and the photographs address a wide range of choices; indeed, they encompass every aspect of life. The first essay is entitled 'The Chittagong Hill Tracts and their Inhabitants'. In this essay, the 'Sak' origins of the Chakmas have been upheld. The Saks (Chak) were a major ethnic group once quite dominating in ancient Myanmar. Loeffler legitimately stressed the accommodativeness of the Chakma people, who, no matter being Buddhists, followed even Muslim usages. Coming to the Marmas, it has been pointed out that they are more orthodox to their Mranma (Burmese) norms, and probably constitute a group of late comers. Their identification with the Buddhists of Myanmar (Arakan in particular) was so deeply rooted, that they turned occasionally withdrew from CHT and went back to Arakan.

The second essay is the description of the 'house' and the 'home'. With excellent photographs of the Mru villages, the essay among other things presents a vivid description of how the Mru people built their home with bamboo with proper arrangements inside and outside. In every step, the consciousness of the people towards their environment is expressed. Thereafter comes the essay on the description of Food and Clothing. Unlike 'more civilized' people, the Mru do not have to depend on imported or factory-made clothes. Instead, in most Gandhian way, they weave their own clothes, grew their own paddy and vegetables by way of slash-and-burn (swidden/jhum) cultivation. The book contains impressive photographs of how the Mrus trapped animals for their consumption. Domesticated animals are seen as part of the family. Furthermore, it is known (p. 130) that dogs are some time needed to ward off evil spirit. Gayals are also domesticated by the Mru people. Women wear jewelleries made of silver, brass and aluminium. During harvest festival men play drums and go around the villages. The third essay is dedicated to a very important subject: 'Kinship and Life Stages'. This is an extremely important essay, for, the structure of the clan, to which a family belongs, has been explained. Details of marriage customs and marital experiences have been enumerated in great detail. What strikes one is the importance of clan-membership of the individual, which, as the author states, is given the utmost importance in the Mru society.

For those, who are interested in tracing back the influence of the Rakhine–Myanmar kinship model among the CHT people, this book remains an essential reading. It is quite significant to mark that in the Mru society, the *karbaris* occasionally use the title *Ruatsa*. In literary sense it means 'village eater', precisely the person who enjoys the tax paid to him by their people. The Myanmar (Burmese) word 'Yva' which means 'village', and which is pronounced in Rakhine/ Arakanese language as 'Rua'. Some of the headmen from the Mru society felt very proud that their forefathers were *Ruatsa*. Though, as the author rightly states, *Ruatsas* are no more representative of their respective clans, rather they act as agents of the state. An interesting information makes the fact that old Indian silver rupees served as bride price in the Mru society. Photographs published on page 185 stand witness to such practices. I may mention in this connection that the entire region called Chittagong–Arakan Front, including Hills of Chittagong and Arakan, occupied close attention of the colonial administrators, for, the clandestine contact between the Bengali revolutionaries based in British Burma and their counterparts based in eastern India went through this area only. A few observations on how the people of the CHT stood in relation to nationalist movements in India and Myanmar, would have been quite illuminating.

The last essay of the book under review is entitled 'Cattle Ceremonies and Feasts of Merit'. Like most of the tribal societies, in the Mru society too, animal sacrifice is practised for the achievement of merit. Pages 231 to 240 are full of details of how the feast-giver family arranges the feast, how all the rituals are followed according to norms prevalent, how sacrifices of chicken and buffaloes are made, how rice beer brings the mood for such grand event, how decorations are made with bamboo, an article which plays a major part in the life of Mrus altogether.

The book has an excellent epilogue, inclusion of which brings a new dimension, i.e. the political dimension in the discussion. Otherwise, in major part, book is more of a historical-ethnological nature. In 1971, when Bangladesh became Independent, the tribal population of CHT had full faith in a future, which would bring a secular state into existence, where their natural and inherent rights over land and environment would be honoured constitutionally. As the work under review rightly points out, two things disappointed them: one was the flight of the Chakma Raja Tridiv Roy himself to Pakistan, and the other is the rise of military rule and Islamic twist in the political culture of Bangladesh. In a very bold language, the book describes the major events of 1970s and 1980s: the involvements of the Mizo rebels when they fought the war against the Indian Nation using the CHT as their sanctuary, the flight of the displaced people of CHT into the bordering areas of India, the state of Tripura in particular, ruthless and aggressive acts of violence perpetrated upon the people of CHT by the then Bangladesh Army, the struggle of the Shanti Bahini guerrillas engaged in fighting for the cause of Human Rights in CHT, the concern of the United Nations for the CHT people, the repealing (in 1989) by the Bangladesh Government the Regulation of 1900 and bringing of new bills for constitution of local government councils in the three districts: Rangmati, Khagrachari, and Bandarban. The councils were entrusted to settle the land questions. We are aware that after the signing of Peace Accord on 2 December 1997 between the then government headed by Prime Minister Sheikh Hasina of Awami League and the Parvatya Chattagram Janasamhati Samiti (PCJSS), headed by Jyotirindra Bodhipriya Larma (also known as Shantu Larma), most of the refugees went back from Tripura, and that several measures were taken by the Bangladesh Government to bring peace and stability in this region. Important steps were taken to settle the land questions, including rehabilitation. CHT cannot be seen as an isolated agenda; the region's prosperity and progress depend much upon the overall situation in Bangladesh. Since Bangla desh is emerging as one of the most important countries of South Asia, the only one besides India, which has a direct border with South-East Asia, this particular work, documenting a unique cultural milieu, a melting pot of South and South-East Asian culture, deserves even closer attention. Both, the author Lorenz G. Loeffler and the photographer Claus Dieter Brauns, of this extraordinary work deserve our salutation.

India–Myanmar Relations: 1886–1948

Swapna Bhattacharya (Chakraborti)
Kolkata: K.P. Bagchi & Company, 2007

KAUSIK BANDYOPADHYAY

From time immemorial, India has had strong historical and cultural ties with Myanmar. The spread of Buddhism has been the most enduring legacy of the Indian connection in Myanmar (Burma). Buddhism came to Myanmar from India in the Asokan era, and since then has permeated every aspect of Burmese life. It was a philosophy which enabled the Burmese to meet the challenges of the outside world with supreme confidence, yet at the same time breeding a strong indifference to the outside world. The subjugation of Myanmar and the end of Burmese monarchy after the Third Anglo–Burmese War was a traumatic experience for the Burmese and resulted in an unprecedented break with the past. However, under British imperialism, both countries suffered the same pain of suppression and economic exploitation, and their sentiments also ran together to get liberated from the yoke of foreign rule. The Indians played a very significant role in the economic life of colonial Myanmar. They were prominent in transport, industry, labour, road construction, banking, insurance and exchange and wholesale and retail trade. Moreover, trade was the vital aspect of Indo–Myanmar economic relations in the colonial period. Geographical proximity, joint administration and the complementary character of the resepctive economies of Indian and Myanmar contributed to a large extent to the development of their trading links. The Indian nationalist movement, on the other hand, was very important in setting the pattern for a direct challenge to British imperial rule in Myanmar, as it not only provided the Burmese people with the basic objectives of constitutional reforms but also gave them the messages of non-violent struggle and boycott methods, which they later employed in their fight for freedom from colonial exploitation. Thus on the cultural, economic and political planes, India and Myanmar had close methodological and ideological exchanges, which proved beneficial to both.

Swapna Bhattacharya's work *India–Myanmar Relations: 1886–1948* delves into this wider trajectory of India-Myanmar relations during the colonial rule. The work is a product of the author's erudite and eclectic scholarship on a subject which has mostly been neglected in Indian studies on colonial South and South-East Asian history and culture. Given the dearth of factual and analytical research on the complexities of a reciprocal relationship between the two neighbours, Bhattacharya realized that 'it is more important to narrate the happenings rather than evaluating the same, let alone giving judgments!' (p. xix). This narrative flavour is the greatest asset of the book, and should inspire younger scholars to qualify this informative narration with historical analysis. However, this does not imply that the work lacks analytical perception. Bhattacharya, 'fond of experimenting with various theories and perceptions', steers clear of the exclusivity of a mutual relationship paradigm and tries to put in place a holistic paradigm, exploring the engaging story of involvement of a number of countries like Japan and Germany in the reciprocal affairs of India and Burma during colonial rule. More importantly, the author's attempt to highlight the continuity and importance of people-to-people relations in any mature appreciation of India–Burma overall relations during the period under review certainly gives the serious researcher a lot to think about.

Bhattacharya's work is divided into eight chapters apart from an Introduction and a Conclusion. She begins with an exhaustive overview of Indian writings on Myanmar. She is right in claiming that the Indian litterateurs and scholars built-up an enduring tradition of Burma studies since the nineteenth century. Discouraging any mystic perception about Myanmar, she urges the scholars 'to nurse a school of Myanmar Studies from the Indian Perspective'. Bhattacharya's instructive description of the Buddhist past of Bengal serves as an exemplar of such a historical initiative. While much has already been written on the impact of Indian immigration in colonial Burma, the author looks at the problematic in Chapter II from a different angle. Even given the inescapable economic imperatives of such immigration, contemporary studies and documents including the riot enquiry committee reports suggest that there existed a serious apprehension in the minds of many Burmese that the Indian immigration was largely responsible for the unemployment in Burma. This was but natural in a society where immigrants play a crucial role. Despite the criticality of the issue of Indian immigration in colonial Burma and the kind of impact it had on mid-twentieth-century India–Burma relations, Bhattacharya rightly emphasizes the need to revisit India's contribution to the making of modern Myanmar. To the extent Indian labour, business groups, professionals and educated groups played a positive role in the country should be accorded due recognition. And one must not forget the close mental bond the Indians cultivated towards their adopted country and the identification of both the Burmese and the Indians with Burma as *their* country. According to the author, the complementarity between the two countries at the political level needs to be analysed in this context.

Chapter III of the book discusses the complexities of colonial penetration and consolidation in Burma. The author explains the British annexation of Burma in terms of a strategic plan prompted by the fear of a possible German penetration into the region as a whole. In her opinion, the fear of Germany as 'a competent rival' haunted the British in many of their actions in Burma during the period under review. On the other hand, how Indian revolutionaries abroad came to forge a close nexus with the Burmese political movement in the early twentieth century is well narrated in her useful discussion on the spirit of Ghadr and its propaganda and activism. The role of Indian revolutionaries in the context of the complementarity of political-nationalist movements of India and Burma is immortally personified in Sabyasachi, the hero of Sarat Chandra Chattopadhyay's celebrated novel *Pather Dabi*. However, Bhattacharya warns that 'any attempt to interpret the novel as an episode of a futile revolt of a *Babu* or *Bhadraloka* class, ignoring the then prevalent state of India–Burma relations, will bring little progress in historical research' (p. 20). In Chapter IV, while analysing Sarat Chandra's novels that deal with the life of Indians in Burma in the context of the then prevailing political and economic situation in colonial Burma, the author on the one hand brilliantly deciphers the underpinnings of immigrants' misery in Burma, and on the other, brings forth the inspirational impact of the Indian revolutionaries of Burma on the Bengali youth. That the

Bengal–Burma contact remained a constant source of concern for the British becomes evident from the continuous proscription of *Pather Dabi* till Sarat Chandra's death. In fact, Bhattacharya devotes an entire chapter (Chapter V) to discuss this strong connection between the Bengal revolutionaries and Burma during the period 1923–39. In the process, she attends to the importance of the old Arakan–Chittagong route as used by the revolutionaries of India and Burma, explores the Burmese connections of the Bengal revolutionaries, and relates the political actions of Bengali and Burmese revolutionaries in Burma to the rise and growth of Extremism in Bengal politics. Although the Thakin movement in the 1930s gave the nationalist movement in Burma a different direction, the author notes the complementarity of the radical political trends in both countries in the 1920s and 1930s. In fact, opposition to a common enemy strengthened the bond of cooperation between the nationalist movements of both the countries.

While it is well known that the nationalist movement in Burma was strongly influenced by the intellectual and political developments taking place in India, there has been no systematic study of the role of Indian leaders like Mahatma Gandhi or Subhas Chandra Bose in the political life of Burma. The present work redresses this imbalance by narrating the impact of these two leaders on Burmese nationalist politics. In Chapter VI, Bhattacharya takes up Gandhi's relations with Burma in the light of his three visits to the country and his speeches during those visits. She also examines the impact of Gandhian ideals on the political agitations of Burma. As in other colonized countries, Gandhi remained an icon in Burmese political life throughout its struggle for national independence. In the next chapter, the author revisits Subhas Chandra Bose's links with Burma and its nationalist leaders. In doing so, she describes Bose's life in Mandalay jail, discusses his observations on Burmese history, culture and society, and focuses on his political vision about Burma and India. She also explains Bose's contacts with Aung San or Ba Maw, especially during the period of Japanese occupation of Burma, in the joint context of the internal rifts within the Indian National Congress as well as the internationalization of the nationalist movements of Burma and India at the onset of the Second World War.

In the last chapter Bhattacharya pays attention to the complexities of political confrontation and negotiation in Burma in the years preceding Independence, in which Aung San played a pivotal role. More importantly, she casts her eye on the India–Burma relations with special emphasis on the Muslims of Indian origin in Burma, which is quite contextual given the recent exodus of a sizeable number of Muslims from northern Arakan to Bangladesh. The roots of this unfortunate happening, as she rightly points out, could be found in the political doldrums of the pre-independence years of Burma and India, if not also in the British government's Bengal-oriented Arakan policy. During the last stage of India's struggle for independence, Indians including the Indian National Congress leaders expressed concern over the independence of Burma while the Burmese nationalists like Aung San and U Saw reciprocated similar sentiments of sympathy towards India's struggle for independence. Post-Aung San, U Nu continued the friendly relations with Jawaharlal Nehru.

In 1990 Aung San Suu Kyi wrote her small but influential book *Burma and India: Some Aspects of Intellectual Life under Colonialism.* Although written from a Burmese perspective, the work went into the psyche of India–Burma intellectual relations with some useful observations on the reciprocality of political and cultural movements of the two countries during colonial rule. Since then an Indian initiative was due to approach the theme from an Indian perspective. Swapna Bhattacharya has done this job admirably. She charts the trajectory of Burma's enduring relationship with India at the political, cultural and economic levels. As already noted, she places before her readers a huge repository of materials which should inspire the younger researchers to take up the more tricky and micro issues of this long-term relation. For instance, taking cues from this work one can debate the notion of the anti-Indian character of Burmese nationalism or assess the long-term impact of Indian immigration on Indo–Burmese relations. The complex background to the separation of Burma from India in 1937 and the exodus of Indians that followed it, as transpires from Bhattacharya's work, can also form a viable subject of historical enquiry. If Bhattacharya's initiative is followed by scholars who would take up such issues with the corroborative use of Burmese sources, her pious wish for an efflorescence of Myanmar Studies in India would certainly be fulfilled.